Star Trek and History

Star Trek and History

Race-ing Toward a White Future

DANIEL LEONARD BERNARDI

Rutgers University Press

New Brunswick, New Jersey, and London

Manufactured in the United States of America

Portions of chapter 2 of the present work appeared as "Star Trek in the
1960s: Liberal-Humanism and the Production of Race," *Science Fiction
Studies* 24, no. 72 (July 1997); and "Infinite Diversity in Infinite
Combinations: Diegetic Logics and Racial Articulations in Star Trek,"
Film & History 24, nos. 1 & 2 (February–May 1994).

Bernardi, Daniel, 1964–
    Star Trek and history : race-ing toward a white future / Daniel
Leonard Bernardi.
        p.   cm.
    Filmography: p.
    Includes bibliographical references and index.
    ISBN 0-8135-2465-2 (alk. paper). — ISBN 0-8135-2466-0 (pbk. :
alk. paper)
    1. Star Trek films.   Star Trek television programs.   3. Race
relations in motion pictures.   4. Race relations in television.
I. Title.
PN1995.9.S694B37   1998
791.45′75′0973—dc21   97-17665
                                                           CIP
British Cataloging-in-Publication data for this book is available from the
British Library

To My Parents:

Yiya, who is also my best friend;
Leonard, who challenges my ideas and beliefs;
Roger, who encourages me to reach
beyond the stars

Contents

Illustrations

Acknowledgments

This book is a revision of my dissertation "The Wrath of Whiteness: The Meaning of Race in the Generation of *Star Trek*." I would like to thank the members of my dissertation committee—Nick Browne, George Lipsitz, Steve Mamber, Chon Noriega, Michael Omi, and Vivian Sobchack—for their valuable feedback. Vivian Sobchack was especially helpful, providing careful and engaging comments and suggestions on each chapter. She is a remarkable scholar and an even better friend. Nick Browne was an ideal chair, providing both the room I needed to figure things out myself and, at just the right moments, brilliant insights into argument and method. I would also like to thank Bob Rosen for his support, both intellectual and moral. I learned more about textual analysis from working as Bob's teaching assistant than I did in any graduate course I ever took. He is both a friend and a mentor, and I know I could not have finished the dissertation or the book without his help.

Scholars, professionals, and fans have also been helpful, particularly John Caldwell, Rick Worland, Henry Jenkins, Brigette Boyle, Jay Badenhoop, and Jeff Mills. I would also like to thank the fans who participated in STREK-L, a listserver on the Internet, from 1992 to 1994. In the true spirit of fandom, they were gracious, funny, and generally quite thoughtful. Finally, I would like to thank Majel Barrett-Roddenberry for allowing me access to the Gene Roddenberry Papers held in Special Collections at the University of California, Los Angeles Research Library. I'm also grateful to Brigitte Kueppers, Arts Special Collections librarian, for her assistance and ongoing work with this collection.

I was lucky enough to secure sufficient financial support throughout the writing of both the dissertation and the book. The Critical Studies faculty in the Department of Film and Television at UCLA awarded me a Plitt Southern Theaters Trust Fellowship that helped with much of the early research. The Ford Foundation provided a much-needed and generous dissertation fellowship. A University of California President's Postdoctoral Fellowship gave me the time and resources to turn the dissertation into this book.

Star Trek and History

1 The Meaning of Race in the Generation of *Star Trek*

Where No Text Has Gone Before

Imaginary time may sound like something out of science fiction, but it is a well-defined mathematical concept. In a sense it can be thought of as a direction of time that is at right angles to real time. One adds up the probabilities for all the particle histories with certain properties, such as passing through certain points at certain times. One then has to extrapolate the result back to the real space-time in which we live.
—*Stephen Hawking*

Data: If you prick me, do I not . . . leak?

In a 1992 parody of the original *Star Trek* (1966–1969), *In Living Color* (1990–1993) has the U.S.S. *Enterprise* and crew speeding toward a hostile planet. Playing James T. Kirk, Jim Carrey sits in the now famous captain's chair. Suddenly, Kim Wayans, playing Communications Officer Uhura, reports a strange message: "Something about intergalactic oppressors." David Allan Grier turns toward the captain, his pointed ears and raised eyebrows a clear sign that he is parodying Science Officer Spock, and warns: "Intruders are approaching the bridge, sir." The music crescendos as three dapper African-American males in suits and bow ties emerge from behind the bridge door. In the staccato delivery of William Shatner, the actor who plays the "real" Captain Kirk, Carrey asks: "Who . . . are . . . you?" "I am the Minister Louis Farrakhan," Damon Wayans responds, and the skit's title, "The Wrath of Farrakhan," is superimposed over the image. The audience roars. "What do you want?" Captain Kirk demands. "I've come to warn your crew of their enslavement aboard this vessel," Farrakhan calls out as his two followers melodically repeat punctuating words.

Kirk orders Uhura to get Starfleet Command on the communicator, but Farrakhan quickly intervenes: "Oh, my Nubian Princess, how long have you placed his calls? I watch this show every week and all I see is the back of your nappy wig." Uhura experiences a sudden epiphany, and responds angrily to Kirk: "He's right! I've been sittin' here for fifteen years with this damn thing in my ear [her small communicator] and ain't got one raise yet. Is that all I'm good for, to be your little secretary or your occasional chocolate fantasy?" Oohs and ahhs from the audience egg the scene on. "You get up off your flat butt and get Starfleet your daaamn self," she brazenly continues, "because I ain't busting."

Kirk turns to Helmsman Sulu, played by an Asian-American guest performer, and orders him to call Chief Engineer Scotty for help. Again Farrakhan intervenes: "Wait a minute, Mr. Sulu. Before you touch that dial, answer me this question: Who does the laundry around here?" "I do," Sulu answers. The helmsman then turns to his captain and blurts out: "You call me Buddha head and pie face in front of everybody. I've been in space all this time, and I haven't had one woman yet," he continues, "My loins are about to explode." With hips gyrating and a prurient smile on his face, Sulu declares: "I wanna' do the nasty." In what seems like a cathartic release, the audience roars.

In search of a faithful crewperson, Captain Kirk turns toward his science officer and frantically urges: "Mr. Spock, my friend . . . we've . . . got . . . to . . . do something." Spock responds calmly and logically: "Why do you say we, Caucasoid? It's obvious, Captain, that Minister Farrakhan is right." Shocked, Kirk retorts with a pun: "Spock, are you out of your *Vulcan* mind?" Again, the audience roars. "Galactically speaking, Captain, I am the strongest and most intelligent person aboard this vessel," Spock continues, "yet I'm only second in command. I should be captain." Farrakhan preaches: "Can't you see, it's discrimination!"

Kirk shoots Farrakhan with his phaser pistol, but nothing happens. The Minister responds confidently: "Put your puny weapon down, Captain. You cannot hurt me. My people have survived four hundred years of slavery, three hundred years of apartheid, and twenty-five years of *The Jeffersons* in syndication." He then orders Kirk to his room, and the powerless captain scurries off the bridge with head down and a whimper. The skit ends with Minister Farrakhan sitting in the captain's chair, flanked by his two followers, supported by the multi-humanoid crew, and ordering the *Enterprise* to return home: "Destination, 175th Street." The audience cheers.

More than a quarter of a century after the original *Star Trek* aired on NBC, the science fiction series is still worthy of parody—still able to evoke laughter and cheers. That this parody occurs on *In Living Color*, a variety show known for satirizing race, is not without due cause or, as Spock might say, logic. The world of *Star Trek* and its spin-offs—a trek that includes *The Animated Series* (1973–1975),[1] eight feature films to date, *The Next Generation* (1987–1994), *Deep Space Nine* (1992–present), *Voyager* (1994–present), hundreds of novels, and thousands of other commodities—is both implicitly and explicitly about the meaning of race: about integrated casts and crew; about anthropomorphic aliens and intergalactic half-breeds; about the discovery and exploration of extraterrestrial worlds and cultures; about space colonies, colonizers, and dissident movements; about a utopian Earth where there is no poverty, no crime, and, contrary to the claim of Damon Wayans's Farrakhan, no racial discrimination. Indeed, the science fiction series often addresses the meaning of race with telling self-consciousness: the original *Star Trek* dealt with bigotry between two oppositely colored extraterrestrials in "Let That Be Your Last Battlefield" (1969); *The Undiscovered Country* (1991), the sixth installment of cinematic Trek, narrativized the end of a cold war between the mostly white Federation and the distinctly dark Klingon Empire; in "Code of Honor" (1987), *The Next Generation* crew visited an all-black world with a tribal government; *Deep Space Nine* has an African-American captain in charge of a space station cramped with odd and exotic aliens and humans fighting to get along; *Voyager* casts a Chinese-American (Garrett Wang) as communications officer, a Mexican-American (Robert Beltran) as a Native-American dissident turned first officer, a Puerto Rican (Roxann Biggs-Dawson) as a half-Latina and half-Klingon chief engineer, and an African-American (Tim Russ) as a Vulcan security officer (figures 1 through 4). As these examples might suggest, and as this book aims to show, the imaginary time of Trek speaks to the real space-time of race relations.

This book traces the shifting meaning of race articulated throughout the Trek phenomenon, specifically the television series, feature films, and fan community. I address the following questions: What are the representational and narrative functions of race in Trek, a series highly regarded for its humanistic treatment of social issues? How is the meaning of race in the science fiction series facilitated or constrained by creative and network decision making, by genre, by intertextuality, and by the fans? What is the relationship between sociopolitical projects like the civil rights and neoconservative movements and the production

1. Garrett Wang as Communications Officer Harry Kim. © 1996
United Paramount Network

and meaning of Trek texts? How did the ongoing series negotiate these
turbulent histories? And, most significantly, why is it important for us
to understand better the articulation of race in this enduring icon of
United States popular culture?

In the first section of this chapter I set out a broad introduction to the
Trek phenomenon. My goal is to illustrate both the remarkable pliabil-
ity and the enduring popularity of the science fiction series. Trek, I try
to show, is more than the particularity or, for that matter, the sum of
its otherwise individual parts. I then offer a brief explanation of why a
systematic study of Trek can lead to a better understanding of the function of race in the science fiction series in particular and in United States
popular culture in general. In the second section of this chapter, I ask
the reader to bear with some necessary abstraction as I elaborate on
what I mean by "race." The theory I use here is based on Michael Omi
and Howard Winant's notion of "racial formation," which, in short,

2. Robert Beltran as First Officer Chakotay. © 1996 United
Paramount Network

sees race as a historically specific system of meanings that has a profound impact on social organization, political movements, cultural articulations, and individual identity. My goal is to lay out the notion of
race that informs this work and to suggest a useful approach to studying race in popular film and television.

The Expanding Trek Universe

Trek is an enduring icon in United States popular culture. For many
people, the science fiction series represents bold exploration of the unknown and humanistic respect of the foreign and the alien. In fact,
many fans—many Trekkers—claim that *Star Trek*'s vision of a utopian
future, where humans no longer engage in racism, sexism, capitalism,
and many other "isms," is a main reason for their loyalty. And, despite
the implication of William Shatner's statement on *Saturday Night Live*

3. Roxann Biggs-Dawson as Chief Engineer B'Elanna Torres.
© 1996 United Paramount Network

(20 December 1986) that they should "get a life," fan loyalty to Trek is informed by the realities of both technological innovation and socio-political experience. It was, for instance, the prodding of thousands of letter-writing fans that prompted then President Gerald Ford to name the first United States space shuttle after the *Enterprise*, the imaginary starship directed "to boldly go where no man has gone before." And fans' passion for Trek's multicultural future prompted Paramount, the Hollywood studio that owns and produces the science fiction series, to continue casting an increasingly diverse group of actors in *Deep Space Nine* and *Voyager*. Indeed, the fans are responsible for *Star Trek*'s (and for that matter, Shatner's) longevity. After all, the science fiction series has informed our imagination of the future for more than a quarter of a century.

4. Tim Russ as Security Officer Tuvok. © 1996 United Paramount
Network

Star Trek has mushroomed into a conglomerate of texts and intertext, becoming nothing less than a *mega-text*: a relatively coherent
and seemingly unending enterprise of televisual, filmic, auditory, and
written texts. In addition to the four prime-time series, the cartoon
series, and the eight films, there is a gushing current of comic books,
magazines, novels, compendia, biographies, and autobiographies. Even
scholars contribute to the mega-text, discussing the science fiction series in their courses and publishing articles, dissertations, and books on
its interpersonal and social significance. Probably the largest group of
producers of Trek texts are the fans, who write and distribute thousands of original stories, known as fanzines, and disperse hundreds of
thousands of comments and criticisms about the mega-text in cyberspace. There is even a group of linguistic-minded fans, including most

visibly the founders and members of the Klingon Language Institute, who are busily translating the Bible, Shakespeare, and other well-known documents into the "imaginary" Klingon language.[2]

Like the physical universe theorized by such cosmologists as Edwin Hubbell and Stephen Hawking, the mega-text is expanding into anything and everything. There are Trek action figures, beach towels, Christmas tree ornaments, coffee cups, models, pins, posters, screen savers, and computer games. There is a Trek MasterCard with a variable interest rate. Paramount is even working with Hilton to build a Trek theme park and casino in Las Vegas, Nevada, intended to attract the gambling-minded fan. The unabashed merchandising of the science fiction series has promoted one fan newsletter, edited by Jeffrey H. Mills, to include a column that lists the more disagreeable examples. Titled "The Ferengi Awards," after Trek aliens known for their garish taste in clothing and their abiding faith in "The Rules of Acquisition" (figure 5), the column recently singled out for special attention a framed 2″ by 4″ piece of the kilt worn by Scotty in "The Savage Curtain" (1969) mounted next to a picture of James Doohan, the actor who plays Scotty, cutting the garment into pieces. The entire package comes autographed, numbered, and accompanied by a certificate of authenticity—and costs only $125.00. "Want it personalized to a friend?" Mills warns, "That'll cost you $25 more!"[3] When it comes to the commoditization of the mega-text, one is immediately reminded of the Ferengi's 202nd rule of acquisition: "The justification for profit is profit."[4]

Despite the unrelenting merchandising of the mega-text, the stuff of Trek can go beyond a bottom-line exchange. Fans who write fanzines often distribute their contributions to the mega-text without a price or only for the cost of production. Most scholars who study Trek are more than willing to share their ideas, connections, and works-in-progress with other scholars—a less than common practice in the larger academic community. In fact, both fans and scholars have generously and rigorously read chapters of this book, providing useful comments and insightful suggestions on everything from the dates of episodes to the relationship between theory and criticism. Even on the information superhighway there are a number of toll-free vehicles: from MUDS (Multi-User Dungeons—a type of electronic role-playing game) to newsgroups, listservers, and home pages on the World Wide Web (WWW). The Ferengi would not approve of such a waste of potential profit.

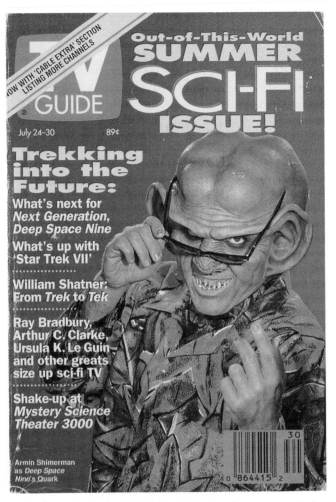

5. Quark on the cover of *TV Guide* beckoning the consumer to buy

The Trek mega-text is going where no television series has gone before. The world of Trek is *flow*, in Raymond Williams's sense of the
term: continuous yet segmented.[5] Williams argues that network television is analogous to electricity, a flow from shot to shot, scene to
scene, program to program, commercial to commercial. The viewer is
taken along the electromagnetic current of media programming toward
a potentially continuous and swelling stream of texts and intertexts.
One of the ways this programming flow is achieved is through the
soundtrack, for instance when the volume of a commercial is markedly

higher than the volume of its corresponding program. As Rick Altman shows, this strategy cues the viewer to remain attentive to the set—in other words, to stay tuned to the advertisements.[6] Analogous to Williams's theory of television, and making as much noise as the soundtrack, Trek is a flow: potentially endless programming for seemingly endless consumption.

Aside from toys and other such commodities, there are 79 episodes of the original series and 177 episodes of *The Next Generation* in syndication. There are six feature films with the original cast in cable, satellite, and television distribution, including *The Motion Picture* (1979), *The Wrath of Khan* (1982), *The Search for Spock* (1984), *The Voyage Home* (1986), *The Final Frontier* (1989), and *The Undiscovered Country*. *The Next Generation* was canceled at the height of its ratings and popularity after a seven-year run so that the cast, following in the footsteps of their successful though aging predecessors, could make feature films. The first two of these ventures, *Generations* (1994) and *First Contact* (1996), are also available in cable, satellite, and television distribution. With all this feature film flow, *Deep Space Nine*, now in its sixth season, and *Voyager*, now in its fourth, are keeping television Trek on the network airwaves—often twice a week. Not unlike Williams's theory of television programming, Trek is flowing from screen to screen, from market to market, saturating television sets and movie theaters with an endless current of Trekdom. If the science fiction series is to collapse in a Big Crunch, it won't be anytime soon.

Due to the technological and economic structure of television (networks, advertising, etc.), Williams also theorizes that television reception is dispersed and simultaneous. For Williams, this makes it a powerful and far-reaching medium. While television reception is no longer simultaneous per se—many shows can now be seen in different time slots, at different and sometimes multiple times each week—it is still widely dispersed, reaching deep into national and international markets. As I noted above, *Star Trek*, *The Next Generation*, *Deep Space Nine*, and *Voyager* are beamed into almost every home in the United States. Most video stores offer for rent and sale video copies of feature Trek; many of these stores also rent and sell episodes from the first three prime-time series. The cartoon series is available for rent and purchase at various specialty shops and bookstores. Finally, VCRs, laser-disk players, and, if all goes according to industry plans, digital video disks (DVD) allow fans to review Trek texts at their leisure. It is relatively easy for consumers of the mega-text to watch and re-watch their favorite episodes.

The Trek universe is even distributed across the planet, giving the mega-text an international flow. The science fiction series is beamed into numerous countries, from Japan, where it earns fairly high ratings, to Brazil, where the fan community is becoming nationally organized. One of Trek's most fertile international markets is the United Kingdom, where, like *Doctor Who* (1978–present), it earns high ratings and its fan conferences are generally well attended. Much to the chagrin of the French, the Ferengi are known even in Paris. As postmodern as it might sound, these and many other countries are being treated to the ways in which Trek and, by extension, United States television imagines a utopian Earth in the midst of a diverse but dangerous galaxy.

Though offering an imaginary time dominated by a United Federation of Planets that commands a fleet of starships that can travel faster than the speed of light, Trek flow draws upon and engages real space-time politics and experiences. The original series was one of the first television programs to use an integrated cast; every spinoff since has also represented a multicultural future. As I mentioned earlier, the original series was also one of the first programs to engage explicitly the politics of racial discrimination; every spinoff has also dealt with bigotry and prejudice. Even the fans read race into and out of Trek, exchanging opinions and engaging in debates about everything from casting to whether or not fictional aliens are metaphors for real space-time nations and peoples. In short, Trek has been willing to take a position on many of the racial practices and experiences that inform contemporary society. Because this willingness spans thirty years of conflict over the meaning of race—from the civil rights movement of the 1960s to the neoconservative movement of the 1980s and early 1990s—the mega-text becomes a valuable site for studying the ways race is produced, performed, and perpetuated in United States popular culture.

Aside from Trek's durability and its willingness to engage the politics of race, the fact that it is science fiction also makes it a telling site for investigating the meaning of race in popular culture. Science fiction offers representations of peculiar aliens, different worlds, wondrous technology, futuristic times, imaginary spaces, and other odd and fantastic tropes. Yet science fiction film and television, as artifacts of culture and products of the Hollywood system, are based on real-world signifiers and myths. Whether metaphorical or allegorical, a myth or an amalgamation of signifiers, the genre and its tropes are necessarily grounded in the real space-time in which we live. As Fredric Jameson argues, science fiction tends less to imagine the future than to "defamiliarize and restructure our experience of our own present."[7] Aliens, for example, can be said to be always already real world peoples—signifiers of nations, cultures, and identities—simply because there are no real space-time referents for living and embodied extraterrestrials.[8] In Trek texts, articulations of race in this regard can be as straightforward as darkening up an alien species in order to make them seem more ominous and threatening. Many evil aliens in Trek are dark. It can also involve whitening an alien race so that they might appear benevolent or godlike. Almost all divine creatures in Trek are white. Science fiction's regime of verisimilitude, its unique spin on the codes of Hollywood realism, draws upon and engages sociopolitical history in order to construct a frightening or an ideal future. What this future looks like vis-à-vis race—the historicity of race—is addressed in subsequent chapters.

The Meaning of Race

Before I address the historicity of race in the Trek mega-text, I want to elaborate on what I mean by "race"—a term that is as cryptic and volatile as it is familiar and unifying. Despite common perceptions, race is not black and white. In laying out what amounts to a theory of race, I hope to draw out and to question the somewhat cumbersome baggage associated with academic writings on the subject as well as to reaffirm the need for scholars, particularly those in the humanities, to forge ahead despite the pitfalls and hazards. Though studies of race in general and of whiteness in particular can earn the author accusations of everything from perpetuating essentialisms to engaging in reverse discrimination, the impact of racist practice and the myth of white superiority on the production, distribution, and reception of cultural works like *Star Trek* and its spinoffs requires both rigorous and self-conscious scholarly attention. To do otherwise is to ignore one of the most ubiquitous and insidious elements of United States culture and history.

This is easier said than done. It is not easy to write about race from within—or, for that matter, outside—the walls of academia, whether one is referring to a category of people, discussing a series of representations, or deconstructing the term. The concept is highly charged in our institutions of higher learning, not only because of the turbulent sociopolitical realities that contextualize our colleges and universities, but also because of the tendency of scholarly work to claim objectivity while masking political and, in some cases, ludicrous assumptions and arguments. Scholarship on race is often reductive and essentialist, especially when it contends that an otherwise heterogeneous group of people have a common biological root or that they share some universal characteristics like temperament or physical ability. This is especially the case with *The Bell Curve* (to name a recent example), which links inheritance, and thus biology, with socioeconomic formations.[9] Moreover, writings on race are often relativistic, especially those that define it as a mere illusion or a fiction we can all overcome. While pointing to the ideology of this term of classification, the notion of race as an illusion or fiction tends to displace and ignore real people's real experiences and identities. Finally, academic work on race is often simplistic, especially those purely polemical writings that fail to go beyond critiques of stereotypes and stories as "racist." It's not enough for scholars to say that a representation or story is racist, because doing so says little about representation, storytelling, race, or the relationship between these practices. Like the Trek mega-text, race is more than the sum of its practices.

Part of the problem is the definition of race, a term that is difficult to pin down because of its multiple and highly charged meanings. Unlike "gender," where the referent in the English language is polar (male/female), "race" is a more slippery term.[10] For some, it refers to a taxonomy of people, a subdivision or subspecies, who share a common gene pool, a physiognomic look, or an innate morality or intellectual capacity. This is often the biological and sociobiological definition. For others, the term refers to a sociopolitical category of people who share a historical relationship to institutional power: from in-groups, or the privileged (whites), to out-groups, or the excluded (nonwhites). This is often the sociological definition of race. The term can also refer to a culture, a category of expressions, behaviors, and a language/vernacular unique to a region, nation, or continent. This is partly the case with Ebonics, which stirred national controversy in 1996 when an Oakland, California school district announced it would make the African-American vernacular part of its curriculum. Similarly, "race" is often used to denote an identity, a sense of self-awareness, such as Puerto Rican or "Spanish." Race as culture and as identity is generally the cultural studies position. All these broad definitions—biological, sociological, and cultural—implicitly inform each other in different and complex ways, making it even more difficult to determine exactly what the term means.

So what do I mean by "race"? In the context of this study, the term does not refer to a natural or objective taxonomy of people that includes, say, caucasoids, mongoloids, and negroids. I agree with Henry Louis Gates Jr., who writes: "Race, in these usages pretends to be an objective term of classification, when in fact it is a dangerous trope."[11] From religious dogma before the Enlightenment to the eugenics movement at the turn of the century, from the infamous Jensen report of the late 1960s to *The Bell Curve* of the mid-1990s, race as a natural or biological category has done more to support and encourage discriminatory and exploitative divisions of humans than it has to further our understanding of nature, biology, or social formation.[12] In what amounts to notions of innate and thus a priori difference and behavior, race in such usages often becomes a rationalization for the production and maintenance of white power and privilege—or racism. More specifically, my rejection of a biological definition stems from what seems to be the suspicious subjectivity of classifying and interpreting genetic data and the subsequent relevance of that data to our understanding of social organization, culture, political projects—to history. On the one hand, most studies of genetic variance among human populations have proven as subjective as studies of skin color and cranial capacity did in the early twentieth century. Ultimately these studies seem more interested in critiquing and supporting sociopolitical problems and policies than in understanding the complexities of genetic difference and its relationship to human experience. On the other hand, sorting people into biological categories seems ultimately arbitrary, since no study has been able to predict how genes will affect behavior outside the realm of history. In fact, many contemporary scholars of genetics conclude that if there are biological races, then there are more than three, and the only way to categorize them is to synthesize data from genetics, linguistics, and archaeology. As evolutionary biologist Luigi Luca Cavalli-Sforza writes: "Recent classifications point to anywhere from three to sixty 'races.' We could count many more if we wanted, but there doesn't seem to be much purpose. Every classification is equally arbitrary." For this reason, Cavalli-Sforza argues that "It is hard, if not impossible, to classify race."[13]

Nor is race a mere illusion, a figment of our collective but false imagination, as many postmodern and poststructural scholars have argued. While studies characterizing the concept in this way acknowledge the ideology of the term, they often fail, like the genetic definition, to recognize that race is a significant material and experiential phenomenon. In other words, "race" as a term of distinction is more than a function of reductive and ideologically laden proscriptions or, for that matter, language. Whether or not there are true biological subspecies, there are historical races: groups of people who share lived experiences ranging from discrimination and privilege to cultural traditions and ways of expression. Race is real—material and experiential—because the meaning of race has consistently had a concrete impact on real people's real lives.[14]

"Race" partly refers to culture, in the sense that the realm of images, tastes, stories, and myths is one of the primary areas in which the meaning of race is produced and perpetuated. Culture clearly informs the significance of race. Yet the term is not simply a synonym for culture, because culture does not adequately describe or explain the sociopolitical or individual force of race. "Race" also refers to identity because people see themselves and express themselves in racial terms: "I" am white; "I" am not white. But the term is not a synonym for identity either, because, like culture, identity does not adequately account for the sociopolitical dimensions of race. Though informing and informed by culture and identity, race is at one level more fundamental and at another more expansive than these other realms of humanity.

In this book, "race" refers to a multifaceted, omnipresent but utterly historical category of meanings: meanings informed by and informing social organization, political struggle, economic viability, cultural traditions, and identity. Rather than referring to an essence or an illusion, or simply a culture or identity, the term "race" names a historical process informed and determined by multiple and interdependent factors. This historically specific process is perhaps best characterized by Omi and Winant as a *racial formation*: "We should think of race as an element of social structure rather than as an irregularity within it," they write, "we should see race as a dimension of human representation rather than an illusion." [15] Race, then, is a system of meanings that shift and change with time and space, with social organization, political movements, cultural tradition, and identity.

Omi and Winant's theory is against subsuming race under the umbrella of ethnicity, class, or nation. For the sociologists, academic paradigms that reduce race to these other phenomena fail "to grasp the uniqueness of race, its historical flexibility and immediacy in everyday experience and social conflict." [16] While a thorough examination of their argument on this point is beyond the scope of this chapter, it suffices to say that the racial formation in the United States crosses class distinctions, supersedes ethnic divisions, and incorporates and moves beyond nationality. As the sociologists note: "From the very inception of the Republic to the present moment, race has been a profound determinant of one's political rights, one's location in the labor market, and indeed one's sense of 'identity.'" [17]

The notion of a racial formation is useful to our understanding of race as a term and as a phenomenon, mainly because it recognizes both the illusion and the subsequent power of race as a biological category, and its significance as a particular sociopolitical process. Simply put, race signifies the historical insistence and subsequent conflict over divisions of real people into biological, sociological, and cultural types. Because of—or despite—its fictitious grounding in nature, it is very real. Moreover, it is a term of distinction that recognizes both the history of discrimination and the history of resistance and struggle. The meaning and function of race has always been challenged and resisted. When we ground the term in social conflict and history, race becomes a more holistic—or less reductive, relativistic, or fatalistic—description of the process by which "racial categories are created, inhabited, transformed, and destroyed." [18]

Omi and Winant's work draws upon the neo-Marxist theories of Antonio Gramsci, particularly his notion of hegemony as it relates to complexities of state activity, the machinations of coercion/consent, and the politics of common sense.[19] Together these concepts form a theory of history specific to formations of power that account for the ways in which ideology functions to both maintain and challenge systems of dominance. It is perhaps useful to lay out in brief Gramsci's abstract notion of hegemony and how it relates to the specificity of race in order to understand better some of the nuances of the racial formation approach. In this regard, the work of Stuart Hall is particularly useful, as he has applied Gramsci's work to the specificity of culture (as opposed to the state, which Omi and Winant concentrate on). Both state activity and cultural practices are primary reasons for the continued prominence of the ubiquitous racial formation in United States history.

Hegemony is best understood as a process, an activity, that moves a group or groups toward the state of total dominance, a highly uncommon historical moment in which a ruling group achieves complete and total power over subordinate groups. As Hall explains: " 'hegemony' is a very particular, historically specific, and temporary "moment" in the life of a society. It is rare for this degree of unity to be achieved, enabling a society to set itself a quite new historical agenda, under the leadership of a specific formation or constellation of social forces."[20] In a state of hegemony, one group achieves top-down dominance over another. Hegemonic activity, then, is the process by which groups at the center of state power and privilege try to solidify and expand their status at the expense of groups at the periphery. As Hall, quoting Gramsci, advises: "what we are looking for is *not* the absolute victory of this side over that, nor the total incorporation of one set of forces into another. Rather, the analysis is a relational matter—i.e., a question to be resolved *rationally*, using the idea of 'unstable balance' or 'the continuous process of formation and superseding of unstable equilibria.'"[21] The state of hegemony, of total dominance, is rarely achieved, because groups at the periphery are constantly vying for inclusion and attempting subversion of the groups at the center, which are resisting and appeasing. The process depends on struggle—both conservative, where power is maintained or expanded, and subversive, where power is challenged and destabilized. For Gramsci and the racial formation approach, this ubiquitous but unstable balance of power relations is the key to the ways in which "advanced" societies perpetuate economic, ideological, and sociopolitical systems of dominance and exploitation.

In order to maintain privilege, and thus avoid messy things like revolutions where the elite can lose all power, hegemonic activity, the preferred strategy in advanced capitalist countries like the United States and the western European nations, relies on an ideology of coercion and consent (as opposed to physical repression and outright force). At times, groups at the margins of power are coerced into accepting their status as natural or inevitable. At other times, peripheral groups are appeased, allowed somewhat closer to the center, as their struggle intensifies and begins to threaten the power of the center. This process is not necessarily passive, with peripheral groups blindly or unconsciously buying into their status. Quite the contrary—consent is generally active and frequently conscious. For example, the pursuit of privilege—toward economic and racial elitism, for instance—is all too often seen as being in one's best interest. Subordinate groups attempt to grab a piece of the pie, to access the higher ends of privilege, rather than baking their own cake or rejecting the center/periphery way of life. Gramsci, ever concerned with the philosophy and social function of religion, sums up the concept: "One can say of coercion what the religious say of predestination: For the 'willing' it is not predestination, but free will."[22]

Coercion and consent result in the common-sense acceptance of a historical moment as natural or in the best interest of all groups involved. For Gramsci, common sense is the linkage of ideas and conceptual categories that make up the consciousness of both center and peripheral groups. Moreover, it is in this domain that the struggle over the state of hegemony occurs. As Hall explains, it is the terrain "on which more coherent ideologies and philosophies must contend for mastery; the ground which new conceptions of the world must take into account, contest and transform, if they are to shape the conceptions of the world of the masses and in that way become historically effective."[23] Thus, common sense is both the site in which coercion and consent penetrate consciousness—indeed, our very identity—and the site in which individuals and groups come to reject and subsequently subvert the power and oppression of a historical moment.

Omi and Winant recognize that Gramsci's model can be used effectively to describe and explain the specificity of United States race relations. First, they see hegemonic activity occurring in all areas of society, not just the economic. Hall agrees with this reading: "This reproduction (hegemonic ideology) is not simply economic, but social, technical, and, above all, ideological."[24] Moreover, Omi and Winant see ideologies of coercion and consent as fracturing groups along multiple lines, such as between whites and nonwhites, and not just via class. Again, Hall seems to agree: "It (racism) translates classes into 'blacks' and 'whites,' economic groups into 'peoples,' solid forces into 'races.'"[25] Finally, Omi and Winant recognize Gramsci's move from a traditional Marxist account of false consciousness, a distortion or ignorance of contradiction and alienation, to a more expansive and yet specific understanding of common sense, a less determinist and fatalistic description of the relationship between ideology and consciousness. Common sense, then, is the terrain where hegemonic activity earns its power and where it ultimately must be challenged. "Race," Omi and Winant write, "becomes 'common-sense'—a way of comprehending, explaining, and acting in the world."[26]

Grounding their work on Gramsci's theoretical project enables Omi and Winant to make the compelling argument that the United States racial formation has been supported by the state and the mass media, and contested by social and cultural movements; and that the trajectory of the racial formation has shifted due to coercion, consent, and resistance. In this way, race becomes a pervasive but ultimately unsteady complex of meanings constantly being transformed by struggle. The racial formation is, above all else, an "unstable equilibrium" susceptible to contestation and rearticulation. Thus, the Gramscian model enables Omi and Winant to offer a path to subverting the racial order, as the struggle over the meaning of race is initiated when the common-sense acceptance of the racial formation is subverted; when, in other words, it becomes common sense—in one's moral and material interest, for example—to disrupt the center.

The meaning of race shifts and reforms under the influence of *projects*, social and political groups and organizations that attempt to disrupt or redirect the ways institutions, social structures, and cultural forms are racially organized. Racial projects seek either to enforce or to rearticulate the meaning of race common to a historical moment. Omi and Winant provide a concise summation: "A racial project is simultaneously an interpretation, representation, or explanation of racial dynamics, and an effort to reorganize and redistribute resources along particular racial lines."[27] There are two major types of racial projects. First, there are projects that function at the macro-level of society, such as those organized on traditionally political grounds. This might include what is commonly referred to as the Left and the Right, liberals and conservatives, Democrats and Republicans. Second, there are projects that take place at the micro-level of everyday experience and individual action. This might include people and groups that engage in racist activity, such as the Ku Klux Klan (KKK), and those that work against such discrimination, such as the Rainbow Coalition. Finally, Omi and Winant stress that these projects draw upon, respond to, and are in some ways extensions of past projects. The KKK, for instance, has given rise to a number of splinter groups, including most recently the militia movement in Montana and other states. For that matter, the Rainbow Collation came from such earlier efforts as the NAACP, the Urban League, and the civil rights efforts of Dr. Martin Luther King Jr.

Two examples of racial projects that are of central concern later in this book are the civil rights movement of the 1960s and the neoconservative movement of the 1980s and early 1990s, moments in which Trek was created, distributed, recreated, and popularized. This would include, for example, the black power, antiwar, feminist, gay, and environmental projects for the civil rights movement; Christian fundamentalism, the new right, and conservative Republican projects for the neoconservative movement. These groups challenged the racial order of things common to their historical moment: de jure segregation and discrimination during the civil rights movement; welfare liberalism and so-called traditional values during the neoconservative movement. These challenges to the racial order of things have had substantial impact on the meaning of race and on the trajectory of the racial formation—and thus on sociocultural life. As I show in chapters 2 and 4, they also had an impact on the articulation of race in the *Star Trek* of the 1960s and *The Next Generation* of the 1980s.

Like state activity, culture plays a determining role in the hegemonic trajectory—the historical significance—of race. Culture is a dominant or dominating site in which the racial formation is both supported and contested, making it the state's number one bedfellow. As such, the symbols, metaphors, expressions, key words, and narratives—indeed, the texts—that make up culture are important sites of analysis for the production and perpetuation of racial projects. As Omi and Winant acknowledge, "From a racial formation perspective, race is a matter of both social structure and cultural representation."[28] Popular culture is the terrain on which the meaning of race most forcefully penetrates common sense. This is especially the case with television, as more than 95 percent of United States homes have one or more sets. Though not completely deterministic, television nevertheless has access to our public mythologies, consciousness, and identity. This is also the case with cinema, as moviegoing has been one of the most popular forms of entertainment since the turn of the century. Simply put: Hollywood, the industry responsible for most popular television and film texts, reaches deep into the collective consciousness of most citizens, and throughout the world. In today's world of news programs ranging from *Nightline*

(1980–present) to *Hard Copy* (1989–present) and films such as *JFK* (1991) and *Malcolm X* (1992), even the state and its politics and policies are interpreted and "clarified" by television and feature films.

I bring up the examples of television and film not only because they have attained a profound level of saturation in Unites States society, but because they consistently perpetuate degrading images and narratives of people positioned and marked as nonwhite while constructing whiteness as the unquestioned ideal we should all naturally and faithfully strive to attain. As I argued in my anthology on early cinema and hope to demonstrate further in this book,[29] Hollywood consistently constructs whiteness as the norm in comparison to which all "Others" necessarily fail. In what amounts to a paradox of assimilation, white film and television tries to be expansive and incorporate Others—to whitewash for our best interest—but ends up ultimately pushing those very Others aside because of a presumed innate difference. How do you assimilate a group of people who are biologically Other? And, when Hollywood television and film isn't telling the story of assimilation, it falls back on constructing people of color as deviant threats therefore in need of punishment or civilizing, or as fetishized objects, and thus no less objects and obstacles. Hollywood film and television is, in a word, racist.

Yet, racist film and television is not in a complete or total state of hegemony. Like the racial formation they help support and facilitate, racist media are contested and subverted. As Herman Gray explains, "television's logic of indifference—normalization, commodification, and absorption—is not always uniform or effective."[30] Though relatively few in number, there are texts that challenge the white rule and attempt to subvert the existing color line. The first few episodes of *Voyager*, for instance, suggested a shift from white-dominated science fiction programming to a multiracial cast complete with a female Captain (Kate Mulgrew) who literally takes charge of both the narrative and the supporting characters. Perhaps this series will be one of those rare challenges popular culture offers up to today's racial order of things. Though informing our common sense, racist film and television is in an "unstable equilibrium." Struggles on the terrain of culture can and do change the trajectory of the racial formation.

In sum, "race" refers to a racial formation, a system of historically specific meanings that have a profound impact on the institutions and systems of representation informing sociocultural life. In contemporary

U.S. race relations, the state and cultural power brokers like Hollywood's rely on a hegemonic strategy of coercion and consent to support a center of white power and a periphery of colored exclusion and degradation. The object of hegemonic activity is to coerce subjects, both those who pass as white and those who do not, into accepting the center/periphery way of life. Yet while race becomes common sense, common sense is not fixed or impenetrable. Racial projects rely on the malleable and unstable "nature" of common sense and the racial formation in attempting to impact—to alter and disrupt—the meaning of race dominant in any historical moment. These projects can be conservative, and thus protective of the status of white superiority, or emancipatory, and thus struggling against the common-sense order of things.

To Boldly Go . . .

There are two overarching objectives to this book. First, I want to addresses the particular ways race is articulated in Trek, or the ways in which the science fiction series is racial. Bringing critical studies concepts to the cultural studies approach, I emphasize five aspects of the mega-text: (1) authorship, or the actions of the key decision makers involved in creating and distributing the series; (2) the diegesis, or the imaginary world of the story; (3) chronotopes, or space-time articulations that are warped by history; (4) intertextuality, or the web of other texts and discourse that keep the mega-text in constant semiotic play; and (5) reading positions, or the interpretation and rearticulation of Trek by actual fans of the series. The second goal of the book is to take a clear and defensible position on the articulation of race in Trek, criticizing and politicizing the different ways in which the mega-text is racial. In doing so, I employ a historiographic approach that seeks to balance critical interpretations with an analysis of the real space-time in which we live. While I strive to be both fair and honest, my criticisms and arguments are less about the true meaning of Trek, if there is such a thing, than about the patterns, trends, and relationships—the textual characteristics and sociopolitical projects—that inform and facilitate the mega-text's significance. By synthesizing critical and cultural studies, I hope to both foreground my methodological assumptions and show how existing approaches to film and television studies, perhaps with only minor tweaking and synthesis, can be effective tools in criticizing, deconstructing, or defamiliarizing the meaning of race in popular United States film and television.

Each chapter addresses both objectives. Chapter 2, "The Original *Star Trek*: Liberal-Humanist Projects and Diegetic Logics," investigates the relationship between the racial project of key decision makers, from producers to writers, and the racial project-in-the-text, or the representation and narrativization of race in various episodes. To reveal the project-in-the-text I focus on several *diegetic logics*, or the political alliances and quasi-scientific theories that make *Star Trek* intelligible and political, including: (1) the United Federation of Planets, an intergalactic government dominated by Earth; (2) the notion of "parallel development," Trek's explanation for why so many alien societies resemble human societies; and (3) the anthropomorphic alien, the individual extraterrestrials that interact with the dominantly human *Enterprise* crew. Relying on the work of cultural studies scholars Tony Bennett and Janet Woollacott, and being careful to avoid the intentional fallacy that assumes a direct correlation between "occupational ideologies" and signification, I argue that the project of key decision makers and the project-in-the-text share a *liberal-humanistic discourse* particular to the 1960s that, while espousing integration and racial equality, is fundamentally and pervasively contradictory.

Chapter 3, "Trek on the Silver Screen: White Future-Time as the Final Frontier," looks at what literary theorist Mikhail Bakhtin calls *chronotopes*, or the fusion of space, time, and history, in the first eight Trek films. To uncover the relationship between feature Trek and history, I focus on the master chronotope of future-time, the space-time most endemic to science fiction cinema, as well as six minor chronotopes: (1) starships like the U.S.S. *Enterprise* and the Klingon Battle Cruiser; (2) alien worlds as different as the Klingons and as human as Khan and his followers; (3) outer space, the royal road to a humanocentric universe; and (4) home, or the space-time of the present world represented in the future-time of the fictional world. I argue that feature Trek perpetuates the longstanding myth of the natural and humane right of white rule and occupation into and beyond the final frontier. In what amounts to a *white future-time*, these films participate in longstanding myths fundamental to the persuasiveness of white common sense in United States culture and history.

Chapter 4, "*The Next Generation*: Toward a Neoconservative Play," analyzes the first prime-time spinoff of the science fiction mega-text, focusing on how it assimilates the ideologies of the 1980s and early 1990s that contextualized its production and initial reception. Relying on the notion of *intertextuality*, or the web of texts and discourse that make up "a" text, specifically as the concept is outlined by semioticians such as Julia Kristeva, Roland Barthes, and Umberto Eco, I argue that the meaning of race articulated in this series is framed by a *neoconservative project*, specifically in relation to such venerable intertexts as: (1) history, or the representation of the past and present; (2) evolution, including genetics, species, and origin intertexts; (3) miscegenation, be it alien to human or white-human to human of color; and (4) assimilation, or the attempt to create a galactic melting pot. The first prime-time Trek spinoff is less cutting-edge when it comes to race than was its televisual predecessor of the late 1960s, even considering the latter's contradictory liberal humanism.

Chapter 5, "Reading Race: Trekking through Cyberspace on STREK-L," investigates the degree to which fans *read and write* race into and out of Trek. Drawing on recent approaches to audience studies by television scholars such as David Morley and Henry Jenkins, this chapter focuses on the writings and debates among fans on a particularly active cyberspace listserver, STREK-L. The categories fans seem most concerned with in this regard include: (1) casting, specifically the employment and symbolic currency of actors of color; (2) geopolitics, or the ways Trek can and cannot shed light on United States foreign policy and vice versa; and (3) alien "races," or the extent to which aliens like the Borg, Cardassians, Klingons, and Ferengi represent real-world peoples and cultures. I argue that fan readings of race on STREK-L suggest an *ambivalent consciousness*, one that simultaneously participates in the mega-text's racism, excuses it, ignores it, and condemns it as "anti-Trek."

I do not look in great detail at the textual practices of *Deep Space Nine* or *Voyager*, except in relation to fan readings analyzed in chapter 5. This is not because race is not a relevant articulation in these programs. On the contrary, each is squarely in the Trek tradition of implicitly and explicitly tackling the meaning of race, specifically in the area of casting and narration. The captain of *Deep Space Nine*, for instance, is played by an African-American actor (Avery Brooks), and many of the stories address his single-parent relationship with his son (Cirroc Lofton). Moreover, the cast of *Voyager* is perhaps the most multicultural group on prime-time television, and is constantly dealing with the problem of difference. Rather, I have chosen not to deal in depth with the texts of these programs, opting to leave them for later work, because such an analysis is not central to my overall thesis about the shifting meaning of race from the 1960s to the early 1990s. Both programs started in the mid-1990s, and thus in a historical moment not fully within the purview of this book. They are also still in the process of finding their racial voice.

As a whole, I try to reveal both the diverse ways in which race is articulated in Trek and the ways in which the question of race can be addressed in critical and cultural studies. I try to handle the rather complex relationship between Trek texts, the historical context, and my critical-cultural approach somewhat like Hawking handles the history and evolution of particles in the universe. Assuming an "uncertainty principle" that suggests I cannot come to a single truth, I "add up" the articulations of race in the imaginary time of Trek in order to "extrapolate the result back to the real space-time in which we live."[31] Conversely, I try to "add up" the histories of the real space-time in order to understand the meaning and significance of the mega-text. What I hope to attain is a balance between these two relationships—text to history; history to text.

2 The Original *Star Trek*

Liberal-Humanist Projects and Diegetic Logics

The approach expresses the "message" basic to the series: We must learn to live together or most certainly we will soon all die together. Although *Star Trek* had to entertain or go off the air, we believed our format was unique enough to allow us to challenge and stimulate the audience. Making *Star Trek* happen was a bonecrusher, and unless it also "said something" and we challenged our viewers to think and react, then it wasn't worth all we had put into the show.
—*Gene Roddenberry*

Spock: Superior ability breeds superior ambition.

In "Let That Be Your Last Battlefield," the U.S.S. *Enterprise* is on an urgent rescue mission when it comes across a stolen shuttlecraft and its thief, a humanoid named Lokai who is half white and half black (Lou Antonio). "Judging by looking at him," Captain Kirk says, "we know at the very least he is the result of a very dramatic conflict." Soon after the crew encounters the odd-looking alien, another humanoid who is half black and half white, Bele (Frank Gorshin), boards the starship. Claiming to be the Chief Officer for the Commission of Political Traitors from a planet named Cheron, Bele demands that the *Enterprise* take him and his "political prisoner," Lokai, back to their world. Lokai, on the other hand, claims that he and his kind have been persecuted by Bele and his kind, and demands asylum. The difference between these two bicolored humanoids, and the cause of their conflict, is that they are oppositely colored: Lokai is white on the right side and black on the left side; Bele is black on the right side and white on the left side (figure 6).

The black and white makeup applied to the guest stars in this episode of *Star Trek* is a clear reference to the racial conflict and struggles that dominated life in the 1960s. During the production and initial reception of *Star Trek*, the civil rights and antiwar movements accelerated

6. Lokai and Bele

the fight against a separate and inherently unequal reality in the hopes of achieving a more egalitarian ideal. Network television, especially the nightly news programs, participated in this struggle, as images and stories of civil rights and antiwar demonstrations—of marches, sit-ins, firehoses, attack dogs, riots, and rebellions—flowed into the homes of millions of viewers. These images and stories forced the vast television audience to confront a persistent, at times violent challenge to the existing color line. In an explicit way, "Let That Be Your Last Battlefield" draws upon and engages this real space-time conflict.

Along with the makeup, the dialogue in "Let That Be Your Last Battlefield" correlates Lokai and Bele's struggle over their physiognomic duality with the real space-time conflict over the meaning of race. In one scene, for example, Chekov (Walter Koenig) remarks: "There was persecution on Earth once. I remember reading about it in my history class." Sulu (George Takei) follows: "Yes, but it happened way back in the twentieth century. There's no such primitive thinking today." In another scene, Kirk informs Bele that the Federation will not extradite Lokai on the grounds of "due process," a Fourteenth Amendment clause used by the Supreme Court in such cases as *Bouie v. Columbia* (1964) and *NAACP v. Alabama* (1964) to help dismantle de jure segregation. Along with the black and white makeup, these references to "due process" and the "primitive" racism of Earth's past, or the real space-time for the makers of the series, clearly indicates an intent behind the production of "Let That Be Your Last Battlefield" to link the imaginary universe of the science fiction series to the racial politics and social movements of the 1960s.

Editing, optical effects, and graphic images of burning buildings add a powerful didacticism to "Let That Be Your Last Battlefield," as the episode systematically associates racial conflict with genocide. The ending of the story has the *Enterprise* arriving at Cheron. Sensor readings of the planet indicate that all humanoid life forms are dead; the inhabitants have killed each other over their bicolored duality. Knowledge of this mass genocide sends Lokai and Bele into a rage. They first attempt to kill each other. Then, after Kirk dramatically pleads for peace, they frantically flee the bridge in search of a way to return to their dead world. Intercut shots of Lokai and Bele each running through the starship's corridors accentuate their eternal struggle. Apocalyptic images of burning buildings, which might very well have come from actual television news footage of the race riots and rebellions in cities like Los Angeles, Detroit, and Chicago, are superimposed over these shots (figure 7), functioning as didactic reminders of the real space-time consequences of racial hatred. The rhetoric of the superimposition seems clear: "We must learn to live together or most certainly we will soon all die together."[1]

I have lingered on "Let That Be Your Last Battlefield" because it reveals many of the ways in which the science fiction series imagines racial difference and conflict. First, it utilizes both the signifier of aliens, in this case bicolored humanoids, and a straightforward allegory of intraspecies conflict to negotiate contemporaneous racial politics and experiences. In fact, *Star Trek* rarely depicts racism among humans, preferring to project it as a problem within an alien culture or between two alien worlds. Nonetheless, the projection is always rooted in the real space-time meaning of race, particularly since aliens are almost always referred to as "races," and inter- and intra-alien bigotry as "racism." Second, the allegory of racial struggle suggests a liberal-humanist intent, especially in the line of dialogue stating that Earth has overcome its "primitive" past. As noted in chapter 1, in the imaginary future of *Star Trek* the people of Earth have united across class, gender, national, and racial lines—the purported goal of liberal humanism. Finally, the

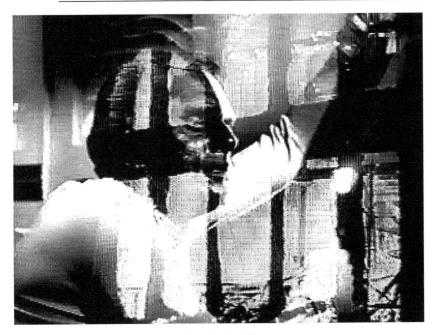

7. Bele's image superimposed over burning buildings

use of stylistic techniques such as cross-cutting and superimposition are overdetermined in their didacticism about the horrific results of racial hatred.

How did the choices made by writers, producers, and executives, or the decision makers involved in the production of *Star Trek*, facilitate or delimit the textualization of race in the science fiction series? In what ways was racial ideology reconfigured in the process from production, or the making of the series, to textualization, or the signification of race in the broadcast texts? How is the *Star Trek* universe organized? In what ways does this organization draw upon and engage the meaning of race that dominated the 1960s?

In addressing these questions, the first half of this chapter focuses on the conditions of production specific to the beliefs, goals, and practices of key decision makers, including network executives, producers, writers, and stars. The articulation of race here has less to do with the actual broadcast texts than it does with the institutional and individual practices—the "real agency," as Raymond Williams might call it[2]—that informed the making of the series. Focusing on scripts, memoranda, and related extant documents, I show how these decision makers were consciously involved in a didactic project to engage the experiences and politics of the 1960s: I argue that this project was inconsistent and contradictory—often participating in and facilitating racist practice in its attempt to imagine what Gene Roddenberry called "infinite diversity in infinite combinations."

The second half of this chapter analyzes the project-in-the-text, or the representational and narrative forms of race—the signs and stories of race—in the broadcast texts. Relying on close textual analysis, I identify the *diegetic logics* that give cohesion and intelligibility to the science fiction universe. These include the United Federation of Planets, an intergalactic government dominated by Earth; the notion of "parallel development," Trek's explanation for why so many alien societies resemble human societies; and the anthropomorphic alien itself, the individual extraterrestrials that interact with the Enterprise crew. In focusing on the ways in which the *Star Trek* diegesis is organized, I show how the racial project-in-the-text is both as didactic and as contradictory as was the project of the key decision makers.

In analyzing both the project of key decision makers and the project-in-the-text, I am not suggesting that network and creative decision makers simply pour their ideology into a *Star Trek* container from which a passive audience then guzzles indiscriminately. In my view, the relationship between the intent to imbed ideology *in* a text and the ideology *of* a text is never direct or without contradiction. Moreover, audiences are anything but passive consumers, as I show in chapter 5. Nonetheless, I also recognize that entertainment institutions and decision makers, network executives and craftspeople, do imbed and attempt to fix meaning. And this agency—the act of writing, directing, performing, and network gatekeeping—has a significant impact on the broadcast texts themselves. As Tony Bennett and Janet Woollacott point out, "the deliberations, calculations, and policies which actually inform the making of a film (or TV series) have a direct and discernible bearing on the processes through which ideologies are worked over and transformed into a specific filmic form."[3] For instance, if, as NBC initially requested, the crew of the *Enterprise* had not included Uhura (Nichelle Nichols), Sulu, or Spock (Leonard Nimoy), then the show would not have conveyed the spirit of a multicultural future for which it is now famous. Indeed, it might have gone the direction of *Lost in Space* (1965–1968; figure 8). In their attempt to affect signification and

8. Cast of *Lost in Space*

fix meaning, television authors both limit and enable reading possibilities; they facilitate and set boundaries to meaning-production.

What the contradictory projects of key decision makers and the project-in-the-text have in common is a *liberal-humanist discourse*, the zeitgeist of the 1960s, that directly and often explicitly informs the strategies of both projects. A value and belief system that espouses political equality and social egalitarianism, liberal humanism emphasizes individual worth and freedom, racial and gender equality, and the importance of secular human values. It suggests that humans, with their rational minds, can comprehend all problems, earthly or galactic, by systematic action from within established institutions such as a united federation of states and paradigms such as liberal democracy. Progress for liberal humanism during the 1960s is determined by the extent to which the government (in the case of *Star Trek*, the United Federation of Planets) and the people (the crew of the *Enterprise*) serve to expand liberty and civility to all people, all aliens. Yet the contradictory aspects of *Star Trek*'s liberal-humanist zeitgeist are perhaps due to what philosopher David Theo Goldberg recognizes as the historic paradox of liberalism: "The more ideologically hegemonic liberal values seem and the more open to difference liberal modernity declares itself, the more dismissive of difference it becomes and the more closed it seeks to make the circle of acceptability."[4] This historic paradox applies to both the racial project of key decision makers and the project-in-the-text.

The Project of Key Decision Makers

The articulation of race in *Star Trek*, from its casting of actors to its metaphors and allegories, was uncommon in the network television of the 1950s and early 1960s. The meaning of race in this period was dominated by a segregationist tone, a separate but unequal trajectory. Television was what television historian J. Fred McDonald called "white." This is evident in the network programming of the period, which was governed by an overt policy of exclusion and segregation. When African-Americans and Native-Americans were represented in such series as *Amos 'n Andy* (1951–1953) and *The Lone Ranger* (1949–1957), they were characterized either as shiftless and unintelligent or as obedient servants to the white man. Representations of Asian- and Latino-Americans were almost nonexistent; when present they received similar treatment. A case in point is Sammee Tong in *Bachelor Father* (1957–1962), a feminized Asian "house boy" who spoke, walked, and expressed himself in stereotypical ways. Unlike his costars, he was more a caricature than a character.

The dominant meaning of race in the 1950s and early 1960s was openly and massively contested in the mid- to late 1960s. Civil rights advocates such as Martin Luther King Jr. and Malcolm X, and the American Indian, antiwar, and Chicano and Puerto Rican movements, among others, struggled to push the meaning of race toward a more egalitarian ideal. As Michael Omi and Howard Winant argue, during the 1960s "new conceptions of racial identity and its meaning, new modes of political organization and confrontation, and new definitions of the state's role in promoting and achieving 'equality' were explored, debated, and fought on the battlegrounds of politics."[5] The civil rights movement had its successes, including the 1964 Civil Rights Act, the 1965 Voting Rights Act, and the 1968 Fair Housing Act.

The mid- to late 1960s was also a time when the National Aeronautics and Space Administration (NASA), the United States government agency responsible for space exploration and the development of space technology, was completing successful flights into outer space and landings on the moon. With the Gemini and Apollo missions, NASA came to embody the hopes and aspirations, the future and potential, of the United States. It also stood in ironic juxtaposition to the contemporaneous domestic and international injustices that dominated the latter part of the decade. United States citizens dying in the rice paddies of Vietnam and in the streets of the nation's cities, protests against the government, and cold war tensions made the future look much bleaker than the optimistic image of Neil Armstrong's "giant leap for mankind" might otherwise suggest. NASA symbolized future hope and represented immediate contradiction.

Images and stories of civil rights and antiwar demonstrations flowed into the homes of millions of viewers from both print and electronic news sources, forcing viewers to confront a contestation over race. At issue was the racism inherent in segregation, the politics of stereotypes, and the ideals of integration. Producers, directors, writers, and network executives capitalized on this sociopolitical struggle. For the first time in television history, programs like *East Side, West Side* (1963–1964), *I Spy* (1965–1968), and *Julia* (1968–1971) employed African-American actors in major roles that were not patently stereotypical. Decision makers responsible for the production of such series drew on domestic and international politics and experiences in the hope of selling their programs and advertisements to an audience sensitive to race relations.

Yet even with the increase in programs that employed African-Americans, integration in late-1960s television was problematic. Network programs with people of color tended to be segregated as "race" shows or hidden at the edges of prime time. Moreover, Asian-, Latino-, and Native-Americans were largely absent from television screens during this period, as civil rights ideals tended to be interpreted by the networks in black and white terms. When these other minority groups were represented—for instance, Hop Sing in *Bonanza* (1959–1973) or any number of European-American actors in redface in other westerns—it was often in the form of desexualized servants, loyal sidekicks, or unthinking savages. Even producers attempting to engage social issues felt they ultimately had to appeal to the majority—the European-American, Protestant middle class—and not "offend." Indeed, the television programming of the period suggests that the goals, values, and ideologies of the networks were conservative, resisting radical change and unrestricted integration in order to maintain a stable—dominantly white—bottom line.

While the majority of network programming remained white, *Star Trek* was among the few series that embraced and consistently spoke to the shifting meaning of race that contextualized its production and initial reception. This effort to engage the politics and experiences of the 1960s can be traced to the practices of a number of creative and network decision makers involved in crafting the series. Of course, the most notable of these was Gene Roddenberry. An outspoken humanist very much concerned with the message of his work, Roddenberry wrote many of the episodes and was involved with almost every other aspect of the show's development (selecting and revising scripts, casting, editing, etc.).

In a 1991 interview with David Alexander for *The Humanist*, Roddenberry acknowledges that he is both a humanist and a liberal. "I think my philosophy," he states, "is based upon the great affection I have for the human creature. I mean a tremendous affection."[6] He also explains that "one of the underlying messages of both series (*Star Trek* and *The Next Generation*) is that human beings can, with critical thinking, solve the problems that are facing them without any outside or supernatural help."[7] This liberal-humanist philosophy is evident in statements more contemporaneous with the original series. "Intolerance in the 23rd century?" he rhetorically asks in 1968,

> Improbable! If man survives that long, he will have learned to take a delight in the essential differences between men and between cultures. He will learn that differences in ideas and attitudes are a delight, part of life's exciting variety, not something to fear. It's a manifestation of the greatness that God, or whatever it is, gave us. This is infinite variation and delight, this is part of the optimism we built into *Star Trek*.[8]

"We must learn to live together," he says with a touch of civil rights and cold war concern, "or most certainly we will soon all die together."[9]

Roddenberry's liberal humanism also surfaces in the primary evidence surrounding the production of the series. In developing *Star Trek*, the creator-producer insisted that a progressive and unified Earth, a single world government, be foregrounded in the science fiction universe. Moreover, racial harmony and tolerance were to be the norm rather than the exception in the ongoing *Star Trek* diegesis. In effect, he called for a multicultural future. For example, the original series treatment, which the creator-producer used to sell the series to various networks, describes a one-hour show with an integrated cast of characters that includes a Latino navigator, a woman as second-in-command, and an alien science officer complete with red skin and a forked tail (a character who eventually became Spock). The treatment goes on to pitch the show as "wagon train to the stars," an action-adventure of optimism fraught with human conflict.[10] Unlike *Lost in Space*, where the main characters are all white, Roddenberry's vision of the future is clearly integrated.

The liberal-humanist vision articulated in Roddenberry's original treatment for *Star Trek* is not without its contradictions, however. This is particularly the case with the description of the Latino navigator, José "Joe" Tyler, which is loaded with stereotypical traits. The lengthy passage from the original treatment is worth quoting in full:

> José (Joe) Tyler, Boston astronomer father and Brazilian mother, is boyishly handsome, still very much in the process of maturing. An unusual combination, he has inherited his father's mathematical ability. José Tyler, in fact, is a phenomenally brilliant mathematician and space theorist. But he has also inherited his mother's Latin temperament, fights a perpetual and highly personalized battle with his instruments and calculators, suspecting that space—and probably God, too—are engaged in a giant conspiracy to make his professional and personal life as difficult and uncomfortable as possible. Joe (or José, depending on the other party) is young enough to be painfully aware of the historical repute of Latins as lovers—and is in danger of failing this challenge on a cosmic scale.[11]

As the parenthetical clause in Roddenberry's description suggests, José is written as a racial half-breed: one part is brilliant, a trait that comes from his Boston (presumably European) paternal line; the other part is irrational, a failed Latin lover, a trait that comes from his Brazilian maternal line. This dichotomy is a familiar one, playing on common racial essentialisms and stereotypes about Latinos. It is also eminently entangled with naturalized gender hierarchies: the maternal side of José is characterized as emotional and the paternal side as intellectual.

With the failed Latin lover on board, Roddenberry attempted to sell *Star Trek* to a number of networks and studios. After the show was rejected by CBS, he pitched and subsequently sold it to Desilu Studios, then in decline from the major-studio status it enjoyed when it produced shows like *I Love Lucy* (1951–1957). Desilu eventually secured interest and capital from NBC, which was looking for the next *Lost in Space*. The eventual result was "The Cage," which featured highly evolved, giant-headed, white-humanoids who literally caged other aliens for their material needs and intellectual pleasures. An allegory for slavery and the arrogance of "superior" intelligence, the pilot provided Roddenberry with an opportunity to "say something" about humanity.

NBC had problems with the pilot, however. Network executives at its screening—which reportedly included Grant Tinker, vice president in charge of West Coast operations, and Mort Werner, vice president in charge of television programming—apparently liked the overall feel of the program, but rejected it as being "too cerebral." They also rejected a few of the characters, including Number One (Majel Barrett, listed in the credits as M. Leigh Hudec), a strong woman character who was the ship's second-in-command, and Spock, now a half-alien with pointed ears and raised eyebrows. According to Stephen Whitfield and Gene Roddenberry, the executives felt neither character would be accepted by the television audience.[12] NBC made the unprecedented decision of ordering a second pilot. This initiated the ongoing tug-of-war between Roddenberry and the network over the programming content of *Star Trek*.

Despite the network's rejection of "The Cage," Roddenberry pursued his liberal-humanist ideals.[13] He cut the character of Number One, but kept the character of Spock. He then cast an even more diverse crew of characters than before, including a female communications officer from the "United States of Africa," Uhura; a Japanese-American helmsman, Sulu; a Scottish engineering chief, Scotty (James Doohan); and a European-American nurse, Christine Chapel (Majel Barrett). He added a character in the second season, a Russian "cosmonaut," Pavel Chekov, who looked strikingly similar to Davy Jones of The Monkees. Throughout the show's three-year run, the crew was headed by a European-American captain, James T. Kirk, and included a cantankerous European-American doctor, Leonard "Bones" McCoy (DeForest Kelley). So one of the characters was Japanese-American, one was African,

9. Cast of *Star Trek*. © Paramount Pictures Corporation

two were European ethnics, one was half-alien and half-human, and three were European-Americans (figure 9). Though predominantly white, for 1960s network television this was an integrated cast.

Roddenberry instructed writers and directors working on *Star Trek* to utilize the multicultural characters in their stories. In "The Guide to Star Trek," a document that explains the series to prospective writers and directors, the *Enterprise* crew is described as "International in origin, completely multi-racial. But even in this future century we will see some traditional trappings, ornaments, and styles that suggest the Asiatic, the Arabic, the Latin, etc. So far, Mister Spock has been our only crewman with blood lines from another planet. However, it is not impossible that we might discover some other aliens or part aliens working aboard our Starship." The Guide goes on to advise: "We like ways of using the crewmen (extras as well as actors) to help suggest the enormous diversity of our vessel." [14]

The science-fiction nature of the series gave Roddenberry and the rest of the creative decision makers space to address contemporary issues while avoiding some network censorship. As John Meredyth Lucas, a writer, director, and producer of several episodes, reminisces:

> It was great to work on *Star Trek*, because working in the science fiction genre gave us free rein to touch on any number of subjects. We could do anti-Vietnam stories, our civil rights stories. . . . Set the story in outer space, in the future, and all of a sudden you can get away with just about anything, because you're protected by the argument that,

"Hey, we're not talking about the problems of today, we're dealing with a mythical time and place in the future." We were lying, of course, but that's how we got these stories by the network types.[15]

Even Leonard Nimoy remarked in 1967 that the character of Spock enabled him "to say something about the human race."[16]

Despite science fiction conventions that privilege metaphor and allegory, however, network decision makers attempted to curtail and control the creative staff's liberal-humanist project. Perhaps the most famous example of this tug-of-war surrounds the production of "Plato's Stepchildren" (1968), in which a pre-shooting script calls for Kirk, manipulated by Greek god–like aliens, to kiss Uhura. According to most speculations, this would have been network television's first interracial kiss between African-American and European-American stars. Apparently, NBC was concerned with the potential fallout from such a "first," especially among its affiliates in the South, and requested some less than subtle changes. A memorandum from Jean Messerschmidt of NBC's Broadcast Standards Department made the network's position explicit: "it must be clear there are no racial over-tones to Kirk and Uhura's dilemma."[17] While many creative decision makers resisted the network's capitulation to racism, NBC insisted on censoring the interracial "dilemma." Apparently they even requested that Spock, the racialized alien half-breed, be the one to kiss Uhura. Nichelle Nichols explains: "Somehow, I guess, they found it more acceptable for a Vulcan to kiss me, for this alien to kiss this black woman, than for two humans with different coloring to do the same thing." She continues: "It was simply and clearly racism standing in the door . . . in suits. Strange how a twenty-third century space opera could be so mired in antiquated hang-ups."[18]

The scene that was aired pairs Kirk with Uhura and Spock with Nurse Chapel. It begins with the telekinetic Greek-like aliens controlling the physical movements of the *Enterprise* landing party, making them walk and dance in contorted and humiliating ways. Soon a chorus of the powerful beings watch as their leader forces Spock to kiss Chapel several times. We actually see the Vulcan kiss the human in three drawn-out medium shots. The chorus also watch Kirk and Uhura diligently resisting their forced coupling. These shots too are drawn out, dramatizing the extratextual tension surrounding their pairing. The Greek-aliens applaud Kirk and Uhura's struggle; some even derive

10. Kirk resists kissing Uhura

prurient pleasure from the anticipation of its "forbidden" outcome. Eventually the power of the aliens overtakes Kirk, and, in a slow dolly into a close-up, moments after Uhura gasps, the captain pulls her closer to him. He turns her body toward the camera, the back of her head taking up most of the bottom half of the screen. Kirk is still shown diligently resisting, his eyes glaring at the omnipotent aliens, his lips pursed in anger and resentment (figure 10). Their mouths are only millimeters apart when the camera cuts to the alien chorus in rapt attention, a seemingly self-conscious play on the imagined attention of the television audience. NBC's Office of Broadcast Standards and the creative decision makers apparently compromised: the interracial kiss was implied.[19] Either way, of course, the coupling between black and white is coded as undesirable and perverse—a thing to be resisted or kept at arm's length.

Contradictions in *Star Trek*'s liberal-humanist project are also apparent in the use of actors of color. In fact, despite Roddenberry's call to use them "to suggest the enormous diversity of our vessel," throughout the series the integrated supporting cast was kept at the margins of most stories and in the background of most shots. This is especially the case in the way the character of Sulu was both conceived and utilized. He is only supposed to look Asian. In "The Star Trek Guide," he is described as a white-identified Japanese-American who prefers French customs over Japanese traditions. Worse yet, he is characterized as being confused and mystified by Asians: "Mixed oriental in ancestry, Japanese predominating, Sulu is contemporary American in speech and manner. In fact, his attitude toward Asians is that they seem to him rather 'inscrutable.' Sulu fancies himself more of an old-world 'D'Artagnan' than anything else."[20] Sulu's intended integration into the space of the starship comes at the expense of a recognizable identity with Japanese culture; that is, the character was conceived as having "successfully" assimilated into the European-American melting pot of humanity's future.

This pattern continues in the actual broadcast texts, where, despite the fact that his position as helmsman places him literally in the foreground of many shots, Sulu is relegated to the background of most stories. Out of the seventy-nine *Star Trek* episodes, Sulu is not once the focus of a main storyline. One of the few times he does make it out of the background is in "The Naked Time" (1966), where he is shown as a rampaging swordsman in search of a duel (figure 11). Sulu's secondary status is especially problematic in the second and third seasons, after Chekov joins the crew. During this period, the Russian character is given substantial roles in comparison to the Japanese helmsman. Chekov is even left in charge of the crew when Kirk, Spock, Bones, and Scotty are off the ship. Though he has seniority, Sulu is left in charge of the ship only once, in "The Omega Glory" (1968), an episode in which he has very few lines and Chekov is not featured. For a show that claims strict adherence to verisimilitude, *Star Trek* breaks its own chain of command when race is a factor.

The description and representation of Uhura also demonstrate the contradictory nature of *Star Trek*'s liberal-humanist project. Like Sulu, Uhura is relegated to the spatial and narrative background for most of the episodes, making her more a token than a truly integrated character. Nichols comments on the use of her character:

> I'd get the first draft, the white pages, and see what Uhura had to do this week, and maybe it was a halfway-decent scene or two, sometimes more, and then invariably the next draft would come in on blue pages and I'd find that Uhura's presence in the show had been cut way down. The pink pages came next and she'd suffer some more cuts, then the

11. Sulu on the lookout for a duel

yellow, more cuts, and it finally got to the point where I had really had it. I mean I just decided that I don't even need to read the FUCKING SCRIPT! I mean I know how to say, "hailing frequencies open." . . .[21]

The utilization of Uhura as "background color" evolved from the character's description in "The Star Trek Guide," one of the earliest extant

12. Uhura's body

documents that mentions the character: "Uhura is also a warm, highly female female off duty. She is something of a favorite in the Recreation Room during off duty hours, too, because she sings—old ballads as well as the newer space ballads—and she can do an impersonation at the drop of a communicator." As a singing, "highly female female" African, Uhura is written as a performance, an icon, of black beauty. This translates to the broadcast text. In "Mirror, Mirror" (1967), for instance, she is eroticized by the camera, as several scenes show her scantily clad body in tight close-ups: her long legs, smooth stomach, and large breasts—scopophilic fragments of her body—are emphasized for their womanly and "exotic" features. It is as if her blackness is made safe and appealing when it is performing in fragmented and fetishized forms—when, in other words, it is as exoticized as it is eroticized (figure 12). In a 1967 interview, the actress commented on the dilemma: "My problem is being a black woman on top of being a woman."[22]

The use of Spock is another site where contradictions can be seen within the liberal-humanist project. The tradition of the alien in science fiction involves the foregrounding of Otherness, particularly in reference to the difficulties and conflicts stemming from physiognomic and cultural difference. Aliens often work as metaphors, as an implicit means by which human experiences and likenesses are imagined and fictionalized. Spock, especially because he is a "half-breed," serves this traditional function. Yet the character is often constrained so as not to be either too literal or too obvious about the nature of the universe and the politics of the 1960s. Even in metaphors and allegories involving aliens, the decision makers often take the racially "safe" way out.

Harlan Ellison's original script for "City on the Edge of Forever" (1967) has Kirk and Spock materialize in 1930s New York. As New Yorkers begin to notice the odd pair, Spock is encircled by an inflamed mob agitated by a bitter racist:

> What kind of a country is this, where men have to stand in bread lines just to fill their bellies? I'll tell you what kind . . . a country run by the foreigners! All the scum let in to take the food from our mouths, all the alien filth that pollutes our fine country. Here we are, skilled workers and they want us to sign up for CCC camps. Civilian Conservation Corps, men—is *that* what we're gonna do? Work like coolies inna fields while these swine who can't even speak our language take the . . .[23]

Later in the script, Ellison's technical directions stipulate that in order to conceal Spock's alien features, "he has been made up to faintly resemble a Chinese."[24] Here the acclaimed science fiction writer is trying to comment on the history of racist discrimination against Chinese-Americans during the Depression, employing Spock as both a connotative and a denotative signifier. His project, it seems clear, is to use the character to reveal the racist elements of class politics during this era of United States history.

In the aired version of "City on the Edge of Forever," the indictment against racism was removed in favor of a comic scene in which a 1930s police officer and a few city people stare curiously at Kirk and Spock. There is no bitter racist trying to incite violence and no angry mob threatened by a "foreigner." Instead, a policeman simply looks at Kirk and Spock, as the captain stammers out an explanation for his first officer's physiognomic difference: "My friend is obviously Chinese. I see you've noticed the ears. They're actually easy to explain." With a slight suggestion from Spock, the captain continues: "The unfortunate accident he had as a child. He caught his head in a mechanical rice picker." As Rick Worland aptly points out, the indictment against racism in this episode of *Star Trek* takes the form of a racial joke.[25] Instead of being foregrounded, the history of racism against Chinese-Americans is deleted. The intended reference to the history of American bigotry is not televised.

Case Study: "The Paradise Syndrome" (1968)

As with "The City on the Edge of Forever," the conditions of production surrounding "The Paradise Syndrome" reveal a contradictory racial project, this time one that stereotypes Native-Americans as noble savages and whites as "normal" and even divine. The basic storyline has Captain Kirk, suffering from amnesia, becoming a medicine chief for a tribe of Native-Americans on a planet far from Earth. The tribe was placed there centuries ago by a "super-race" who wanted to "preserve them." Primary evidence surrounding the production of the episode indicates that the incorporation of the noble savage stereotype was a direct result of the liberal-humanist ideals and practices of Roddenberry and other creative decision makers. In other words, regardless of the tug-of-war between Roddenberry and the network, in this episode of *Star Trek* it was the creative decision makers that participated in and facilitated racist practice.

Originally titled "Pale Face," the story outline by Margaret Armen uses well-worn racialized adjectives and clichés to construct the Native-American tribe as noble savages. Kirk, Armen writes, "has found this tribe gentle, kind, and in complete attune with nature."[26] Armen has Kirk being accepted into the tribe and marrying one of the women, Miramanee. This emphasizes the mythical structure of the story, that of the so-called paradise syndrome, which typically involves a white man escaping civilization or getting lost in the wild, befriending a wise but simple tribe of natives, falling in love with a submissive and often scantily clad native girl, and, after saving the natives from an event or person bent on destroying them, eventually determining that living among them is not his life's mission. The white man, not the native, has evolved, and he must accept his role as a complex, civilized human. In Armen's outline, Kirk realizes that Miramanee "can never fit into [his] world. Simple and gentle as she is, her only place is the idyllic tribal environment of her people. Gently, he tells her that he no longer fits into her world either, that the ancient prophecy has been fulfilled and he must go on to fulfill his further duty." The outline concludes: "He knows a part of him—the part of man that is always pagan—will always remain behind, that a poignant longing for the idyllic life of the noble savage will never leave him."[27]

The noble savage stereotype found in the development of "The Paradise Syndrome" functions as a sort of fetish, much like its eighteenth-century predecessor, analyzed by metahistorian Hayden White: "belief in the idea of a Noble Savage was magical, was extravagant and irrational in the kind of devotion it was meant to inspire, and, in the end, displayed the kind of pathological displacement of libidinal interest that we normally associate with the forms of racism that depend on the idea of a 'wild humanity' for their justification."[28] All three aspects of White's noble savage fetish are played out in Armen's outline. First, the Indians are associated with magical qualities, especially in the representation of them as being mysteriously connected to—"in complete attune with"—nature. Second, the representation of the Indians as existing in some pristine and unchanging condition—on another planet, no less—reveals an irrational devotion to a particular image of Native-Americans as "noble," an image "fixed" in time like the fetish. This is perhaps most prominent in both the super-race's efforts to preserve them and Kirk's nostalgic longing to become one of them. Finally, the stereotype is strongly suggestive of a libidinal displacement, perhaps most clearly projected in the relationship between Kirk and Miramanee—in which the captain, after falling in "love" with the beautiful native, has nothing less than a "wild" time.

The use of the noble savage theme in the conceptualization of "The Paradise Syndrome" ultimately has less to do with the lifestyle and customs of Native-Americans than with the evolution of whiteness. In his analysis, White goes on to argue that the noble savage fetish ultimately "draws a distinction, in the nature of an opposition, between normal humanity (gentle, intelligent, decorous, and white) and an abnormal one (obstinate, gay, free, and red)."[29] The "abnormality" of an otherwise noble humanity cannot be understood outside the notion of a wild/savage humanity (Indians), which itself cannot be understood outside the notion of a "normal"—and, at least rhetorically, superior—humanity (whites).[30] Such an opposition thus becomes a way to define the superior "civility" of whiteness, which in the making of "The Paradise Syndrome" is especially evident in Roddenberry's efforts to ensure that the Indians, despite centuries of unencumbered evolution on a far-off planet, haven't really evolved. In a memorandum to Fred Freiberger, the producer of *Star Trek* during its third season, Roddenberry states his case in explicit terms:

> if the Indians were brought here many centuries ago, it is likely that even though they retain much of their terrible custom, they would have advanced somewhat along the scale of civilization. Perhaps not to firearms, or not that fast, but perhaps added on to the Indian culture, it is a growing mastery of mechanics, which has resulted in the wheel, possibly the crossbow. . . . Not enough to deprive our tale of the wonderful simplicity of life here, but enough to stay true to the premise and to logic.[31]

Roddenberry's insistence on representing the tribe as having advanced only far enough to invent the wheel reveals a hierarchy of cultures that has whites "naturally" on top of an evolutionary ladder—a telling contradiction in his liberal-humanist project.

Roddenberry's interest in representing Kirk and crew as more advanced than the Indians stems from his interest in the myth of the "paradise syndrome" (it was Roddenberry who insisted that the original title be changed to "The Paradise Syndrome"). He writes:

> Our story here, the essential and I think the most interesting and different one for our series, is whether a Herman Melville theme, i.e., modern man finding his "Tahiti", that natural and simple and happy and untroubled life all of us dream about some day finding—and having found it and having held it in his hand, he learns he's incapable of closing his hand around it and keeping it because all of us are innocent prisoners of our own time and our own place. And, as with Melville's "Typee," neither can our modern man (or his clerk from Boston) take his woman from this simple life back to his land and his time, since she would be as destroyed by it as he would be if he stayed there. This is the premise and theme, a strong one if used properly and certainly a most powerful and enduring one in Western literature.[32]

Roddenberry's interest in defining the problems of whites in a modern world, here both metaphorically and literally represented by Kirk, is ultimately pursued at the expense of Native-American peoples and cultures.

The NBC censor was also concerned with the notion of the "paradise syndrome," but in the way in which it might affect the star persona of Captain Kirk. A letter from Stanley Robertson, manager of film programming, noted:

I think that it is a major mistake to have our star, Kirk, "marry" the lovely native girl, Miramanee, to have a child by her and then to return to "his world" with the *Enterprise* when a rescue is affected [*sic*]. I realize that your feelings are that you can "justify these actions" by establishing Kirk as a man engrained in the customs, mores, and social patterns of the planet's culture. However, I think that we must remember that even though our series takes place at a time in the future, we still have contemporary people with contemporary views on morals, manners, etc., viewing our shows and, while we are able to portray others than our heroes in opposition to these conventional points of view, we should not ever depict our leads as having such thoughts.[33]

Clearly mindful of the twentieth-century audience, the NBC censor, though aware of the logic of science fiction, was less interested in the stereotyping of Native-Americans than with maintaining the "superior" morality of the white hero—another instance of network conservatism protecting a white bottom line.

This interest in representing whiteness as morally atop the evolutionary ladder goes beyond the goals of the network censor. In the memorandum to Freiberger, Roddenberry goes to great lengths to rationalize the benevolent super-race:

We are saying arbitrarily for purposes of this script that there was once, or still may exist somewhere, a race of highly advanced and kindly humanoid aliens, who had great love and affection for all forms of life and all levels of civilization and hated to see the fresh and different potential of primitive cultures absorbed and changed, such as happened on Earth with the Egyptians, Crete, American Indians, etc. Undoubtedly, the same sort of thing happens on other planets, too—it is a demonstratable law of progress in civilization that richly interesting primitive cultures die out and their particular values are lost when stronger cultures absorb or destroy them.[34]

Roddenberry's interest in the super-race, a logic derivative of the social Darwinian notion of "survival of the fittest," continues, as he makes a weak effort at explaining why the Indians believe Kirk is godlike: "it is obvious that the Indians have never seen an *Enterprise* landing party member before and, therefore, more believable they believe Kirk is a sort of god."[35] The "demonstratable law of progress" implicitly assumes that "white" phenotypes, which is all that separates Kirk from the Indians at this point in the story, would be construed by "primitive cultures" as godlike, thereby linking Kirk not to the Indians, and thus to members of his own species, but to an alien super-race: Kirk is more alien super-race than human Indian. The discourse of white superiority, "not there as a category and everywhere as a fact," as Richard Dyer argues about whiteness,[36] is stretched into the future by the science-fiction notion of an alien super-race and a heroic white captain.

The Kellam DeForest Research Company, hired by Roddenberry to verify facts in preproduction stories, cites errors in "The Paradise Syndrome" script that would ultimately produce an essentialistic representation of Native-Americans, indicating that Roddenberry was made aware of at least some of the problems in the script. The report suggests changing the tribal mixture of the peaceful Indians, which already had been changed from simply "Mohicans" in the story outline to a "mixture of Navajo, Mohican, and Mandan" in the script, in order to be more authentic: "The Mandans were among the most violent, intransigent of all the American Indian tribes. They made war on everyone, on any excuse. Suggest Pawnee or Cherokee." The report also notes that " 'Mohican' is a very bad tribal name to use for several reasons: it is not really an Indian name (Mohegan or Mahican is close). It brings to mind immediately 'Last of the . . . ;' and they were also very war-like. Suggest: Delaware. (The Delaware were related and sets and props would be correct for either culture.)"[37] Finally, the research report notes that the script is not authentic in its call for Indian costuming: "feathered cloaks are associated with the natives of Polynesia and with the Aztecs. Some feathers were used by the California tribes in particular, as decorations. Use by northern and eastern tribes is not valid."[38]

Despite the Kellam report, the aired version of "The Paradise Syndrome" reproduces the noble savage stereotype with little change. The episode begins with Kirk, Spock, and McCoy beaming down to a planet that lies directly in the path of a huge asteroid—an ominous collision that will ultimately kill all the planet's inhabitants, "a mixture of Navajo, Mohican, and Delaware," Spock describes. Upon seeing the Indians, Kirk fantasizes about their "peaceful, uncomplicated" nature, and Dr. McCoy chimes in: "Typical human reaction to an idyllic natural setting. Back in the twentieth century we referred to it as the Tahiti syndrome. It's particularly common to over-pressured leader-types like starship captains." Soon after the landing party finds evidence of the conscientious super-race who "preserved" the Indians—the Noahs of the galaxy, as it were—Kirk accidentally hits his head, gets amnesia, and is subsequently separated from his friends. After diligently trying but failing to rescue their captain, Spock and McCoy return to the *Enterprise* to deal with diverting the asteroid. Back on the planet, the captain, unaware that he is a "more evolved" human than the Indians, befriends the tribe, eventually "rising to the top" apparently due to his "natural" ability by becoming a medicine chief and, as the paradise syndrome would have it, marrying—in a feathered cloak no less!—the beautiful Miramanee (Sabrina Scharf).

As in the production documents, the noble savage stereotype in the broadcast text emphasizes the "superiority" of whiteness. In one scene, for example, Miramanee cannot figure out how to pull Kirk's shirt off, as she cannot find any lacing. She is portrayed as simpleminded, not that bright. This is not the case with Kirk. Moments before, he had fashioned a lamp from an old piece of pottery and saved a boy by using mouth-to-mouth resuscitation. Despite his amnesia, he is shown as naturally superior. The text seems to say: while you can take the white man out of civilization, you can't take civilization out of the white man. Given the impossibility of the white man's return to the simplicity of paradise, the ending in particular plays out the morality of whiteness and, in the process, resolves Kirk's Tahiti syndrome. When the Indians realize Kirk is not a god, they stone both him and Miramanee (it's the Indians who are violent in this version of the noble savage stereotype). Spock and McCoy eventually intervene, but only Kirk survives. In this take on a standard white/red miscegenation narrative, the native girl dies so that Kirk, the white male hero, isn't shown unheroically and immorally leaving her and their unborn baby behind. In accordance with both the network censor's goal and Roddenberry's vision of paradise, the starship captain is left unencumbered in his trek toward a white future.

The Project-in-the-Text

The following analysis of the racial project-in-the-text builds upon the previous analysis of the articulation of race in scripts, memoranda, and related production documents. However, the "project" analyzed here has less to do with the beliefs and practices of creative and network decision makers than with the representational and narrative substance that is the byproduct of their conscious or unconscious decisions. In other words, I am now interested in the specific forms of ideology that, as Bennett and Woollacott show in their analysis of *The Spy Who Loved Me* (1977), have been "worked over and transformed" from "the deliberations, calculations and policies" that informed the making of *Star Trek*.[39]

A liberal-humanist articulation of race in the broadcast texts is contextualized and facilitated by the show's diegetic logics—that is, the political alliances and quasi-scientific explanations that give coherence and intelligibility to the Trek universe. As I noted at the beginning of this chapter, these logics include: (1) The United Federation of Planets, an intergalactic federation dominated by Earth; (2) "parallel development," Trek's explanation for why alien societies resemble human societies; and (3) the anthropomorphic alien, the individual extraterrestrials that interact with Kirk and the crew. In the rest of this chapter, I will show that these historically analogous alliances and quasi-scientific explanations not only tie the imaginary universe of *Star Trek* to the real space-time of the 1960s, but also perpetuate a contradictory racial project-in-the-text that ultimately advocates the evolutionary hegemony of whiteness.

The United Federation of Planets: NATO or Bust

Star Trek takes place in Earth's future, specifically the twenty-third century. In this imaginary time, Earth belongs to the United Federation of Planets, a powerful interplanetary body that unites a vast collective of worlds. The Federation is similar to the federalist government of the United States (its power is centrally controlled) as well as to the United Nations (each member has an autonomous government). Given the structure of the *Star Trek* universe and the 1960s context in which it was produced, however, the interplanetary organization more closely resembles the North Atlantic Treaty Organization (NATO), the real space-time alliance whose main purpose at that point in international relations was to deter communist expansion. The Federation's main exploratory and military resource is Starfleet Command, which includes the United Space Ship *Enterprise* as one of its flagships. Their mission: "to explore strange new worlds, to seek out new life and new civilizations. To boldly go where no man has gone before."

The main enemies of the Federation include the Klingons, a warlike dictatorship—an "evil empire"; there are also the Romulans, a more mysterious though equally merciless regime. The three intergalactic superpowers are separated by a neutral zone, a kind of "iron curtain" that prohibits one power from crossing into the territory of another. This obvious parallel to the nonfictional world is direct, drawing on the contemporaneous cold war polarity. As Worland summarizes: "Like the Soviet Union with regard to the United States, the Klingon Empire is a vast system roughly equivalent in power and influence to the Federation. Like China in the two decades following the communist revolution, the Romulans are a secondary but nonetheless formidable regional power."[40] The Federation is stereotypically honest, mostly white, and ostensibly democratic. Their charter is based on universal cooperation, free trade, and mutual defense. The Klingons, positioned as the Soviets, are evil, dark, and underhanded. They are a totalitarian and imperialist regime who deem battle glorious. The Romulans, positioned as the Chinese, are stereotypically mysterious and ruthless. They rarely involve themselves in skirmishes with the Federation, but when they do they are cunning and unscrupulous.

Issues like balance of power and imperialism are narrativized in *Star Trek* via the diegetic logic of a democratic federation and totalitarian empires like the Klingons and the Romulans. This is evident in the narrative situations into which the *Enterprise* and crew are thrust, such as covert battles across the neutral zone. In "Errand of Mercy" (1967), for instance, the Federation and the Klingon Empire plan for war in a disputed area close to the neutral zone. At stake is the only inhabitable planet in this strategically important sector of the galaxy, "ideal for either side." On the one hand, the Federation's goal is to defend the Organians, the "primitive" people living on the planet, in order to deter Klingon encroachments. The Federation intends to arm the Organians so that they can defend themselves. The goal of the Klingons, on the other hand, is to put the peaceful people into slavery for the benefit of their Empire. The episode's title is a clue to the Federation's mission, "an errand of mercy," as the Organians are believed to be technologically unequipped to deal with the imperialistic Klingons.

The correlation between the Federation as NATO and the Klingons as the Soviet Union is expressed in the dialogue, a site well suited to didacticism. Spock describes the Organians as "friendly people, living on a primitive level. Little of intrinsic value." Kirk mumbles to himself: "Another Armenia, Belgium." Kirk's sentimentality continues: "The weak innocence, those who seem to be located on natural invasion routes." As with the dialogue in "Let That Be Your Last Battlefield," Kirk's lines associate geopolitical history, in this case the Soviet expansion into Eastern Europe, with the imagined world in which the Klingons invade the defenseless Organians. More specifically, it reveals the liberal-humanist project's efforts to rationalize NATO's agenda of deterring Soviet expansion. *Star Trek* in the 1960s takes the side of liberal democracy and late capitalism.

Toward the end of the episode, the Organians reveal themselves to be omnipotent gods who choose to present themselves as humanoids so as not to upset visitors. They magically stop the Federation and Klingons from waging war, imposing what is known in the Trek canon as the "Organian Peace Treaty." What is problematic about these malevolent beings is that they choose to materialize as white males who are identical to the white-humans, as opposed to Klingons, Vulcans or, for that matter, humans of color. They seem to be the manifestation of the super-race that was linked to Kirk in "The Paradise Syndrome."

There are many *Star Trek* episodes like "Errand of Mercy" that draw upon the global polarity that defined the 1960s international stage. "The Trouble with Tribbles" (1967), "Friday's Child" (1967), "A Private Little War" (1968), "Day of the Dove" (1968), and "Elaan of Troyius" (1968) also engage cold war policies and events. The science fiction series goes as far as using time travel to twentieth-century earth to address the escalation of the arms race between the Soviet Union and the United States in "Assignment: Earth" (1968).

As the Federation interacts with the Klingons and Romulans, xenophobia becomes a polemical topic. The ideological spin on this form of bigotry smacks of liberal humanism, as Trek explains it as individual and irrational rather than sociopolitical and systematic. "Balance of Terror" (1966), for instance, uses the conflict between the Romulans and the Federation to draw upon the national and racial biases between East and West. In this episode, the Romulans pose a threat to the Federation. Shown covertly crossing the neutral zone and attacking defenseless outposts, the Romulans are positioned as a mysterious enemy with insidious ambitions. As a consequence of these and past actions, they are hated by a member of the bridge crew, Lt. Stiles (Paul Comi). When Stiles discovers that Romulans and Vulcans "look alike," he irrationally turns his hatred toward Spock (Romulans are descendants of Vulcans in the *Star Trek* universe). Thus bigotry is foregrounded as an irrational transference of the fears and hatred of one group, the Romulans, onto another, the Vulcans, whom they happen to resemble.

What is particularly compelling about "Balance of Terror" is that the construction of Stiles as xenophobic and racist is enhanced by the rhetorical aspects of visual style. The episode employs tight framing, quick dollies, rapid cuts, and key long shots to add to the tension and conflict created by a narrative event that reveals that the Romulans, the ominous enemy of the Federation, resemble the Vulcans, a loyal Federation society. For example, in the opening scene, after Uhura secures a clandestine picture of the enemy ship's bridge, we see for the first time in *Star Trek* history a Romulan (Mark Lenard). A jarring cut takes us to a medium shot of Kirk standing in the foreground with Stiles sitting directly behind him. The camera dramatically dollies into a tight medium shot of the two just as Stiles stands, intently glaring at the image of the Romulan commander. The abrupt editing and pronounced dolly foreshadows the impending conflict and tension. After a reestablishing shot of the commander, we then see the same tight medium shot of Kirk and Stiles. This time, Stiles turns and glares at Spock. His eyes act as vectors leading the viewer to the similarities between the Romulans and Spock; his facial expression, pronounced in the tight medium shot, suggests mistrust and disgust. Without dialogue, the silence actually adding to the tension, the scene eventually fades to black after another reestablishing shot of Stiles, who continues to glare at Spock. Through these stylistic set-ups, the scene makes it clear that Stiles's bigotry against the Romulans is intense, individual, and includes Spock.

The next scene opens with a long shot of the entire bridge. Stiles is still intently glaring at Spock. We also see Kirk, Sulu, and Scotty staring at Stiles, distancing themselves from the implications of his glare (figure 13). This long shot and the composition serve to isolate Stiles and his irrational biases from the rest of the crew. The next shot is of Spock, who, sensing the glare, slowly turns his chair to confront the hate-filled crewman. In a close-up, we see Spock bite his lip, a rare show of emotion from the logical Vulcan (figure 14). The close-up accentuates his concern as well as his precarious condition; his facial expression makes the problem evident. Later, Stiles utters a sarcastic statement questioning Spock's loyalty, prompting a warning from Kirk: "Well, here's one thing we can be sure of, mister," as the camera quickly dollies into a medium shot and the captain pulls Stiles's chair toward him, "Leave any bigotry in your quarters. There's no room for it on the

13. Stiles looking disgustedly at Spock

14. Spock biting his lip

bridge." The quick dolly acts as a kind of rhyme with the dolly that opens the previous scene. As a rhetorical set-up, the cuts and dollies establish both the bigotry that consumes Stiles and the intolerance of his bigotry that motivates the rest of the crew. The dialogue makes clear what the visual style articulated in the previous shots: Prejudice is individual, irrational, and apparently unacceptable to the rest of the crew (save when it is expressed in one's own quarters). The use of a Stiles rather than a regular character as the vehicle for engaging bigotry allows the liberal-humanist vision of a "colorblind" multicultural crew to remain intact, a symbol of humankind's potential.

"Balance of Terror" is one of many *Star Trek* episodes that deals explicitly with bigotry. As I discussed earlier, "Let That Be Your Last Battlefield" uses humanoids who are half-white and half-black to address the causes and consequences of racial oppression. In "The Galileo Seven" (1967), Spock is again used to address prejudice, as he is forced to prove his "humanity" to a stranded shuttle crew before gaining their trust and loyalty. In these and other episodes, creative decision makers utilized the notion of the United Federation of Planets and Starfleet Command to create an imaginary universe that could draw upon and didactically engage contemporaneous politics.

Parallel Evolution: A Humanocentric Universe

The *Star Trek* universe is populated with a wide variety of alien civilizations. Aside from Klingons, Romulans, and Vulcans, there are Andorians, Ekosians, Tellarites, and many others. Given the potential diversity of the real space-time universe and the possibilities of the creative imagination, these alien societies are strikingly similar in morphology, social development, and moral disposition to us Terrans. The diegetic logic that rationalized all this similarity in a galaxy arguably as populated with diverse sentient life forms as there are known galaxies in the universe is the notion of "parallel evolution," or the "similar worlds concept." Gene Roddenberry considered this notion a valid scientific theory, and thus felt it made the Trek universe both coherent and believable: "We depict many humanoid aliens," the creator-producer rationalized in *The Making of Star Trek*, "because we (along with Cal Tech studies and others) do believe parallel evolution is a distinct probability. Natural laws undoubtedly govern life development just as other natural laws govern time, space, and atoms."[41] Of course, the notion of parallel evolution also made sound business sense. As the original

15. An original Klingon

story outline for the science-fiction series acknowledges, "Normal production casting of much of this alien life is made practical by the SIMILAR WORLDS CONCEPT. To give continual variety, use will, of course, be made of wigs, skin coloration, changes in noses, hands, ears, and even the occasional addition of tails and such." [42] In short, the diegetic logic of parallel evolution allowed the creative decision makers to construct alien societies with which both the audience and the network could identify.

The notion of parallel evolution facilitated the depiction of a Eurocentric universe that privileged and lionized the evolution of whiteness. Despite claims by Roddenberry that *Star Trek* represented a diverse universe, most parallel worlds are similar in look and culture to white-Western society. Indeed, strikingly few *Star Trek* episodes deal with the parallel evolution of nonwhite Earth peoples or cultures. When parallel societies are dark in complexion, such as the Klingons, the color of their skin cues their sinister threat to the mostly white Federation. In fact, the actual makeup used to depict Klingons is often so disproportionately applied as to overdetermine their nonwhiteness (figure 15).

Many parallel evolution episodes represent real space-time societies and belief systems. In these episodes, history is the topic for liberal-humanist polemics. Yet because of its tendency to celebrate the hegemony of white evolution, the contradictory nature of that ideological project remains consistent. This is especially the case with "The Omega Glory," which uses symbols of United States patriotism and myths about both Asians and Native-Americans to prophesy the white world's "superiority." The story begins with the *Enterprise* discovering a vacant Federation starship orbiting a distant planet. Transporting to the starship, Kirk, Spock, Bones, and an unnamed crewman find, instead of a live crew, the crystalline remains of human bodies. They also discover a message left by one of the crew members minutes before he was crystallized. The doomed crewman warns them not to return to the *Enterprise* because they are now infected with whatever killed his crew. He also tells them that they should immediately go to the planet below, which will provide some sort of immunity. Once on the planet, the *Enterprise* landing party finds Tracey (Morgan Woodward), the captain of the unmanned starship, and two species of humanoids: the Yangs, a "white" race, and the Comms, a "yellow" race. (Casting is clearly intentional in this episode, as the Yangs and Comms are played by actors with phenotypically European and Asian and features, respectively—figure 16). Tracey characterizes the Yangs as uncivilized barbarians and the Comms as "friendly enough once they got over the shock of my white skin."

In the early scenes of "The Omega Glory," the culture and civility of the *Enterprise* crew is more closely aligned with the Comms, the "yellow race." This is because the Yangs are seemingly more animal-like, constructed as savages who attack without, as Spock notes, "logic." They wear bearskins, do not seem to know how to speak, and, like the representation of "wild Indians" in Hollywood westerns, hoot and holler when they attack. The Comms, on the other hand, are more civilized. They live in an organized community and appear to be rational. Like the Federation, the Comms have full command of the English language (although they speak with a homogenized "Asian" accent). The beginning of the episode thus shows that those with white skin can be uncivilized savages and those with yellow skin can be civilized and rational. This construction of the whites and the yellows suggests that the project-in-the-text is playing with racist essentialisms and stereotypes,

16. Yangs and Comms

a reversal on the common representation of the colored Other as savage and the white as civilized. This would be counter to the hegemonic representation of Asians in United States media; that diverse collective of peoples are consistently constructed in film and television as a menacing "yellow horde."[43]

"The Omega Glory" is not, however, a counter-hegemonic episode. In fact, the episode not only reveals an unwillingness to be critical of the hegemony of racist representations, but also systematically participates in the stereotyping of Asians. As the story progresses, the Yangs are constructed as noble savages; their cause to annihilate the Comms is established as justified. The Comms, on the other hand, are constructed as brutal and oppressive; their drive to suppress the Yangs is established as totalitarian. This more hegemonic articulation of race is made evident when Kirk and Spock realize the extent to which the Yangs and Comms parallel Earth's civilizations. They find out that the Yangs are actually "Yankees" and the Comms are "Communists," both cultures having slurred the pronunciation of their names over the years. The world of the Yankees and Communists is literally a parallel to Earth, except, as Spock notes, "they fought the war your Earth avoided. And in this case the Asiatics won and took over this planet." The *Enterprise* crew also determines that the Yankees have been fighting for generations to regain their land from the conquering Communists. In this light, the Yangs are no longer savages, but noble warriors fighting for a just and honorable cause. They want to regain the land they lost in a war with the Asiatics. And the Comms are no longer a civilized community, but an oppressive empire determined to run the planet. They are the frightful image of a "yellow horde" that succeeded in its quest for world domination. The initial play on racist essentialism ends up repeating that common stereotype.

The use of Native-American referents in the construction of the Yankees reinforces and complicates the noble savage characteristics ascribed to the white race and its cause to regain its land. The attempt to parallel real space-time Native-Americans in this episode is quite explicit. For example, the leader of the Yankees (Roy Jensen) is named "Cloud William." Further, the Yankees, like the Indians in "The Paradise Syndrome," wear typical homogenizing Indian garb, such as feathers and animal furs. Finally, the dialogue between Kirk and Spock makes the association overt. Kirk begins by acknowledging the parallel: "If my ancestors were forced out of their cities, into the deserts, the hills." "Yes, I see, Captain," Spock responds. "They would have learned to wear skins, adopted stoic mannerisms, learned the bow and the lance." Kirk concludes: "Living like the Indians. Finally even looking like the American Indian." In short, the Yankees are constructed as stoic, tall, muscle-bound blonde men in animal skins beating drums and speaking of worship—a melange of racial signifiers that combine to mark their cause—to massacre the "yellow" Communists—as noble. The irony here, of course, is that in the real space-time universe, it was a horde of white Yankees that massacred millions of Native-Americans.

"The Omega Glory" ultimately celebrates nationalism, intermixing the Yankees' noble fight to recapture their land with symbols of United States patriotism. Their words of worship include "freedom" and "We The People." Instead of a totem pole, they have a torn United States flag. In the last sequence, the restoration of the Yankees to power is celebrated as if it were the Fourth of July. The first scene of this sequence begins with Kirk and crew prisoners of the victorious Yankees. Soon a United States flag is brought in, inducing a respectful silence from both

17. Yangs holding up the American flag

the captors and the Federation representatives (figure 17). The flag is shot from a low angle, connoting its importance. We hear the opening of the United States national anthem, which reinforces the significance of the patriotic icon. Kirk and crew place their right hands across their chest, as Cloud William recites his people's worship words: "I pleglion nectumflagen fu pep like for stand." Kirk, in low angle shot, chimes in: "Unto the republic for which it stands, one nation under God, indivisible, with liberty and justice for all." With Kirk and the Federation crew on the side of the noble Yankees, the project-in-the-text cannot be more clear about what side of the racial hierarchy it feels is best for humanity's future.

The Anthropomorphic Alien: Black, Brown, Red, Yellow, and White

There are aliens in *Star Trek* whose meanings are designed to be more implicit and analogous than explicit or directly linked to actual peoples and events. This is especially the case with aliens that are absolutely foreign in morphology to humans, such as the creature known as the Horta in "The Devil in the Dark" (1967). The Horta, a sentient rock-

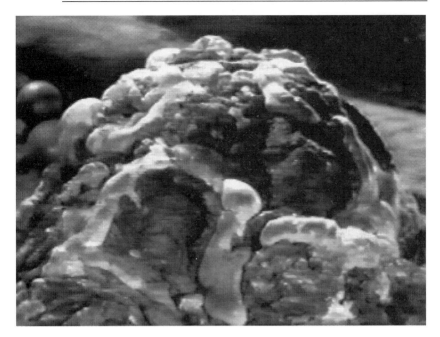

18. The Horta

like being that sought to protect its metallic egg-like young from min-
ers, does not signify a particular group like Native-Americans or Asians
(figure 18). The Horta's referent is not clearly specified by its signifiers,
the narrative context, or symbols like feathers and bearskins. Rather,
the purpose of the Horta is to comment on humanity's battle with difference and prejudice in a decidedly abstract manner.

But the use of aliens that are not anthropomorphic by design is relatively rare in *Star Trek*. Because meanings ascribed to these more
abstract extraterrestrials are not explicit, and thus the potential for didacticism less direct, the project-in-the-text relies on aliens that are
morphologically similar to humans, like Vulcans and Klingons. Anthropomorphic aliens generate less interpretive play than alien figures
like the Horta because they are iconic, clusters of signs that represent
humans and humanity by means of resemblance and similitude. This
includes creatures coded as aliens by either physiognomic or cultural
signifiers; both types are grounded by their clear reference to humans.
As I have suggested throughout this chapter, *Star Trek* is less concerned
with imagining the "infinite variety" of the universe than with drawing
on and instructively engaging the politics and experience of the 1960s.

Iconic aliens often signify the difficulties posed by physiognomic difference and the plight of racial struggle and conflict. However, the figure of the anthropomorphic alien, for all its humanistic sentiment, often ends up supporting the persistence of racial hierarchies. This is a common function of the alien in science fiction films since the 1960s. As Vivian Sobchack suggests, the "articulation of resemblance between aliens and humans preserves the subordination of 'other worlds, other cultures, other species' to the world, culture, and 'speciality' of white American culture. We can see this new American 'humanism' literally expand into and colonize outer space."[44] In sum, anthropomorphic aliens in *Star Trek* are the most consistent forms employed by the liberal-humanistic project to espouse egalitarianism and infinite diversity. They are also the most obvious site of contradiction once reconfigured into a textual form.

Spock is perhaps the quintessential alien of this type. Though a humanoid, he is clearly coded as an extraterrestrial: his pointed ears, raised eyebrows, and slightly different skin tone cue his alien difference. The character is consistently shot in profile, usually in close-ups and medium shots, thereby emphasizing his devilish ears. His seven-year mating cycle, known as Pon Farr, and his suppression of emotions in favor of logic are designed to further support this difference. Yet Spock is actually half human—or, as the Guide to *Star Trek* describes, "biologically, emotionally, and even intellectually a 'half-breed'"[45]—making him even more useful to a project fixated on the sociopolitical meaning of race. Episodes that feature the character often emphasize his experiences as mostly Vulcan among a mostly human United Federation starship. Dr. McCoy, for instance, is constantly reminding him—and thus the audience—of his "green blood" and "pointy ears."

Not unlike Tonto in *The Lone Ranger*, Spock is an Other that is depicted as stoically and loyally withstanding the prejudice of others in the interest of serving the manifest destiny of the Federation. He signifies the alien who can pull himself up by his bootstraps and steadfastly serve the interest of his white captain and the mostly human Federation. Most of the episodes that feature the half-breed construct him as highly competent and extremely trustworthy. This devotion is represented as logical; his service to the Federation and Kirk is rational. By making Spock logically loyal in this way, the program's creators use the racial project-in-the-text to displace the liberal-humanist ideal of the rational man onto the half-breed alien so that he poses little or no

THE VENGEANCE OF FU MANCHU
CHRISTOPHER LEE   DOUGLAS WILMER   TSAI CHIN

19. Christopher Lee as Fu Manchu

threat to the Federation or white television. He is the ideal and idealized alien, assimilated into the dominantly white world of the United Federation of Planets.

Anthropomorphic aliens like Spock are composites or condensations of many ideological projects. For instance, Klingons, while certainly signifying Soviets, are assigned racial signifiers that include cosmetically darkened skin and sinister goatees cut in the fashion of stereotypes of the Chinese. In fact, Klingons in the original Trek bear a striking resemblance to the diabolical Fu Manchu character made famous by Warner Oland in the early 1930s and revived in both the serials of the 1940s and in such 1960s films as *The Vengeance of Fu Manchu* (1968), in which the character was played by Christopher Lee (figure 19), and *The Blood of Fu Manchu* (1968), in which the character was played by horror film star Boris Karloff. The striking similarity between Fu Manchu and the Klingons made the fictional aliens more readily identifiable and acceptable as a vile enemy.

The composite nature of the alien form is especially evident in "Elaan of Troyius," where race and gender are conjoined in the figure of a female alien played by an Asian-American actor (France Nuyen). In the episode, Kirk and crew are charged with transporting two diplomats from one "Federation controlled planet" to another in a star system close to the neutral zone. The two planets have been at war for centuries, and with the advent of interplanetary flight, the fear is that the conflict will escalate to the point of their mutual destruction. Moreover, because the Klingons claim the star system as their own, it is in the Federation's best interest for the two worlds to make peace and then cooperate in their resistance to Klingon encroachment. In order to ensure peace between the two worlds, Elaan, the female Asian-alien, is to be wed to the male leader of Troyius. The *Enterprise* is charged with bringing Elaan to her new suitor. Because she is perceived as uncivilized and barbaric, Elaan is to be instructed on the customs and amenities of the Troyan people. A classical narrative journey, the story's ultimate purpose is for Kirk to tame the shrew in order to stop a war and keep the Klingons from expanding their empire.

"Elaan of Troyius" is a Vietnam allegory that brings into play two stereotypes of the Asian female—the manipulative dragon lady and the submissive female slave—in order to support the myth of the superiority of NATO (the Federation) and the white male hero (Captain Kirk). In fact, sex becomes the means by which the captain establishes his control and dominance over the Asian-alien. This is a common use of Asian female characters in Hollywood. As Marchetti remarks: "Hollywood narratives are part of what Edward W. Said has described in *Orientalism* as 'a Western style for dominating, restructuring, and having authority over the Orient.' They create a mythic image of Asia that empowers the West and rationalizes Euroamerican authority over the Asian other. Romance and sexuality provide the metaphoric justification for this domination."[46] Captain Kirk, the "white knight" of *Star Trek*, articulates his and the Federation's moral superiority and authority over the Asian-alien and her people through sexual conquest.

As a representation of Vietnam, often portrayed by the United States military and the media during this period as a "damn little pissant country,"[47] Elaan is both irrational and primitive. She throws temper tantrums, eats with her hands, and drinks from the bottle. She spits and snarls. "That's another one of your problems," Kirk tells her, "Nobody's told you that you're an uncivilized savage, a vicious child in a woman's body, an arrogant monster." She is a worthy student of Captain Kirk. Early in her education she throws a knife at him; later, she slaps him. Like the representation of North Vietnam in the late 1960s, she puts up a good fight. However, Kirk is a worthy instructor. He slaps her back and then threatens her like a father would threaten a child: "If I touch you again, your Glory," he arrogantly states, "it'll be to administer an ancient Earth custom called a spanking, a form of punishment administered to spoiled brats." Like the representation of the United States' efforts in Vietnam before 1968, Kirk is sure to win.

As the story progresses, Kirk wins Elaan's heart through force and charm. Indeed, it is only after the captain physically and sexually dominates her that she respects and eventually falls in love with him. "Captain, there's one thing you can teach me," Elaan says to him after he threatens to get her another tutor. "I don't know how to make people like me." After giving in to Kirk's power, Elaan, like the cunning and manipulative dragon lady of classical Hollywood cinema, returns the favor by capturing his heart. The Asian-alien's tears contain a biochemical agent that, when touched by a man (apparently even aliens like Kirk), forces him to fall deeply in love with her. "Captain," she alluringly asks after Kirk wipes her tears, "that ancient earth custom called spanking, what is it?" Elaan uses her mysterious sexuality to finalize her control over the very white Captain, and apparently gets a spanking in the bargain. Moments later we are cued to their lovemaking.

After she manipulates Kirk into desiring her, Elaan becomes submissive, gentle, loyal, even willing to die with him, by his side, as the Klingons ruthlessly attack the *Enterprise*. It is at this point in the narrative that the other stereotype of the Asian female comes into play—that of the submissive Asian slave. In the end, Elaan does anything Captain Kirk requests, politely and adoringly obeying his demands and orders. Her dragon lady tactics were only used so that she could assume a position she truly desired: the submissive mistress of a white knight. She becomes civilized and docile only when servicing the dominant and dominating masculinity of the paleface protagonist. Thus, the myth of the white hero functions not only as a political legitimization of U.S. dominance over Vietnam, but also as a sexualized justification for traditional Asian female roles.

The contradictory nature of the racial project in "Elaan of Troyius" is further evident in the way Elaan is shot. In much of the shooting and

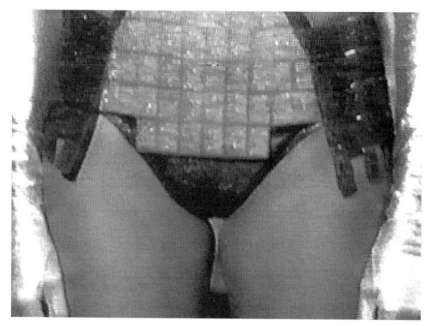

20. Close-up of Elaan's waist

21. Close-up of Elaan's face

22. Kirk and crew kneeling before Elaan

costuming, her body is fragmented into parts and fetishized: feet, legs, waist, breasts, face, and hair. Her costuming is consistently revealing, in the tradition of *Star Trek* females. In the process, her "Asianness"— her nonwhite skin, petite stature, and strong accent—is highlighted and eroticized. For example, in the scene where Elaan arrives on the *Enterprise*, a panning shot slowly reveals her fetishizable parts. Not unlike Uhura in "Mirror, Mirror," we see close-ups of her feet, her bare brown legs, her groin, delicately accented by bikini-type shorts, her small waist, her breasts, and, as the camera finally comes to rest, her stern but striking face (figures 20 and 21). This pronounced camera-work reveals a female Asian-alien with phallic black braids. The music crescendos, italicizing her worthy-of-fetishism presence. After some reaction shots from the men, we then see the *Enterprise* crew, having been treated to the body of the Asian-alien erotic, kneel before her (figure 22). She becomes worthy of their "respect" only after her body is fragmented for their visual pleasure. She is an object of exotic desire—a to-be-looked-at-Other.

Live Long and Prosper

What the *Star Trek* universe looks like vis-à-vis race—the racial pro-ject-in-the-text—speaks to the practices of creative and network deci-sion makers. This is not to suggest that the Trek universe is determined by the makers of the series. Like the physical universe theorized in cos-mology, *Star Trek* is informed by a curved and evolving sociopolitical context with a diverse group of observers who bring distinct levels of interest and histories to the meaning-making process. Rather, the rec-ognition of authorship suggests that the creators of *Star Trek*, while not singularly determining the meaning of the text, nonetheless inform its form and its trajectory. To do away with or ignore the agency of these decision makers is to undermine their responsibility in the ideological project of texts—and thus in the *history* of racism.

The liberal-humanist projects behind the production of *Star Trek* and in the text are patently contradictory. Story outlines that call for an integrated cast are whitewashed; scripts that call for a radical critique of racism are diluted. The science fiction series brings extraterrestrial nations and dissimilar aliens together, yet it also marks and segregates difference as Otherness. Spock is a loyal alien. Elaan is a cunning or submissive fetishized object. Both of them function to support the myth of the white hero. Indeed, in episodes like "The Paradise Syndrome" and "The Omega Glory," *Star Trek* offers a systematic racial hierarchy: whites on top, all Others at the bottom. The results of these practices are liberal compromises that reveal that the project of the creative deci-sion makers and the project-in-the-text are anything but egalitarian. The paradox of *Star Trek* is that, despite or because of its liberal hu-manism, it supports a universe where whites are morally, politically, and innately superior, and both colored humans and colored aliens are either servants, threats, or objects of exotic desire.

3

Trek on the Silver Screen

White Future-Time as the Final Frontier

When a body moves, or a force acts, it affects the curvature of space and time—and in turn the structure of space-time affects the way in which bodies move and forces act. Space and time not only affect but also are affected by everything that happens in the universe. Just as one cannot talk about events in the universe without the notions of space and time, so in general relativity it became meaningless to talk about space and time outside the limits of the universe.
—*Stephen Hawking*

Kirk: Spock, you want to know something? Everybody's human.
Spock: I find that remark . . . insulting.

Nearly ten years after the original *Star Trek* was canceled by NBC, Paramount, the owner of the series after it acquired Desilu Studios in the late 1960s, released *The Motion Picture* to movie theatres across the country. The event was a long-awaited triumph for fans who had fought hard to see their favorite crew and starship once again exploring unknown worlds and new civilizations. Though today it seems like there's a new Trek film every other year, the science fiction juggernaut actually had a bumpy journey from its cancellation as a television series to its reemergence on the silver screen. In the early 1970s most of the original cast lent their voices to *The Animated Series*, but the Saturday morning cartoon lasted only a few seasons. In the mid-1970s Paramount drove the fans into a frenzy by vacillating between bringing the original *Star Trek* back either as a feature film or as the anchor television series to what at the time would have been a fourth network.[1] The making of *The Motion Picture* was itself somewhat tumultuous, with directing responsibilities shifting in preproduction from Philip Kaufman to Robert Wise. Nevertheless, in 1979 James T. Kirk and crew resumed their trek in *The Motion Picture* (figure 23), a film whose tag line, "The human adventure is just beginning," proved amazingly prophetic. Indeed, there have been seven sequels to date: *The*

23. Cast of *The Final Frontier*. © 1989 Paramount Pictures Corporation

Wrath of Khan, The Search for Spock, The Voyage Home, The Final Frontier, The Undiscovered Country, and, with a next generation of characters, *Generations* and *First Contact*. For the first time in Hollywood history, a canceled television series reemerged as a money-making mega-text.

Perhaps the most cathartic scene in Trek's long-awaited return from the ordinarily sure death of television cancellation involves the first time we actually see the Phoenix-like *Enterprise* in *The Motion Picture*. Surprisingly, this scene does not come at the beginning of the story; the film initially teases the spectator's anticipation before it actually releases the prized icon. Instead, the first cinematic Trek opens to an enormous intergalactic cloud easily destroying three Klingon Battle Cruisers and immobilizing a sizable Federation spacestation as it heads toward Earth. Because of the impending threat, Starfleet Command orders their most heroic captain, James T. Kirk, now an admiral with a desk job, to resume command of the recently remodeled *Enterprise* and stop the ominous cloud from reaching its target. Eager to get back to action, Kirk joins Chief Engineer Scotty on board a small shuttle heading for the storied starship. But Scotty is concerned that the *Enterprise* is not ready: "She needs more work, sir, a shakedown," he complains. Kirk tersely explains the urgency of the mission, and orders: "Ready or not, she launches in twelve hours." The feminine personal pronoun the spacemen use in identifying the *Enterprise* recodifies their romantic affections for the vessel. It also works to intensify the spectator's anticipation. Kirk sentimentally admits his pride in the fact that Starfleet "gave her back" to him, and Scotty responds gently: "Any man who can manage such a feat I would not dare disappoint. She'll launch on time, sir, and she'll be ready." The theme music crescendos slightly as the shuttle, a stubby short-range craft, makes its way to the new and improved *Enterprise* (figure 24).

The scene continues for almost five minutes without dialogue, temporarily halting the progress of the story.[2] The fans waited a long time to see their favorite starship back in action, and *The Motion Picture* provides them with a long and uninterrupted look. We first see the *Enterprise* in the distance, surrounded by a kind of scaffolding used in remodeling starships (figure 25). Kirk and Scotty are shown looking out the shuttle's front window against the backdrop of a bright blue planet Earth, a stunning visual effect enhanced by the elongated wide-screen format. As the shuttle approaches the starship, slowly moving outside the scaffolding to track along its body, we begin to see glimpses of "her"—the impressive stern, the two outstretched warp nacelles, the magnificent hull. These fragments of the *Enterprise* are sensualized by both the gentle rhythm of the musical score and the warm, almost glowing facial expressions of Kirk (figure 26). Many of the shots are also from the captain's point of view, thereby allowing the spectator to experience the spectacle of a perfectly white and subtly rounded starship through his eyes.

As the shuttle gradually moves from the port side of the masked starship to the bridge, the music crescendos dramatically as we see for the first time since the television series an unobstructed view of the entire *Enterprise* (figure 27). Lights on the top of the scaffolding highlight the vessel, producing a sort of glow around the bridge. The shuttle moves between the scaffolding and the starship, slowly caressing its way across the top of the craft. It moves though the warp nacelles, around the rear, and back to the port side where it finally docks at a perfectly circular porthole (figures 28 and 29). The long journey around the *Enterprise*—from the stern, around the port side to its bow, back around the starboard side to the stern, and back around the port side to the porthole—is entirely motivated by the vessel's magnificent features. We hear "pressure equalized" from a male voice-over, and Kirk boards his beloved starship and begins his urgent mission to save Earth from the threatening space cloud. The catharsis is complete, the scene ends, and the story resumes.

The depiction of the *Enterprise* in this scene is strikingly similar to the representation of women in Hollywood cinema discussed in Laura Mulvey's groundbreaking essay, "Visual Pleasure and Narrative Cinema." Mulvey writes: "The determining male gaze projects its fantasy onto the female figure, which is stylized accordingly. In their traditional exhibitionist role women are simultaneously looked at and displayed, with their appearances coded for strong visual and erotic impact so that they can be said to connote to-be-looked-at-ness."[3] Like the representations of women in Hollywood cinema, the *Enterprise* is a feminized figure eliciting scopic desire. The starship is literally a show-stopper, temporarily halting the progress of the story. "She" is fragmented into parts by both the composition of the close-up shots and the design of the scaffolding. These views result in fetishizable fragments of the starship, phallic symbols Kirk and Scotty gaze upon with disavowing familiarity and voyeuristic pleasure. These shots are also from the spacemen's point of view, facilitating the spectator's identification with the object of their desire. In this way, the *Enterprise* connotes to-be-looked-at-ness.

Yet, the starship *Enterprise* is also the vehicle that carries Kirk and crew through space and time, enabling them to travel faster than the speed of light, visit distant planets, journey to Earth's past, and, of course, fight off intergalactic oppressors like the Klingon Empire. Without this objectified vessel, Kirk and crew would be unable to explore the vast unknown of the future and the oddities of extraterrestrial worlds. They would be unable to save Earth from enormous space clouds, putting a spin on a common cliché: behind every Trek hero is a beautiful starship. In this way, the *Enterprise* is a specularized figure of a particular kind: a *chronotope*, or what literary theorist Mikhail Bakhtin, loosely borrowing from Albert Einstein's special theory of relativity, recognizes as the "intrinsic connectedness" of space and time. In the chronotope, Bakhtin argues, "spatial and temporal indicators are fused into one carefully thought-out, concrete whole. Time, as it were, thickens, takes on flesh, becomes artistically visible; likewise,

24. Shuttle leaving station

25. *Enterprise* surrounded by scaffolding

26. Kirk glowing with anticipation

27. Full frontal view of *Enterprise*

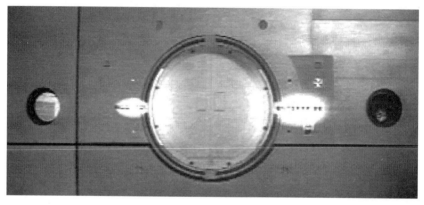

28. *Enterprise* porthole

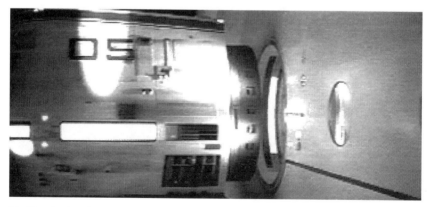

29. Shuttle docking with *Enterprise*

space becomes charged and responsive to the movements of time, plot and history." [4] As a chronotope, the *Enterprise* is simultaneously a spatial marker, a curvaceous curvature of matter, and a temporal indicator, guiding diegetic adventure and assimilating history in the process.

Chronotopes impact all aspects of the science fiction genre, including the meaning of race. They are the means by which diegetic logics like the United Federation of Planets, parallel evolution, and the anthropomorphic alien become meaningful and relative to history: to ideology. The Asian-alien in "Elaan of Troyius" (discussed in chapter 2) would not be a to-be-looked-at Other if not for both her alien spatiality, her eroticized and exoticized look, and her narrative function, a discursive formation that weds a stereotype of Vietnam as primitive with that of Asian woman as sexually mysterious. White starships like the *Enterprise* and aliens of color like Elaan enable us not only to apprehend where and at what time story events occur, but to experience the eventness of narrative and the significance of characterization. They allow us to see stories as politicized allegories and characters as potent symbols. Thus, they are not simply the background for a diegetic universe, but, as Vivian Sobchack shows, a fundamental element that shapes genre, empowers narrative, brings characters to life, and, most importantly, provides for the incorporation—what Bakhtin calls "historicity"—of real space-time politics and experiences. [5]

What can the chronotope as a critical studies concept tell us about the meaning of race in the science fiction genre in general, and in cinematic Trek in particular? What are the defining or recurring chronotopes in the *Star Trek* films? In what ways do these chronotopes assimilate real space-time history, particularly the shifting and reforming meaning of race? In short, what does the future-time of feature Trek look like, and where does it take us?

In addressing these questions, I have divided this chapter into two sections. The first section outlines Bakhtin's notion of the chronotope and how it might apply to our understanding of the science fiction genre. Relying on key films from the genre but also pointing to cinematic Trek, this section focuses on two of the oldest and most common science fiction chronotopes—starships and aliens—to show how the genre in recent years has systematically engaged and extended myths about race in its quest to imagine the final frontier. The second half of the chapter analyzes the minor chronotopes that make up cinematic Trek's future-time, including: outer space, alien worlds, and the space-time of home, or the real world represented in the fictional world. I argue that the history that warps these chronotopes, the history-in-the-text, is the extension of a manifestly white destiny into and beyond the future. In what can best be described as *white future-time*, the minor chronotopes in Trek extend the history of white superiority into and beyond the final frontier.

Science Fiction Chronotopes

Specific chronotopes define specific genres: from saloons in the western to jungles in recent war movies. As I noted above, among the more recurrent science fiction chronotopes are starships, outer space, alien worlds, and planet Earth. Often visualized through art direction, makeup, costuming, and special effects, most of these chronotopes have dominated the genre since Georges Méliès's *A Trip to the Moon* (1902). In this early cinema classic, we see scientists utilizing a starship as the catalyst for an adventure, a trip in space. We also see an exotic alien world, the moon, populated with mischievous and threatening extraterrestrials. Méliès employs stop-motion photography, an innovative special effect of the period, in order to make the moon-people appear to vanish in puffs of smoke when struck by the scientists. The scientists eventually flee for their lives, returning home more familiar with the diversity and dangers of the world beyond Earth's borders. Clearly chronotopes like these, particularly starships and alien worlds, continue to dominate today's science fiction films.

Starships: Where We Come from; Where We're Going

The chronotope, Bakhtin writes, "makes narrative events concrete, makes them take on flesh, causes blood to flow in their veins."[6] The ship in *A Trip to the Moon*, which almost seems like a template for the shuttle in *The Motion Picture*, is what enables the French scientists to experience alien worlds and extraterrestrial threats. In feature Trek, the *Enterprise* is the catalyst for "action-packed" adventures from one unknown space-time to another. The starship enables Kirk and company to explore the depths of the intergalactic cloud in *The Motion Picture*, fight off a Klingon Warbird in *The Search for Spock*, travel back in time to twentieth-century San Francisco in *The Voyage Home*, experience the depths of the galaxy in *The Final Frontier*, and, most symptomatic of contemporaneous politics, secure for the Federation a peace accord with the Klingon Empire in *The Undiscovered Country*. In the Trek sequels with a next generation of characters, yet another remodeled *Enterprise* enables Captain Jean-Luc Picard (Patrick Stewart) to both convince Kirk to leave a dream-like energy ribbon, the Nexus, in order to save a planet's primitive inhabitants in *Generations*; and, like *The Voyage Home*, return to Earth's past to save the future in *First Contact*. Chronotopes like the starship are the vehicles that take science fiction's heroes—and spectators—on journeys from narrative event to event, from beginning to climax to dénouement.

Chronotopes like the starship are a kind of grid, a synthesis of space and time that link the fictional with the real; they are, in other words, graphic signs of history. As Bakhtin notes, "Out of the actual chronotopes of our world (which serve as the source of representation) emerge the reflected and *created* chronotopes of the world represented in the work."[7] For instance, the *Enterprise* is drawn from and extends the history of the American wagon train. Like the starship, the wagon train conveys both an adventurous tone and a Puritan ethic: the conquest and civilizing of the frontier. The wagon train brought European and European-American settlers from the East to the West, "civilizing" the wilderness in its pursuit of manifest destiny. Similarly, the *Enterprise*— a "wagon train to the stars," as Roddenberry was fond of saying—explores the unknown and the uncivilized. It too brings a cast of explorers and settlers to distant spaces, often under the guise of spreading the word of a democratic humanity. Both wagon train and starship are threatened by the uncivilized Others they meet in their adventures: wild Indians in the West; strange-looking aliens in the future. Finally, both wagon train and starship succeed at geographic and intragalactic dominance. Both enable their occupants to dominate and domesticate the frontier.

What we experience in chronotopic history in science fiction film is myth. The historiographic honesty of the wagon train is not told in the Trek films; rather, the myth of the wagon train is extended and expanded via the *Enterprise* chronotope. This does not mean that chronotopic myths like the wagon-train-to-the-stars are simply a lie or only fiction. Rather, it means they are longstanding and ever-present modes of historical knowledge about the past and the future, about where we come from and where are going. As Richard Slotkin notes, myths provide "the broadest-based and most pervasive means for canvassing the world of events and the spectrum of public concerns, for recalling historical precedents, and for translating them into the various story-genres that constitute a public mythology."[8] Myths like the wagon train and its science fiction extension, the starship, are dominant ways we understand the past and, clearly in the case of science fiction films, envision the future. They are assimilations of history that have less to do with historical honesty than with myth-informed common sense.

Most myths work their stuff by subsuming the telling inherent in *history* under the umbrella of natural or divine cause and effect. They naturalize the ideology inherent in historiography. Myths are common-sense "truths" about past events that rationalize the present and justify a particular future. They usually involve binary arguments—good versus evil; white versus black—that are easily digestible and sensible. Through mass retelling, these binary "truths" become conventionalized and commonplace, downsized to graphic markers, codes, and signifiers that make them easily understandable and repeatable. It is these common markers that can be said to be always already chronotopic.

A dominant myth retold and recast in the science fiction genre in general and in the Trek features in particular involves the United States' deep obsession with the frontier, or the untamed wilderness that continues to be "our" civilization's imagined future. The frontier, as Slotkin notes, "is our oldest and most characteristic myth, expressed in a body of literature, folklore, ritual, historiography, and polemics produced over a period of three centuries."[9] Dramatically and drastically informing the culture, economics, and politics of the United States, this myth is based on a history of European and European-American colonization of the "New World" and, later, the "wild West." The purpose of this expansion was to map and civilize the wilderness in order to make room for white settlers. It was the settlers' quality of life, their entitlements to economic and ideological well-being, that was imperative and divinely inspired. Nothing and nobody could stop this westward trek, and if a non-Western people got in the way—like the Native-American nations that populated the so-called New World—they were assailed with a cavalry of atrocities. The myth of the frontier describes and justifies this violent history, what Slotkin names the "savage war," as something natural, divine: inevitable.

The myth of the frontier continues to inform and shape the culture, economics, politics, and identity of the United States. Since the end of the physical colonization of North America, this myth has been used to defend such diverse practices as slavery, imperialism, segregation, and military and economic interventionism. Ultimately legitimizing and advocating a white-dominated hemisphere, the hegemony of this myth is largely due to its political flexibility and binary simplicity. As Slotkin summarizes:

> [The myth] . . . serves with equal facility the requirements of progressives and conservatives, of political managers and movie scriptwriters, of academic historiography and bureaucratic apologetics, of warfare and child's play; that is rooted in history but capable of transcending the limitations of a specific temporality, to speak with comparable authority and intelligibility to the citizens of eighteenth-century colonies, a nineteenth-century agrarian republic, and a modern industrial world power; that originated in tales told by, for, and about rural White "Anglo-Saxon" Protestant heroes, which nonetheless became the preferred entertainment of the audience of the ethnically heterodox population of the twentieth-century "megalopolis." [10]

The myth was especially potent in the 1960s, the period that gave birth to *Star Trek*. Slotkin points to President John F. Kennedy's political rhetoric about "the new frontier," i.e., the impetus for the space race with the former Soviet Union, as a contemporary articulation of this myth. He also points to instances in which United States troops described Vietnam as "Indian country," and search-and-destroy missions as "Cowboys and Indians." [11] The myth of the frontier carried on with Reagan's "cowboy diplomacy," when South and Central America became the space-time in need of conservative civilizing. From the Monroe Doctrine to manifest destiny, from the politics that promoted the United States as the leader of the "free world" after World War II to former President George Bush's "new world order" after the invasions of Panama and Iraq, the myth of the frontier has informed the country's national*ized* identity.

Perhaps the clearest example of the frontier myth in Hollywood cinema occurs in the western, a genre that has consistently retold the story of a white hero who domesticates or obliterates "wild" Indians, "dirty" Mexicans, and "heathen" Chinese in his quest to tame the West. Yet this is also the case with science fiction. At least since the all-white worlds of Fritz Lang's *Metropolis* (1926), the story of a white future has reigned supreme. In *Dune* (1984) and *Star Wars* (1977), for example, there are no visible actors of color, hero or villain. Only in the two sequels to *Star Wars*, *The Empire Strikes Back* (1980) and *Return of the*

Jedi (1983), is there a character of color, Lando Calrissian (Billy Dee Williams). Nonetheless, white rule is still hegemonic in these two films; Lando takes a back seat to the heroics, the force, of the leading white characters, Luke Skywalker (Mark Hamill), Han Solo (Harrison Ford), and Princess Leia (Carrie Fisher). Not unlike Sulu and Uhura, Lando is background color in a time when humans were almost all white. This is further emphasized when the main villain, the treacherous Darth Vader, who wears nothing but black, finally returns to the good side of the force. About to die, Vader takes off his face-covering helmet and reveals, not James Earl Jones, the African-American actor whose distinctive voice gave the character depth, but a white man. In other words, once Vader returns to the force, to the side of good, he literally turns white. The restrictions and stereotypes imposed on characters of color like Lando and Darth Vader and the subsequent reliance on white heroes like Luke Skywalker, Han Solo, and Princess Leia—or for that matter, Kirk and Picard—are fundamental to the extension of the frontier myth into and beyond the stars.

The future is systematically whitewashed in recent science fiction films. In this space-time, the immense distances of outer space do not hinder manifest destiny. Neither do treacherous or primitive aliens. In the future-time of such contemporary science fiction stories as *The Last Starfighter* (1984), *Total Recall* (1990), *Stargate* (1994), and *The Fifth Element* (1997), specifically Western and mostly white-humanoids manage to traverse the profound distances of space and navigate the frightening dangers of alien (or mutant, as the case may be) worlds. Moreover, time is not a barrier in the genre, especially when white history is at stake. Many science fiction films have their heroes escaping the linearity of time to return to the past in order to save the future. In such time-travel features as *The Terminator* (1984) and *Terminator 2: Judgment Day* (1991), the *Back to the Future* trilogy (1985, 1989, 1990), and *Time Cop* (1994), time is the path to a better—often whiter—future. This is also the case with cinematic Trek. In *The Voyage Home*, for example, Kirk and crew journey to present-day Earth to save the planet from a dark alien probe. In *First Contact*, Picard returns to Earth's multicultural past to save the planet from the threatening Borg—the mechanistic beings who, somewhat ironically, intend on assimilating humans into their collective. Despite all the dark matter in the universe, whiteness is ultimately privileged in this myth-extending genre.

Extraterrestrial, Cybernetic, and Human Aliens:
A Strange Yet Familiar Universe

Aliens like the moon creatures in *A Trip to the Moon* are another common science fiction chronotope. This is not to say that chronotopes are synonymous with characters, often the basis for an alien. On the contrary, aliens are chronotopic, notwithstanding the alien world from which they emerge or their dual function as characters, because they are grounded by a particular spatiality—usually physiognomic difference—that is inseparable from both a sense of time—a past, future, or alternative universe where aliens exist—and a sense of history—particularly, in recent versions of the genre, the meaning of race. More specifically, aliens are a fusion of both spatial and temporal indicators that, for all their alienness, more often than not incorporate the myths and ideologies—the exaggerations and distortions—ascribed to the physiognomy and culture of real-world peoples.

Some genres, as Gary Morson and Caryl Emerson note, "come closer to an accurate understanding of the 'actual historical chronotope' than others." [12] Perhaps ironically given the genre's obsession with extraterrestrial existence and the future, this is especially the case with science fiction. And in this regard the genre has been more reactionary and paranoid than progressive. A quick count of alien invasion films, a mainstay of Hollywood science fiction, shows that more were made during the 1950s, a particularly xenophobic and conservative period of United States history, and the 1980s, a period marked by neoconservatism and the politics of reverse discrimination, than in any other decade. [13] Coupled with Hollywood's tendency to shock and titillate rather than challenge spectators, this pattern suggests that the genre has taken advantage of shifts in the real space-time preoccupation with national or physiognomic differences in order to tell frightful stories of alien invaders. This trend has actually accumulated enough critical mass to generate parodies of itself, as can be seen in both *Mars Attacks!* (1996) and *Men in Black* (1997). In the former, hundreds of short, big-brained Martians arrive at a welcoming ceremony on Earth, only to misinterpret the release of a dove, humanity's sign of peace, and begin systematically attacking our cities, monuments, and politicians. The Martians also perform odd medical experiments, such as transplanting the head of a starlet (Sarah Jessica Parker) onto the body of a small dog, thereby making the aliens the least odd-looking creatures in the film. In

Men in Black, K (Tommy Lee Jones), a member of a top-secret organization established to monitor alien activity on Earth, stops a band of Border Patrol agents who are in the process of deporting a few "illegal" Mexican immigrants. Disguised as one of the Mexicans is the true threat to our sovereignty, an illegal extraterrestrial.

While chronotopes like the alien become generic conventions spanning decades of filmmaking, their significance shifts and changes with real space-time. For example, aliens in 1950s science fiction films like *Invasion of the Body Snatchers* (1956) and *Killers from Space* (1954) bear a striking resemblance to Communists or Soviets, as many critics have shown and as *Mars Attacks!* parodies.[14] This makes chronotopic sense given the widespread "red menace" invasion fears of both the United States government and the Hollywood industry during this era. After all, this is the period that saw both the McCarthy hearings and Hollywood blacklisting—two interrelated events that had a significant impact on film production and distribution. In contemporary science fiction films, on the other hand, aliens are less international invaders than domestic and cultural threats. As *Men in Black* parodies, this is perhaps due to a historical moment more concerned with immigration, English-only laws, and the ramifications of multiculturalism than with an "evil empire." As Charles Ramírez Berg suggests: "the movie alien now symbolizes real-life aliens—documented and undocumented immigrants who have entered, and continue to attempt to enter, the United States."[15] While Ramírez Berg is mostly concerned with the representation of Latinos, I will argue that a variety of human colors are segregated by the chronotopic prisms of the alien.

The alien chronotope in contemporary science fiction film ultimately functions to define the purity and civility of whiteness. In *Aliens* (1986), for example, the queen of the monstrous extraterrestrials, whose numerous children literally use the bodies of humans to grow in, is not simply a mother—a representation drawing upon ideologies of gender, as many film scholars have pointed out[16]—but a black mother (figure 30). This, it seems to me, is a common-sense use of the well-worn myth that equates the color black, the look of darkness, with evil. It is also a symptom of the stereotype of overpopulating black women represented in the 1980s as "welfare queens." In contrast, the film's human heroine, Ripley (Sigourney Weaver), an unmistakably white character, is a nurturing mother to Newt (Carrie Henn), the orphan she rescues (figure 31). In the binary tradition of myth-extending

30. Alien from *Aliens*. © 1986 Twentieth Century Fox Film Corp.

31. Ripley and Newt. © 1986 Twentieth Century Fox Film Corp.

32. Khan and crew. © 1982 Paramount Pictures Corporation

chronotopes, not to mention the norms of Hollywood casting and art direction, the overpopulating evil of blackness helps define the nurturing civility of whiteness.

Science fiction cinema is often less than discreet when it comes to the intended meaning of its aliens. In *Blade Runner* (1982), the Replicants—the "skin jobs"—are manmade aliens, white-androids who are expressly correlated with African-Americans. As Deckard (Harrison Ford) tells us in voice-over about his captain's hatred of Replicants: "In history books, he's the kinda cop used to call black men niggers." An example less challenging to the history of racism is *The Wrath of Khan*, which features Noonian Singh Khan (Ricardo Montalban), a genetically enhanced human who, thanks to cryogenics, has come from Earth's twentieth century to take charge of the future (figure 32).[17] In the film, Khan is alien, or at least not a "normal" human, because of his superhuman abilities, his vindictive temper, and his Latino accent—traits that are uncommon among naturally-evolved Trek humans. In

33. Dennis Quaid and Louis Gossett Jr. in *Enemy Mine.* © 1985 Twentieth Century Fox Film Corp.

fact, Khan is an overdetermined bearer of meaning in this regard, not only because of his spatio-temporal look—his post-apocalyptic clothes reveal a super-sized chest—but also because the story casts him as a part Latino/part Indian mix-match from the Eugenics Wars of Earth's past/our future.

The symbolic relationship between aliens and nonwhite humans, or humans who do not pass as white, is particularly evident when considering the relationship between alien chronotopes and the star persona of actors. The way actors are positioned by Hollywood often factors into the significance of the alien. For instance, *Enemy Mine* (1985) features European-American actor Dennis Quaid playing a white-human trapped on a desolate and dangerous planet with an alien enemy, a lizard-like extraterrestrial played by African-American actor Louis Gossett Jr. (figure 33). Both actors bring to their characters star discourses charged with racial subtexts. This is perhaps most obviously the case with Gossett, whose screen credits include *An Officer and a Gentleman* (1982), for which he won an Academy Award for best supporting actor, and *Roots* (1977), one of the most popular mini-series in television history. In both of these films, the actor's identity as an

African-American star is central to both the characters he plays and the stories being told. Similarly, in *Enemy Mine* Gossett's blackness, his identity outside the theatre, seems intended to cue or support his alien-ness. The film is actually science fiction's version of an interracial buddy film, in that it tells the tale of how a black-alien and a white-human become friends in an effort to overcome the dangers of a hostile planet. Like the chained convicts played by Sydney Poitier and Tony Curtis in the classic interracial buddy film *The Defiant Ones* (1958), the two distinct humanoids—one alien, one "normal"—must work through their difference if they are to survive.

Visual style also has a role in the significance of the alien chronotope. Many shots in *Enemy Mine* are devoted to exploring the lizard-like alien's physical difference, with an eye toward segmenting the Other-ness of his body. And, like the relationship between the starship *Enterprise* and Captain Kirk in *The Motion Picture*, these shots are often cued from the Quaid character's point of view, thereby facilitating a fetishistic distance for the identifying spectator. The alien's to-be-looked-at body is dissected for all the humans to ogle. Moreover, the black-alien, clearly coded as hyper-masculine, is pregnant and dies during birth, forcing the Quaid character to raise the lizard-like child as his own. In this light, the ideology embodied in the alien chronotope reveals the interconnectedness of sexism and racism, in that, in the troubling traditions of the Hollywood style, it feminizes the nonwhite male in order to make him safe and befriendable. As I have argued about the early films of D. W. Griffith, men of color, and now aliens of color, are not only demonized and brutalized, but also feminized and fetishized as a means of turning them into pacified yet eroticized Others. Whether nonwhite or alien or both, the end result remains the idealization of whiteness.[18]

While alien threats more often than not come in the form of extraterrestrials, androids, and super-humans, they also come in the form of nonwhite humans in general. In other words, the genre's interest in representing aliens slips from a metaphoric or symbolic association to a literal ascription, from resemblance to actuality, as it collapses the extraterrestrial and nonwhite human signs into one narrative function. This is especially evident in films that represent the future inner city. For example, *Blade Runner*, despite its metaphoric challenge to the history of racism in the ironic form of the white Replicants, depicts an over-crowded, polyglot, and violent Los Angeles (figure 34)—a real space-

34. *Blade Runner*'s Los Angeles. © 1982 The Blade Runner Partnership

time chronotope known outside the theatre for both its diversity and its racial conflicts. In the film's dark and dingy future, the "aliens" include the Asian and Latino immigrants who dominate the crime-infested, techno-pop streets of Los Angeles. The trend of representing nonwhite humans in this way extends into the latter 1980s and 1990s in such urban science fiction films as *Escape from New York* (1981), the *Robocop* trilogy (1987, 1990, 1993), *Freejack* (1992), *Judge Dredd* (1995), and *Escape from Los Angeles* (1996). In these films, the nonwhite humans, like their extraterrestrial counterparts, aspire to destroy the white way of life.

The tendency for contemporary science fiction films to collapse the narrative function of extraterrestrials and humans is especially revealing in Trek's *First Contact*, which features cybernetic aliens, the Borg collective, many of whom are part human. Bent on assimilating human civilization into its mechanistic way of life, the Borg actually start with the *Enterprise*—a small city itself. They then proceed to "assimilate" the *Enterprise* crew in hopes of changing the past to dominate the future. The result is a multiracial mass that threatens the humanistic

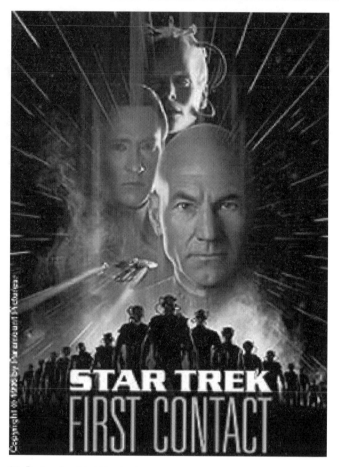

35. Poster for *First Contact*

world of the democratic Federation and its all-too-white heroes. As the composition of the poster advertising the film rhetorically warns, Picard and Data (Brent Spiner)—the white representatives of humanity's next generation—are threatened by an "alien" collective whose components end up all looking alike (figure 35). The contradiction here, of course, is that while the Federation and the U.S.S. *Enterprise* represent pluralism and individual rights, standing in dramatic contrast to the Borg, their pluralism and individuality are humanocentric, Western: white.

The racial essence of the alien chronotope is as obvious in *The Fifth Element* (1997) as it is in *Blade Runner*. Yet, unlike *Blade Runner*, the plight of the "skin jobs" in this film is not an allegory for racism, but an uncritical yet blunt capitulation to the racist myths and stereotypes that plague the genre. First, *The Fifth Element*'s futuristic New York City is diverse, overcrowded, and crime-ridden. Further coding this chaotic and multicolored space-time is a bed of fast-paced Arabic music. More to the point, the film tells the tale of how Earth responds to a dark and evil moon that has come from the recesses of the universe to destroy all life. The dark moon, its only color coming in the form of reddish-orange streaks of molten rock, is aided by a diabolic human, Jean-Baptiste Emmanuel Zorg (Gary Oldman), a devious economic imperialist who is coded as a multiracial Fu Manchu, complete with a little hair under his lower lip, buck teeth, and just enough straight black hair atop his head to make him look the sight of an Asian-white. He represents the misguided result of a multicultural present. In turn, Zorg enlists the help of a violent band of extraterrestrial-aliens, known as Mangalores, whose grotesque faces are dominated by big lips and big noses. These space-faring yet unintelligent aliens have the ability to shape-shift, and often choose to pass as human. The racial coding involved in this explicit form of passing is most obvious in the scene in which the leader of the monstrous aliens presents himself to Zorg—and the audience—as a black-human, only to receive Zorg's scorn: "What an ugly face," Zorg scoffs at the black-human. "It doesn't quite suit you." The leader then shifts back to his natural/extraterrestrial form, and Zorg concludes: "Never be ashamed of who you are." Both the dialogue and the special effect of morphing codify the similar function of extraterrestrials and nonwhite humans as threats to whiteness in what is one of the most blatantly racist moments in the genre's history.

The meaning of race in *The Fifth Element* incorporates and relies upon a perverse homophobia in order to articulate its vision of the future. As the story progresses, the spectator is introduced to one of the future's most popular performers, Rubi Rohd (Chris Tucker), a black-human DJ whose penchant for drag-like clothes and phallic wigs, let alone his name, makes him racially overdetermined in too many ways. Indeed, Rohd is stereotyped as a flamboyant black homosexual who nonetheless spends many moments in the depths of off-screen space apparently performing cunnilingus on a stewardess. In this comic scene, which is cross-cut with the overplayed representation of a spaceship taking off, he only pops his head up to quell the moaning stewardess's fear of getting caught. Moreover, after the Mangalores begin indiscriminately killing passengers on a posh cruiseliner, Rubi spends the rest of the story screaming and panicking in a histrionic style reminiscent of Harvey Fierstein's over-dramatic performance in *Independence Day* (1996). In short, Rubi Rohd is perverse, queer, and black. Embodied in his costuming, performance, and name, not to mention his narrative function, is a sexualized racial essence that is coded as perverse, obnoxious: anything but pure/white.

The function of extraterrestrials and nonwhites in *The Fifth Element* supports the myth of a biologically assured white superiority. The ideal of perfection in the film, the so-called fifth element (after water, fire, earth, and wind), is also so racially overdetermined—so overtly supremacist—as to be obnoxious itself. The fifth element, which is needed to defeat the evil moon, happens to be a genetically "perfect" white woman, Leeloo (Milla Jovovich), whose bright red hair is highlighted by its very blonde roots. According to the film, she is a genetic and physignomic paragon. As Korben Dallas (Bruce Willis), the film's male hero, describes her: "5'9", blue eyes, long legs, great skin. You know, perfect." Her perfection is due in no small measure to such physiognomic characteristics as "blue eyes" and "great [white] skin," apparent results of her "perfect genes." Even Dallas is an overdetermined sign of whiteness, complete with a fluffy white cat that purrs at his feet and blonde toupee atop his head. His romantic coupling with Leeloo, depicted no less than pure as the driven snow, takes place in the glowing white light that ends up destroying the evil moon, and stands in climactic contrast to the perversity of Rubi Rohd, the grotesqueness of the Mangalores, the treachery of the multiracial Zorg, and the darkness of evil.

The tendency of fictional aliens in science fiction cinema to signify real peoples is poignantly satirized in *The Brother from Another Planet* (1984), which chronicles the experiences of a mute alien (Joe Morton) who, looking like an African-American, finds himself marooned in race-conscious New York City. The alien-brother is actually a renegade galactic slave who can sense, literally hear, the voices of the past: from the echoes of past immigrants on Ellis Island to the vibrations of a barstool where an African-American man was recently murdered. Early in the film these voices are extremely painful for the alien, causing him to contort his body and face. Desperate for silence, he gets relief from the painful echoes of the past only after he experiments with drugs. In this way, the film is self-conscious not only about the genre's tendency to simultaneously displace race onto aliens and aliens onto race, but also about its intimate concern with sociopolitical history. *The Brother from Another Planet* is ultimately about history—about the echoes of a forgotten past in a present-time that is economically depressed and scarred by drug use. As one of the regulars at the bar reminisces: "I remember when it was history here. Harlem was the place." In the end of the film, the alien-brother is cornered by two galactic—and very white—slave traders, only to be rescued by his own kind: brother-aliens who have overcome but not forgotten their history.

White Future-Time

Future-time in recent science fiction films is similar to what Bakhtin calls "adventure-time," a master chronotope of ancient Greek romance novels.[19] In this larger organizing chronotope, heroes and heroines journey from one locale to another. Geopolitical space is expansive and abstract, serving the interests of the journey. En route, characters encounter odd and dangerous alien worlds that hinder their quest and endanger their lives. Moreover, chance and accidental occurrences are the mechanism for meetings and confrontations in adventure-time; narrative events such as surprises and captures are almost all random. Finally, characters in adventure-time do not change; they are the same at the end of their journey as they were at the beginning. All these elements make up the future-time of science fiction cinema, even when the text is a sequel. Other than chronological aging, which the Trek stars usually do with grace and a lot of makeup, those who are heroic remain heroic and those who are villains remain villainous.[20] Whether it is the beginning of the story or the end, the first film or the sixth, Kirk, Spock, and Dr. McCoy continue to lead the loyal multiracial crew of Scotty, Chekov, Uhura, and Sulu on journeys across great distances where they are sure to run into threatening aliens. In the next generation of feature Trek, Picard, Data, and Riker (Jonathan Frakes) are the heroes who boldly lead a new multiracial and multi-alien crew from beginning to end, from film to film.

Other elements Bakhtin stresses about adventure-time are not present in science fiction cinema, indicating the degree to which chronotopes shift from ancient romance novels to modern science fiction films. First, Bakhtin argues that the contemporaneous context is irrelevant in the adventure-time of the Greek romance novel. In that story-genre, it is not the real that is important, but another time altogether: a time of fantasy. This is not the case with future-time, which is not only rooted in the shifting codes of realism, and is thus not fantasy, but is, as I argue in chapter 2, often both implicitly and explicitly concerned with real-world conflicts and struggles. Second, aliens are not "exotic" in Bakhtin's conception of adventure-time, for exoticism, as Morson and Emerson note, "implies a constant measurement against a native standard, which is therefore an active and evaluating force."[21] In future-time, however, alien worlds are especially exotic, juxtaposed against the normality of our white heroes. As I also argued earlier, aliens are racialized Others, and are thus evaluative. Partly due to the genre's concern with history, they form the difference necessary to define humanity—white humanity—as normal and thus superior.

Thanks to myth-extending starships and evaluative aliens, the meaning of race is the gravitational force warping contemporary articulations of future-time. In the rest of this chapter, I show how feature Trek represents a space-time where paleface heroes brutalize and civilize dark aliens in an effort to both explore the galaxy, the final frontier, and protect the sanctity of Earth, the mythical center of the universe. In what amounts to a white future-time, the Trek films rest on several minor science fiction chronotopes: (1) outer space, science fiction's royal road to manifest destiny and its discontents; (2) alien worlds, evaluative space-times that ultimately reveal the whiteness of the Federation and its crew; and (3) home, or the space-time of the present world represented in the future-time of the fictional world—from contemporary San Francisco in *The Voyage Home* to the allegory of the break-up of the Soviet Union in *The Undiscovered Country*. Together, these chronotopes perpetuate a final frontier that is explored and domesticated for a dominantly white imagination.

Outer Space: Meetings and Missions

The cold and dark expanse of outer space is where the crew of the *Enterprise* initiate their adventures, their journeys to faraway sectors of the galaxy. It is also where thrilling and suspenseful narrative events occur, most notably meetings with aliens. As such, outer space is an extension of what Bakhtin calls the road chronotope. "On the road," he writes, "the spatial and temporal paths of the most varied people—representative of all social classes, estates, religions, nationalities, ages—intersect at one spatial and temporal point."[22] Outer space becomes science fiction's path to adventure, a road filled with dangerous and unknown alien potholes that our heroes must carefully yet boldly traverse in their mission to explore and dominate the galaxy.

Like the adventure-time of the Greek romance novel that contextualizes Bakhtin's road chronotope, meetings in outer space occur by chance. And like the frontier myth, these chance meetings almost always result in violent confrontations with aliens, fierce encounters in which our heroes must triumph if they are to fulfill their mission. In *The Search for Spock*, for example, the Klingons mount a surprise attack against Kirk and crew, endangering their mission to both find Spock and make sure their evil enemy does not capture the Genesis Project (a torpedo that can create life from lifelessness and replace existing life with its new matrix). In fact, the Klingons go so far as to kill Kirk's son (Merritt Butrick) after he, Saavik (Robin Curtis), and a regenerated-but-young Spock (Stephen Manley) are captured on the Genesis Planet. Threatening to kill more hostages, Kruge (Christopher Lloyd), the commander of the Klingon starship, demands that Kirk allow his men to board and take charge of the *Enterprise*. Fearful of what the Klingons might do to his starship, Kirk secretly initiates a self-destruct sequence. The white captain would rather destroy his beloved starship than have it boarded by the dark and animalistic Klingons. To enhance the threat, and in keeping with the feminization of the famous starship, the voice that counts down the self-destruction, the voice of the *Enterprise*, is unmistakably female. The blackface Klingons eventually beam over to the white starship, but, like Flora (Mae Marsh), the white woman who jumps off a cliff instead of facing a blackface renegade (Walter Long) in *The Birth of a Nation* (1915), the *Enterprise* self-destructs before anything improper can happen. In the end, Kirk thwarts Kruge and saves Spock, remaining heroic despite/because of his command to destroy his beloved starship.

Kirk's missions are about the manifest destiny of Earthlings, making outer space a bumpy road toward a more "humane" future. As Bakhtin suggests, "this is the source of the rich metaphorical expansion on the image of the road as a course: 'the course of life,' 'to set out on a new course,' 'the course of history' and so on; varied and multi-leveled are the ways in which road is turned into a metaphor, but its fundamental pivot is the flow of time." [23] The flow of the human species into a dominant position in the universal order of things is of paramount significance in Trek, with narrative resolutions often ending in a godly evolution. In *The Motion Picture*, for example, Decker (Stephen

Collins), the blonde executive officer, literally melds in an explosion of bright light with V'ger, the unmanned primitive twentieth-century space vehicle (a.k.a. *Voyager*) that, having reached a planet populated by machines, returns to Earth evolved into an all-powerful space cloud. After V'ger and Decker's metamorphosis into an omnipotent human-thing, Kirk asks: "Spock, did we just see the beginning of a new life form?" "Yes, Captain," Spock responds, "we witnessed a birth. Possibly a next step in our evolution." In *The Wrath of Khan*, Kirk thwarts Khan, and in the process a gaseous part of space is turned into a life-rich planet complete with its own sun. In less time than the Biblical God took to create the heavens and Earth, Kirk in the future-time of Trek creates a planet full of life in just one big bang. Outer space, science fiction's road to the future, is the place where our white heroes do their stuff in an effort to ensure a divine destiny. This is the course of *their* history.

Alien Worlds: Others and Us

If outer space is the place for confrontations with alien worlds, these worlds are where Otherness is located and defined. We know an alien is "alien" and what that means because of the chronotopes they inhabit, and those that inhabit them: their starships and their odd yet familiar appearances. Klingons are an excessive example. Even before they attack the *Enterprise*, we get a sense that they are threatening because of their dark and dirty starships, their dark and oily skin, and their dark and sharply spiked clothing. In *The Motion Picture*, we first see their battle cruiser, sharply phallic in comparison to the *Enterprise*. It has a long shaft with a small bridge at the end, making it graphically penis-like (figure 36). In one shot, the camera tracks along its body, emphasizing its sizable potential. In *The Search for Spock*, we see another Klingon starship, the bird of prey. This starship has the capacity to cloak itself (to bend light around it so that it appears invisible), making it even more ominous. The bridge is dingy and misty, and comes with a small dragon-like pet with large fangs, mucus-like slobber, and a considerable appetite. The Klingon commander, who actually resembles Gossett's lizard-like character in *Enemy Mine* thanks to a ridged forehead and a scaly complexion, is deliberately and naturally ruthless. On his bridge, he orders attacks and kills crewmen who make mistakes. This is a dirty, totalitarian space-time.

36. Klingon battle cruiser

The cinematic Borg are similar to the Klingons in that they are both markedly different from humans in physiognomy and just as treacherous as any alien rival. A colonizing collective, half humanoid and half machine, the Borg are as dirty-looking and indifferent to the values of the Federation as the Klingons.[24] When they take over the lower decks of the *Enterprise* in *First Contact*, the occupied area becomes as dark and dingy as the bridge of the Klingon bird of prey. And, like Kluge in *The Search for Spock*, the Queen Borg, the leader, is focused on revenge and power. The only individual in the collective, the Queen tries to use her overpowering sexual prowess to get Picard and Data to help her in her quest to assimilate Earth (figure 37). She is ruthless in her lascivious desire for galactic domination. Finally, like the Klingon battle cruiser, the Borg ship is profoundly different from the *Enterprise*. It's stark and purely functional. Its perfectly cubic shape emphasizes its size; its technological sophistication demonstrates its potential for destruction.

The alien worlds of the Klingons and Borg clearly differ from the world of humans and the Federation. For example, the starship *Enterprise* is markedly feminine—smooth, circular, and fetishizable. In contrast to the alien starship, this space-time is bright, clean, and comfortable. There are no pets allowed. The white starship cannot cloak

37. Borg Queen and Picard. © 1996 Paramount Pictures
Corporation

itself, relying instead on boldly trekking through outer space for all to
see. It also does not have the stand-alone ability to manipulate the time-
line and thus journey to the past as the Borg ship does. In *First Contact*,
the *Enterprise* must follow in the cubic ship's temporal wake. In *The
Voyage Home*, Kirk and crew use a Klingon bird of prey to return
home. Moreover, on the bridge of the *Enterprise*, the Federation crews
do more than fire phasers and launch torpedoes. They analyze, social-
ize, and engage in pleasantries. Captain Picard even asks his junior
officers for advice, revealing a more democratic-minded leader. Indeed,
both the original and the next generation crews are civilized, never
choosing to mount an unwarranted surprise attack or seek totalitarian
domination. Crew members are not killed if they make a mistake. And
the captain is not the only character allowed individuality. In explicit
contrast to the alien and its starship, the *Enterprise* and its crew present
us with a clear image of what we ought to be and where we ought to
go: a purified space-time.

Home: In-Your-Face Historicity

Home, or the space-time of our contemporary world, is where feature
Trek's heart is. In order to ensure that the science fiction series is realistic and widely accessible, Trek periodically returns to planet Earth and
writes history in the process. In other words, the space-time of home enables the historicity of the chronotope to rise to the surface of the text
in the form of historiography. At times this Hollywood historiography

is literal, mainly because Trek is a representation of the future based on the history of the real world. It is our future, and we're constantly cued to understand that fact. At other times, Trek historiography takes the form of allegory, or a more implicit use of real-world events and experience. As I argued in chapter 2, the tension between the United Federation of Planets and the Klingons is an allegory of the cold war between the United States and the former Soviet Union; despite the differences in name, we are constantly cued to understand that as well.

There are several types of history in feature Trek. First, there is the history that takes place in the Trek universe. In what Trek fans call the "canon," this history primarily involves each film drawing upon elements from the original television series and past Trek films, including "back stories" (e.g., a character's history) and arcs (storylines that go from one episode to another). For instance, actors reprise characters from previous installments, as when Mark Lenard, who played Spock's father in "Journey to Babel," returns to his original part in both the feature films and *The Next Generation*. The films and spinoff television series maintain the tension between Sarek, the full Vulcan, and Spock, his half-breed son, that was brought out in the original series.[25] Moreover, the films constantly make reference to narrative events that occurred in previous episodes. For instance, *The Voyage Home* opens with a Federation court projecting the scene of the *Enterprise*'s self-destruction in *The Search for Spock*. In fact, most Trek features are based on events that occurred in past episodes. Kirk's battle with Khan in *The Wrath of Khan*, itself a carryover from the original television series, leads to his search for Spock in the film's immediate successor. His actions in *The Search for Spock* are what prompt his trial, and his adventure through outer space and back to Earth, in *The Voyage Home*. Thanks to the Nexus, Captain Kirk of the twenty-third century is able to hand Captain Picard of the twenty-fourth century the helm of the *Enterprise* in *Generations*, thus paving the way for another era of Trek stories and movie stars. The adherence to the Trek canon, the history that takes place in the Trek universe, ensures that the mega-text and its chronotopes are relatively coherent and consistent, a more or less smooth flow from television to film, film to film, future-time to future-time.

The second type of history in the Trek films is that specifically and overtly drawn from the real world in which we live. This history is also part of the Trek canon simply because the representation of the future in Trek is based on the history of the real world. Events such as the civil rights movement and the cold war have taken place in both the fictional and the real universes, making the Trek present a clear representation of our future. As is the case with "Let That Be Your Last Battlefield" and "Errand of Mercy" (discussed in chapter 2), one way Trek links the two universes is by having characters make direct reference to artifacts and events from our shared histories. For example, in *The Voyage Home* Captain Kirk quotes Lewis Carroll's *Alice's Adventures in Wonderland*. He cites such novelists as D. H. Lawrence and, for contemporary readers, Harold Robbins and Jacqueline Susann. In *The Undiscovered Country*, a title actually drawn from a line in Shakespeare's *Hamlet*, Kirk and crew have a conversation with the Klingons about the famous British playwright: "You have not experienced Shakespeare," Chancellor Gorkin (David Warner) says, "until you've heard him in the original . . . Klingon." In the same film, Spock mentions a "Vulcan proverb" based on a 1970s Earth event: "Only Nixon could go to China."

Basing the fictional universe in the real universe's past is fundamental to Trek's ongoing commitment to a humanist project, making the space-time of home a clear form of didacticism. This is most obvious in *The Voyage Home*, which features Kirk and crew returning to the space-time of present-day Earth, our home, in order to save the planet from a threatening probe in the twenty-third century, their home. This installment of cinematic Trek relies on numerous real-world chronotopes, including shots of a polyglot San Francisco (figure 38). In one scene, for example, Dr. McCoy, Scotty, and Sulu watch with amusement a Chinese woman run screaming out of her shop after a Chinese man. There seems to be no motivation for this scene other than to show the chaotic, multicultural space-time of our contemporary inner city. Moreover, the film's premise, that humpback whales are extinct in the future, is drawn from the common real-world concern over the rapid rate of species extinction. *The Voyage Home* actually critiques and ridicules such contemporary experiences as pollution, nuclear fusion, the reliance on money, "modern" medicine, bad language (what Spock calls "colorful metaphors"), and punk rock music. While riding on a city bus, Spock is actually forced to give the Vulcan neck pinch, which renders a person unconscious, to a punk rocker (Kirk Thatcher) who refuses to lower the volume of his boom box (figure 39). Apparently, even "white trash" needs to be reminded of the wrong and right ways

38. *Star Trek*'s San Francisco. © 1986 Paramount Pictures Corporation

39. Spock giving Vulcan neck pinch

to behave. Before the crew leave their starship to venture out into "old" Earth, Kirk warns: "This is an extremely primitive and paranoid culture." The didacticism of this statement and of the film as a whole seems straightforward: where we come from is bad; where Trek is taking us is where we ought to go.

Another way Trek writes history is through allegory, a less literal and more abstract form of historiography. Nevertheless, allegorical articulations of the past are similar to the direct reference form discussed above in that they are straightforward and didactic. Partly because the Trek films aim to be popular, and thus comprehensible by a wide demographic, feature allegories also tend to hit the viewer over the head with their political projects. This is especially the case with *The Undiscovered Country*, a film that explicitly draws on the collapse of the Soviet Union—a historical event that was contemporaneous with the making and initial reception of the film.[26] The premise of the story is that a Klingon moon called "Praxis" explodes like a Chernobyl due to over-mining and poor safety procedures. The explosion initiates the economic breakdown of that "evil empire." The Klingon chancellor, Gorkin, a Klingon version of Mikhail Gorbachev, proposes a peace treaty with the Federation for, as Spock informs us, "the dismantling of our space stations and starbases along the neutral zone. An end to almost seventy years of unremitting hostility, which the Klingons can no longer afford." Due to the impending economic crisis, the Klingons no longer want to be cold-war enemies with the Federation. Kirk is apprehensive about the peace treaty, calling the Klingons "animals" and suggesting that the Federation "let them die." Spock invokes the past: "Jim, there is an historic opportunity here." Again, the didacticism seems clear: the real United States of America should take advantage of the opportunity the fictional United Federation of Planets is about to embark upon. This is the undiscovered country.

Like "Balance of Terror" (discussed in chapter 2) or *Enemy Mine* (discussed in the first section of this chapter), Trek's historicity transfers the meaning of race, specifically the notion of prejudice based on cultural and physiognomic difference, onto intergalactic/international conflicts in *The Undiscovered Country*. In what amounts to a racial displacement, this practice is nonetheless forthrightly expressed in the scene in which Klingon emissaries eat dinner with Kirk and crew aboard the *Enterprise*. Upon hearing of the invitation, Chekov mumbles the title of a famous 1967 interracial social problem film:

"Guess who's coming to dinner." After the Klingons transport onto the starship, two anonymous crew members comment: "They all look alike" and "What about that smell." During the dinner, the Klingons and the Federation crew observe the foreignness of each other's cultures. The Klingons seem to have the most trouble with using napkins; they are, as the Trek canon goes, uncivilized. The Federation crew, on the other hand, has the most trouble with watching the Klingons eat with their hands. They are civilized.

The scene smacks of self-conscious criticism when the arrogance of the Federation is discussed by the characters. "We do believe all planets have a sovereign claim to inalienable human rights," Chekov preaches. Gorkin's daughter, Azetbul (Rosanna DeSoto), responds: "Inalienable! If you can only hear yourselves. Human rights! Why the very name is racist." She goes on to comment: "The Federation is no more than a *Homo sapiens* only club." In the end, Kirk and crew embrace their humanist ideals by overcoming their "racism" in favor of a "brave new world" (the line is Gorkin's). They eventually get along with the Klingons. With such an ending, as well as the dialogue and the dinner scene itself, the film fuses the meaning of racial conflict onto the breakdown of the Soviet Union as a critique of Trek's humanocentrism and the practice of "white" superiority—a potentially counterhegemonic and, at least, self-conscious articulation. Like *The Brother from Another Planet*, this Trek text seems to want to point out the contradictory aspects of its own canon.

The Undiscovered Country ends up being more like "The Omega Glory" (discussed in chapter 2) than it is like *The Brother from Another Planet*. The film ends up perpetuating more stereotypes than it challenges and questions. First, the whiteness of the Federation ends up morally supreme, as the critique of humanocentrism fails to hinder the manifest destiny of white superiority. The Klingons and humans get along because the Klingons agree to be more like the Federation. Second, stereotypes of real-world peoples of color are employed in the construction of the Klingon chronotope. As with past episodes, the Klingons look like an outer-space Fu Manchu race, goatee and queue included. One Klingon, General "Chang," actually looks like Ming the Merciless of the planet Mongo in the science fiction parody *Flash Gordon* (1980) (figures 40 and 41). However, General Chang is not a parody, a self-conscious spin on an all-too common-trope, but an unquestioned throwback to the stereotype of the diabolical Chinese, the

40. General Chang. © 1994 Paramount Pictures Corporation

"yellow horde," which the history of film and television has consistently told us to fear and guard against. As the story progresses, we find out that Chang actually wants the cold war to continue; he organizes a series of assassinations and conflicts to ensure that peace will not succeed. In this way, the history-in-the-text transfers and extends the stereotype of the diabolical Fu Manchu and the myth of the "yellow horde" onto the Klingons in order to make the fictionalized aliens more treacherous and the mission of the fictionalized whites more heroic and humane. The continued use of stereotypes and myths like these contradicts the film's critique of Trek's canon. Self-conscious change ultimately remains undiscovered country in cinematic Trek.

No Matter Where You Go, There You Are

Like the relationship between the force of bodies and the curvature of space-time discussed in the Stephen Hawking quote that opens this

41. Ming the Merciless. © 1980 Universal City Studios, Inc. and
Famous Films Production

chapter,[27] fictional chronotopes are relative to the forces of history. Cinematic Trek, like the trajectory of particles and planets in the real universe, does not escape the determinacy of history. Indeed, history, be it the stereotypes that dominate the sociopolitical context or myths that span decades, is the gravity that directs Trek's meaning-making trajectory. And not only is the fictional universe affected by what happens in the real world; the real world is affected by what happens in the space-time of fiction. To keep with the quantum physics analogy, as the particle moves along its path it affects the curvature, the gravitational pull, of space-time. As I argued in chapter 1, meanings like race, whether mythical or otherwise, inform who we are, how we see ourselves, and how we experience the world. In terms of the relationship between texts and real people, perhaps this latter effect is not as determining as the former when it comes to an individual film or even a single television series, but cumulatively—taking in the entire spectrum of texts—

the effect is, well, astronomical. This is why it is important to critique and historicize the meaning of race in the Trek mega-text—an ever-expanding series of chronotopes that is informed by and informs our public mythology.

Because the Trek canon is rooted in real space-time events, the vision of the future in the mega-text is realistic, as in realism: a specific set of codes based in the classical Hollywood style. Though set in imaginary time, feature Trek is not fantasy. And this realism, while grounded in such science fiction chronotopes as starships, outer space, and alien worlds, is, like all generic codes and tropes, susceptible to a naturalizing rhetoric—in this case, an unquestioned interpretation of past frontiers and a common-sense vision of future frontiers. That is, because cinematic Trek is a representation of our future, and because it so earnestly sticks to a coherent and intelligible diegesis, it is particularly adept at naturalizing the ideology in its historicity, and thus perpetuating myth. This myth is ultimately about a humanocentric universe that casts aliens as dark and treacherous Others whom our white heroes must battle, civilize, and overcome in the name of manifest destiny, divine evolution: white future-time.

4 The Next Generation

Toward a Neoconservative Play

> The particle is not supposed to have a single history or path in space-time, as it would in a classical, nonquantum theory. Instead it is supposed to go from A to B by every possible path. With each path there are associated a couple of numbers: one represents the size of a wave and the other represents the position in the cycle. . . . The probability of going from A to B is found by adding up the waves for all the paths.
> —*Stephen Hawking*

> *Captain Picard transformed into Locutus of Borg:* Worf, Klingon species, a warrior race, you too will be assimilated.
>
> *Worf:* The Klingon Empire will never yield.
>
> *Locutus:* Why do you resist? We only wish to raise quality of life for all species.
>
> *Worf:* I like my . . . species the way it is.
>
> *Locutus:* A narrow vision. You will become one with the Borg.

In the 1970s and early 1980s the original *Star Trek* earned cult status through its constant rerunning in syndication. Even Gene Roddenberry became a cult figure, earning the nickname "The Great Bird of the Galaxy"—a rare accomplishment for a former police officer turned television writer.[1] Responding to the popularity of the science fiction adventure and its creator, Paramount in 1987 brought Roddenberry back to television Trek as executive producer of *The Next Generation*. Banking that fan loyalty would spin off the old series and onto the new one, the studio went so far as to bypass the major networks and offered the series to independent television stations across the country. Unlike the original Trek, *The Next Generation* had no network middle-man. And although the science fiction spinoff initially struggled for an audience, it rated among the top three syndicated shows for most of its seven-year run. Fans were indeed loyal, as The Great Bird of the Galaxy's second television Trek soared to unprecedented syndication heights.

The Next Generation universe is organized by the same diegetic logics that shaped the 1960s series, except that it is set eighty-five years
into the original crew's future. There is still a United Federation of Planets bound by the same Prime Directive against interfering in the culture
and politics of alien worlds. The striking similarity between anthropomorphic aliens and humans is initially explained through the notion of parallel development, the "similar worlds concept" outlined
by Roddenberry some twenty years earlier. The starship *Enterprise*, yet
another new and improved model, is still a key chronotope in the
show's future-time. And like its television predecessor, the new science
fiction series both casts and narrativizes a multicultural crew. There is
a French captain with a British accent, Jean Luc-Picard; a European-
American commander, William T. Riker; a white-android, Lieutenant
Commander Data; an Irish doctor, Beverly Crusher (Gates McFadden);
an empathic half-human and half-Betazoid ship's counselor, Lieutenant
Commander Deanna Troi (Marina Sirtis); a white female Security Officer, Lieutenant Tasha Yar (Denise Crosby); a blind African-American
helmsman, Lieutenant J.G. Geordi LaForge (LeVar Burton); a Klingon
who was raised by humans, Lieutenant J.G. Worf (Michael Dorn); and
the young son of Dr. Crusher, Wesley (Wil Wheaton).[2] There are several recurring characters, including a black-alien bartender, Guinan
(Whoopi Goldberg) and an Irish transporter chief, Miles O'Brien
(Colm Meaney). With this otherwise diverse crew of humans and aliens
(figure 42), *The Next Generation* continued the Trek tradition of representing and narrativizing the experiences of physiognomic and cultural difference particular to its space-time.

One of the first episodes where the meaning of race is a clear formation is "Code of Honor." In this third episode of the first season, the beginning of the story has the *Enterprise* crew heading for Ligon II, an
alien world, to pick up a rare vaccine they are to deliver to an another
alien world stricken with a deadly virus. Their mission of mercy is
urgent and potentially dangerous. Ligon II is populated by a technologically sophisticated culture, the Ligonians, that the *Enterprise* crew
has never visited. "This should be an interesting experience," Captain
Picard says to Commander Riker and Counselor Troi. "Agreed," Riker
responds, "Not only are they closely humanoid, but their history has
remarkable similarities to ours." "A highly structured society," Troi
interjects, "and they're exceedingly proud." After the three bridge offi-

42. Cast of *The Next Generation.* © 1992 Paramount Pictures Corporation

cers join Security Chief Yar in the cargo bay, five Ligonian males beam aboard, all of whom are played by African-American actors. Unlike the original series or the films, this installment of the mega-text introduces us to a black world.

Although the Ligonians have the capacity to beam or transport themselves through matter, and are thus technologically more advanced than present-day humans, they carry spears and staffs. The men have deep scars on their faces and chests, suggesting hand-to-hand combat and primitive tribal rituals. They wear turbans, poufy pants, and sashes cut in the figure of an "X" so that their dark, muscular bodies are plainly visible (figure 43). The planet is ruled by a bombastic chief, Lutan (Jessie Lawrence Ferguson), whose followers are prone to beating sticks in rhythmic response to his emphatic proclamations. The Ligonian world is reminiscent of the African safari, as we see silhouettes of trees and shrubs against a saturated reddish-orange sky. Even the music-bed, with its heavy bass and slow beat, is reminiscent of classic Hollywood jungle movies and National Geographic documentaries of the "dark continent." The representation of these "closely humanoids" in this way suggests that Ligon II is not only a black world, but one that "parallels" real African tribes.

43. Ligonian men

After Captain Picard compliments Lutan for his people's "unique similarity to an ancient Earth culture we all admire," the chief requests that Yar demonstrate her training regimen. Yar's fighting ability impresses the Ligonian ruler, who grows enamored of her and kidnaps her to the planet below. Rather than using the *Enterprise*'s superior weapons to get her back, as Kirk would likely have done, Picard, ever the diplomatic and democratic leader, asks his crew for insight into why the Ligonian chief would abduct his crewperson. Troi reports that she senses in the chief certain "needs." "What kind of needs?" Riker indignantly interrupts. "Some sexual attraction from all the males," she calmly responds, "but with Lutan I felt something else. Something more like avarice or ambition." Lieutenant Commander Data then advises the captain to be patient, a trait the Ligonians respect. Riker agrees: "You can see it in the precise . . . ritualistic way they do things," he scoffs. Later, Data provides an impassioned analysis of the Ligonian culture: "It is a highly structured society in which people live by strict codes of honor. For example, what Lutan did is similar to what certain American Indians once called counting coup." With dialogue that references "ritual" and "sexual attraction," not to mention "American Indians," this episode of *The Next Generation* perpetuates a common racial stereotype: a primitive, homogeneous, dark people ruled by a self-serving, pompous chief who desires white women and is indifferent to missions of galactic mercy.

Picard immediately understands his precarious position, and politely asks for the vaccine and Yar's safe return. He is anxious to leave Ligon II, even if it means acquiescing to Lutan's ego. Lutan remains deviant, however, and declares that he cannot possibly let Yar go. He wants her to replace his existing "First One," Yareena. In other words, the chief wants the blonde human to be his new queen. "This is not an act of war," he passionately proclaims, "but of love." Picard and Yar are shocked. Yareena is outraged. At this point in the story, the plot takes a dramatic turn: will the black-alien chief have his way with the white-human female? Or will the white-human captain save his damsel in distress?

The parallel to the story of race relations does not end here. Before the men can act, Yareena invokes an ancient Ligonian ritual, the Rite of Supersedence, whereby a sitting First One challenges a prospective First One to a fight to the death. If Yareena wins, she will retain her present position; if she loses, Yar will supersede her. Yareena's challenge pleases Lutan, as he is confident Yar will win. In fact, this has been his ulterior motive all along. He wants Yar to kill Yareena not only because he desires the Security Chief, but also because he wants to acquire Yareena's land. On Ligon II the women own the land and men merely rule, unless the woman dies in the Rite of Supersedence. This explains Counselor Troi's sense of Lutan as having "avarice or ambition." The chief wants to use the white-human female to acquire more power at the expense of the black-alien female. Of course, Picard figures out the chief's lascivious plan and organizes a ruse of his own. He allows Yar to fight Yareena, knowing that he can use the *Enterprise*'s technology to revive the loser.

Yareena and Yar battle each other in a small ring demarcated by multicolored lights. As Yar warms up in the ring, swinging her spiked glove with the precision expected of a member of the Federation, Yareena enters the larger room in a glittery and hooded pink robe. Looking like a prizefighter, she's confident and determined. Her entourage takes off her robe, revealing a jerry-curl hairdo, a shiny headband, and

44. Yareena ready to box

a skintight pink leotard reminiscent of a 1970s disco get-up (figure 44). The Ligonian queen then saunters into the ring and begins her cool but focused attack. Yar counterattacks. At times, Yareena has the advantage; at other times, Yar takes control. The two women grunt and groan with each punch, kick, and fall. Though the match is close, Yareena loses. She is pricked with the poisonous spike affixed to Yar's glove. Lutan proudly pronounces the security chief victorious, and thus his new First One. He has made it—or so he thinks!

Picard beams both Yar and Yareena's body to the *Enterprise*. Thanks to the starship's advanced technology, Dr. Crusher brings the loser back from death. Anxious to reveal the success of his ruse, Picard then beams Lutan and Hagon, the chief's assistant, to the *Enterprise*. Upon seeing the revived Yareena, Hagon is relieved; the Chief, however, is outraged, and calls it "witchcraft." Yet, with Yareena alive, he is no longer a wealthy man. Even worse, Yareena, now aware of his avaricious intentions, decides she no longer wants him as her First One, and chooses Hagon instead. To add insult to injury, she then offers Lutan to Yar. The security officer looks the former chief over, then refuses:

"There would . . . be complications," she says, with some hesitation. In keeping with the rituals of Ligon II, Yareena allows the rejected Lutan to be her Second One. "As you see," Hagon, the new chief of Ligon II, says to Picard, "you may excel in technology, but not in civilized behavior." On that, the episode ends and the trek continues.

I have opened this chapter with a critique of "Code of Honor" not only because of its obvious overdetermination of race, but for two additional reasons. First, it reveals another strategy of the mega-text for articulating race: intertextuality. By intertextuality, I mean the ways in which a text is made up of and subsequently transforms other texts and discourses, becoming what Julia Kristeva calls "a mosaic of quotations."[3] A film or television program, for instance, is not one text; it is many texts in one. The intertexts that make up "Code of Honor" include spears, "counting coup," images of the safari, and disco-like clothing. Even Picard's accent is an intertext, particularly as it might connote British aristocracy and European colonialism. These and many other quotations suggest ways the articulation of race in *The Next Generation* is multifaceted, encompassing nothing less than a mosaic of quotations.

My second reason for starting this chapter with an analysis of "Code of Honor" is that the episode reveals a dramatic shift in the articulation of race in the Trek mega-text, perhaps due to a sociopolitical context less concerned with the practices of the civil rights movement than with a neoconservative ideal. The mid-1980s through the early 1990s, the period of the production and initial reception of *The Next Generation*, is marked by a sociopolitical climate quite different from that of the 1960s, the period of the original Trek's production. In what is now commonly referred to as the Reagan-Bush years, the civil rights movement was no longer the dominant arbiter of the meaning of race. With its roots in the 1970s and earlier, the neoconservative movement came to power during this period with the stated goal of curtailing and even rolling back many of the sociopolitical inroads that had been made in the 1960s. As Michael Omi and Howard Winant note, "The racial reaction initiated in the late 1960s and early 1970s developed in the 1980s into a pervasive ideological effort to reinterpret once again the meaning of race in the U.S. As the Reagan administration adopted its major themes, the racial reaction achieved legitimate, if not hegemonic, status in 'normal' politics."[4] Though capitulating to the notion of a colorblind society, the neoconservative movement claims that whites are the victims in the aftermath of the civil rights era. It also urges non-whites to either assimilate into the traditional values of the American way, becoming "model minorities," or step (or be pushed) aside. "Code of Honor," for example, offers us a view of humanity, proudly embodied in Picard and his bridge crew, that is merciful, sophisticated, and still very white. It also presents us with a black world that is primitive, petty, and menacing despite their advanced technology and codes of honor.

What can the notion of intertextuality tell us about the meaning of race in *The Next Generation*? What are the main intertextual references, the texts and discourses, informing the science fiction series? How do these intertexts make the Trek spinoff racial? Finally, in what ways does *The Next Generation* draw upon and engage the racial formation dominating the 1980s and early 1990s?

In addressing these questions, I have divided this chapter into two sections. The first section briefly lays out both the theory of intertextuality and the basic elements of neoconservatism. More specifically, I show how the theory of intertextuality can be used as a tool to describe and explain the relationship between texts and context. I then describe some of the fundamental aspects of the neoconservative movement. The second half of the chapter investigates the ways in which intertextuality works to articulate race in *The Next Generation*. In doing so, I point to the major intertexts that guide the meaning of race in the science fiction spinoff, including: history, or the representation of the past; evolution, particularly biological determinism; miscegenation, its dangers and limitations; and assimilation, specifically the problems and ultimately the paradox of creating a galactic melting pot that is in the midst of a biologically determined universe. I argue that these discourses make up a neoconservative montage, particularly a future-time that capitulates to multiculturalism while continuing with Trek's tradition of securing—perpetuating and naturalizing—the superiority of whiteness.

Intertextuality and Neoconservatism

Like the chronotopes discussed in chapter 3, intertextuality is necessarily a condition of textuality. Texts are always already intertextual, in that they draw upon and are part of the multiplicity of meanings that circulate within culture and history. In other words, texts are in a constant dialogical relationship, a give and take, with other texts and their historical contexts. As Roland Barthes explains:

> Any text is an intertext; other texts are present in it, at varying levels, in more or less recognizable forms: the texts of the previous and surrounding cultures. Any text is a new tissue of past citations. Bits of codes, formulae, rhythmic models, fragments of social languages, etc. pass into the text and are redistributed within it, for there is always language before and around the text.

Thus, intertextuality is more than a matter of an author consciously borrowing from another author or text, such as an homage or form of plagiarism. Although encompassing such practices, intertextuality goes beyond direct references to other texts.[5] As Barthes concludes, "Intertextuality, the condition of any text whatsoever, cannot, of course, be reduced to a problem of sources or influences; the intertext is a general field of anonymous formulae whose origin can scarcely be located; of unconscious or automatic quotations, given without quotation-marks."[6] Because of the necessary condition of intertextuality, texts like "Code of Honor" are less tangible things—a book, a piece of celluloid, an electromagnetic wave, a series of digital bits—than complex processes of signification, or systems of processes, involved in perpetual articulation. Barthes call this process of meaning production—indeed, this theory of the text—"play."

There are two underlying principles of the theory of texts as intertextual and in play that are key to this study of race in *The Next Generation*. First, the theory exposes the rhetorical conventions and deterministic conclusions that make up the more traditional aspects of scientism, Freudianism, Marxism, and other structuralist paradigms. If a text is intertextual and thus in play, the theory argues, then it cannot be seen as a static structure behind which lies a single truth or fixed meaning. Each text, then, encourages a plurality of meanings and readings, becoming a facilitator and processor of signification. Second, history, or the space-time of materiality and experience, "frames" (to extend Umberto Eco's term) the plurality of the text.[7] Because a text is intertextual and in play does not mean it can mean anything to anyone at any time. History is always present in and contextualizing texts, not only in the form of the diegetic logics discussed in chapter 2 and the chronotopes discussed in chapter 3, but also in the form of intertexts.

As Kristeva recognizes, "History and morality are written and read within the infrastructure of texts. The poetic word, polyvalent and multi-determined, adheres to a logic exceeding that of codified discourse and fully comes into being only in the margins of recognized culture."[8] In "Code of Honor," historical frames include not only spears, but primitivism, blackness, miscegenation, evolution, and, of course, whiteness. As I will show, these frames are key to the neoconservative movement's articulation of race.

Neoconservatism or Bust

In the Reagan-Bush years, the civil rights movement is no longer the dominant arbiter of the meaning of race. Instead, it is the neoconservative movement that steers the course. As I noted earlier, a central goal of neoconservatism is to curtail and "roll back" the accomplishments of the 1960s. In what amounts to a systematic sociopolitical project, the rallying cry of this movement is the constitutional legality of a colorblind society. Yet, the contradiction of the notion of "opposition to race thinking" rests in the fact that the United States has been and continues to be a color-conscious society—a space-time where those who pass as white are materially and ideologically privileged over those who do not. In fact, for many minority groups, living conditions actually got worse during the 1980s and early 1990s, "measured," as Omi and Winant point out, "by indicators such as unemployment rates, number of families falling below the poverty line, and the widening gap between white and black infant mortality rates."[9]

Omi and Winant point to three political projects that were central in organizing the movement: (1) the far Right, which includes the KKK; (2) the New Right, which includes such religious figures as Pat Robertson and Jerry Falwell; and (3) neoconservatism, symbolized most clearly by former President Ronald Reagan and current Speaker of the House Newt Gingrich.[10] For the sociologists, each project maintains distinct tactics, with the far Right being the only one that systematically engages in overt and violent racism. The New Right and neoconservative projects engage in more subtle tactics, always under the banner of individual rights, traditional values, opposition to big government, and other democratic ideals. In this chapter I will use the term 'neoconservative' to refer to the practices and dominance of the New Right and neoconservative projects, because they openly rely on each other. As for the far Right, while it might be fair to consider *The Next Generation* symbolically violent, it must be emphasized that its racial play is seldom explicit and its goals are not to exclude, terrorize, or murder but to assimilate, inculcate, and "move beyond" race.

The shift in the sociopolitical meaning of race that came to power in the 1980s did not result in a complete and successful backlash, a return to the overt racism of the past. Most political leaders supporting the movement did not advocate the "separate but equal" inequalities of the 1950s and earlier. Rather, racial equality was given "lip service," an ideal more in the form of a rhetorical appeasement than a concerted practice. As Omi and Winant note: "Racial equality had to be acknowledged as a desirable goal. But the meaning of equality, and the proper means for achieving it, remained matters of considerable debate." [11] The use of code words, which make indirect reference to the racial politics of the past but do not explicitly challenge democratic ideals such as justice, equal opportunity, and colorblindness, became the central strategy for the neoconservative movement. These code words include "busing," "reverse discrimination," "immigration,"and, of course, "affirmative action"—those practices that were intended to make integration a reality.

The Next Generation is not just in dialogue with this sociopolitical rearticulation of race; it takes a definitive position. Indeed, the ideology of neoconservatism is systematically woven into the spinoff via intertexts that, while revealing a diverse universe where humans and aliens of color coexist, ultimately proffer a space-time where integration succumbs to either assimilation (which is usually only possible to the degree to which one "acts white") or exclusion based on a primitive or unappealing evolution. In "Code of Honor," for instance, the intertextuality of race offers us a group of humanoids who "closely" resemble "an ancient earth culture" and have evolved into a technologically advanced but tribal, polite but patriarchal, disco-wearing and spearchuckin' alien "race" dominated by males who are more pomp than character. Picard and crew first consider the Ligonians almost equals, then appease their primitive egos, only to continue on their mission of mercy to save the universe without them.

There are several intertexts framing *The Next Generation*, not just those specific to the racial formation. The meaning of gender—specifically, the position of women in the future—is a dominant discourse interwoven in and guiding Trek's play. [12] As in the original *Star Trek*, women in *The Next Generation* are consistently positioned as either helpers or fetishized objects. This is the case with both Dr. Crusher and Counselor Troi—their Federation jobs are suggestive of their role as nurturers. The doctor and the counselor rarely if ever give orders and almost always serve the men. Moreover, while the women of *The Next Generation* are generally not as loosely clad as the women in the original series, shot during the sexual revolution, they are still systematically objectified and fetishized. Troi, for instance, wears clothes that tightly hug her body and reveal her breasts. As Lynne Joyrich comments about the relationship between Troi's gender and her costuming, "TNG's presentation of Troi's outfits mimics the women's fashion industry in terms of the promotion of seasonal change: a constant adjustment of wardrobe constitutes femininity in terms of both consumerism and commodities, not only identifying the woman with the body but identifying the female body as never quite good enough, always in need of further improvement."[13] Not unlike women in the original series, many of the shots she is in show Troi exiting a scene, thus revealing her backside, or bending over, thus revealing her cleavage. Her not-quite-perfect accentuated parts are nonetheless to-be-looked-at and consumed.

Heterosexism is another discourse framing the plurality of *The Next Generation*'s neoconservative play. Gay fans like the Gaylaxions discussed by Henry Jenkins have argued that the show's vision of a utopian future where all people are accepted regardless of their difference is contradicted by the almost complete absence of gays in the fictional universe. As Jenkins notes:

> They looked around them and saw other series—*LA Law, Heartbeat, Thirtysomething, Quantum Leap, Northern Exposure, Days of Our Lives, Roseanne*—opening up new possibilities for queer characters on network television, while their programme could only hint around the possibility that there might be some form of sexuality out there, somewhere beyond the known universe, which did not look like heterosexuality.[14]

The few times homosexuality is suggested in the spinoff, the series takes the heterosexist way out. In "The Host" (1991), for instance, Beverly Crusher falls in love with a Trill, a life form that consists of a symbiotic relationship between a humanoid host and a small parasite. In the episode, the male humanoid host dies, forcing the parasite to be temporarily put into Riker's body. Crusher's love extends to Riker, whom up until that point she apparently considered to be like her brother, and their romantic relationship continues. Yet, when the parasite is put into a woman's body, Crusher draws the line and ends the relationship—no lesbianism allowed. Similarly, in "The Outcast" (1992), Commander Riker falls in love with a member of the J'naii, an androgynous (albeit not gay) race. As in "The Host," heterosexuality is affirmed when the person Riker falls in love with is revealed to be, deep down inside, more female than male. Adding to the narrative discourse about the true sexual identity of the "androgynous" alien is the obvious fact that the character is played by a female actress (Melinda Culea). The hint at Riker having an open sexuality is negated: the commander—and the series—remain secure in their heterosexism. Indeed, nowhere in the Trek imagination does a sexuality other than heterosexuality exist.

The Paradox of Assimilation

In the rest of this chapter I try to show how the intertexts framing the next installment of prime-time Trek advance the neoconservative project that was the zeitgeist of the 1980s. More specifically, I argue that the science fiction spinoff capitulates to a utopian future where "race" is determined by biology, miscegenation is still a taboo, and difference is either whitewashed or exaggerated and punished. In *The Next Generation*, humans and aliens of color are either on their way to living the white way, or rejected and marginalized for their inability to assimilate. Indeed, this marks the paradox of assimilation, a discourse that tries diligently to bring people of color into the fold but ultimately restricts or qualifies their equality because of a presumed biological difference. The intertexts framing the neoconservative spin on race in this way include: (1) historiography, or the representation of past people, places, and events; (2) evolution, including genetics, species, and origin intertexts; (3) miscegenation, be it alien to human or human to human; and, most symptomatically, (4) assimilation, or the qualifications for entering the United Federation of Planets' melting pot.

Historiography: Past, Present, and Future

If Trek speaks with one voice, it is the voice of history. While intertextual references of this kind are more often "of unconscious or automatic quotations," this is perhaps most clear in *The Next Generation*'s representation of the past. In fact, like the original series and the feature films, *The Next Generation* represents three historical periods: pre–twentieth century, the past in both the fictional universe and the real world; twentieth century, the present in the real world and the past in the fictional world; and post–twentieth century, the future of the real world and the immediate past or present of the fictional world. As I suggested in chapter 3, these voyages to the past often smack of a didacticism that wants to warn the audience about where we are going and how we're going to get there. *The Next Generation* is mindful, even fearful, of the adage that "the past is prologue," and tries diligently to show us a better way. What is neoconservative about this historiography, this wedding and alteration of historiographic intertexts, is that it seems most concerned with warning us against the dangerous ramifications of a multicultural present. For the Trek spinoff, the future is an uncertain space-time that, if we are not careful today, will be less Western and white than a utopian future apparently can be.

Historical intertexts in *The Next Generation* can be as straightforward as real-world people playing themselves. For instance, Joe Piscopo, the comedian of *Saturday Night Live* (1975–present) fame, plays a hackneyed holodeck comedian who tries to teach Data how to be funny in "The Outrageous Okona" (1988). Even more memorable, Stephen Hawking, the cosmologist responsible for the theory of "imaginary time," plays himself in "Descent" (1993). Even real-world non-actors have cameo roles, such as the time NASA astronaut Mae Jemison appeared on the bridge as a member of the engineering crew (figure 45). Trek is brimming with the representation of real-world figures like Piscopo, Hawking, and Jemison, although most are played by actors rather than the real people. For instance, Data not only plays cards with the real (albeit represented as imaginary) Hawking in "Descent," but also with Albert Einstein (Jim Norton) and Isaac Newton (John Neville). Even Sigmund Freud (Bernard Kates) makes an appearance, helping Data to psychoanalyze his dreams in "Phantasms" (1993). Explicit quotations such as these are also indicative of Trek's concern with a multicultural future. This is perhaps most obvious in the names given to starships. Along with the U.S.S. *Enterprise*, there is the U.S.S. *Crazy Horse*, the U.S.S. *Gandhi*, the U.S.S. *Potemkin*, and the U.S.S. *Zapata*.

The Next Generation's concern with the ramifications of history is established in the premier episode, "Encounter at Farpoint" (1987). The story begins with the *Enterprise* heading toward Farpoint Station,

45. Astronaut Mae Jemison. © 1994 Paramount Pictures
Corporation

a distant part of the quadrant. En route they encounter Q (John de Lancie), a sarcastic and omniscient being who can manipulate the space-time continuum with the snap of a finger. Q first materializes on the bridge of the *Enterprise* as a pre-twentieth-century British naval officer, complete with epaulettes and wig. Looking at Picard, he charges: "Thou art notified that thy kind have infiltrated the galaxy too far

46. Q as World War II soldier

already. Thou art directed to return to thine own solar system immediately." He then instantaneously changes into a U.S. World War II pilot,
and proceeds to call humans a "dangerous, savage child race" with
little indication they "will ever change" (figure 46). Agitated but confident, Picard defends human history by arguing that by World War II
humanity "had already started to make rapid progress." Q then turns
into a twenty-first-century soldier from Picard's past but our immediate
future, and continues his charges about the genocidal history of the human race. With intertextual quotations ranging from costuming to dialogue, the episode uses history to criticize the violence of humanity's
past, with the warning that God, in the figure of Q, is concerned it
might continue indefinitely.

Q grows tired of the captain's claims of progress, and literally puts
the human race on trial for "crimes against humanity." The judgmen-
tal being instantly selects Picard, Data, Yar, and Troi as the representatives of humanity, and transports them to a twenty-first-century Earth
courtroom—the space-time of the Eugenics War that begot Khan and
which is depicted in *First Contact*. In contrast to Q's selection of four
very white representatives of humanity, the space-time of our future is

47. Twenty-first-century bailiffs

filled with a multiracial chorus of courtroom spectators who cheer each act of violence as if they were at a carnival. The people in this history represent the dangers and atrocities of a diverse, multicolored reality. Thus, the whiteness of Federation representatives is juxtaposed against not only dark aliens of the present, as it was in "Code of Honor," but multicolored humans from our immediate future.

The two bailiffs who call the court into session are specific and over-determined references to this motley past/our future. One is a small person, a "midget," who does not talk but carries a large cow bell. The other is an Asian male (Cary-Hiroyuki) who, like the Comms in "The Omega Glory," speaks with a stereotypical accent. Both bailiffs wear sinister-looking goatees, an overused intertext in the mega-text that suggests the horror of a potentially Asian future-time (figure 47). Adding to the difference of the bailiffs is the fact that they are shot in close-ups and low angles—set-ups that exaggerate their already demented and contorted facial expressions. Their difference is intended to be frightening, and the visual style helps us see that. This is a strange and brutal history humanity ought diligently to avoid.[15]

In contrast to the diversity and its dangers represented in the premier episode, "Time's Arrow, Part I" (1992) and "Time's Arrow, Part II" (1992) ignore the racism shared by both the real and the fictional worlds. In an embrace of traditional values, this two-part episode has the *Enterprise* crew traveling back in time to late-nineteenth-century San Francisco, where they meet, among other historical figures, Mark Twain (Jerry Hardin). The episode also features Guinan, a long-lived alien apparently interested in American literature. Because Guinan's species resembles humans, she easily passes as an Earthling and is accepted without reservation. What is striking about this is that Guinan, played by African-American actor Whoopi Goldberg, is treated as if she were white. There is no mention of the racism and segregation so prevalent during this period of American history. The world of old Earth is apparently colorblind. Indeed, in this historical space the reality of racism is elided in favor of a clean and traditional narrative. In this case, race is not relative to the values of Trek historiography.

Neoconservative Trek wants to forget the past it shares with us in order to continue with the model of colonialism that is our future. Like the liberalism of the original Trek, the institutions and paradigms that organize the past and present are left uncriticized and in fact are supported in the future-time of the spinoff. As Katrina G. Boyd comments: "Even in acknowledging the past and celebrating Western culture, the show takes great pains to distance itself from certain aspects of that culture: conquest, colonialism, class distinction, racial discrimination, and exploitation."[16] To emphasize that today's models of organizing the world are effective if unencumbered by race, "Encounter at Farpoint" shows us an immediate future where multiculturalism and diversity are dangerous and totalitarian. In the space-time of "Time's Arrow, Part I" and "Time's Arrow, Part II," not to mention the future-time of Picard's world, racist brutality is elided under the successfully superior world of whiteness. This is apparently where we should be going: back to the far past of traditional values and white domination.

Evolution: Genetics, Species, and "Lucy"

Evolution is an overarching discourse framing the play of meaning in *The Next Generation*. The spinoff explicitly grapples with the subject, as well as such related discourses as genetics, species, and human origins. This is perhaps most obvious in the titles of various episodes, including "Evolution" (1989); "Unnatural Selection" (1989), which puts a spin on Charles Darwin's notion of natural selection; and "Genesis" (1994), which involves the crew of the *Enterprise* "de-evolving" into primitive life forms. In this last episode, Lieutenant Barclay (Dwight Schultz) becomes a prehistoric arachnid, Riker becomes a Neanderthal, Troi becomes an extinct amphibian once indigenous to her home world, and Worf becomes a vicious predator from the recesses of Klingon evolution. The cause of their "de-evolution" is a "synthetic T-Cell" that, upon invading their bodies, activates certain "introns" that lurk in primal "DNA." Grounded in the science of T-cells and DNA, irrespective of their more fictional elaborations, "Genesis" plays to today's notions of evolution.

The intersection of evolution and *The Next Generation* takes on a neoconservative edge as the spinoff ultimately explains behavior and social differences by way of genes. In what amounts to biological determinism, humans and aliens in the spinoff are programmed by nature. In "The Icarus Factor" (1989), for instance, Data explains Worf's temperament in biological terms: "There is, of course, a genetic predisposition toward hostility among all Klingons." While I will discuss the Klingons and Worf in more detail later in this chapter, it is clear from this one line, given authority because it is uttered by the most "objective" scientist in Trek since Spock, that Klingons, and by extension all species, cannot escape "nature." Such a notion has informed real-world science from social Darwinism and eugenics to today's neoconservative studies of the inheritance of intelligence seen in such popular academic books as *The Bell Curve*.[17] Of course, this "science," whether of the fictional or the real world, serves to minimize or absolve the government and the social formation of responsibility for the production and maintenance of social and ideological inequalities. While these institutions and social formations are uncontested in Trek, remaining the vehicles that lead us to a utopian history, in the real world they are, of course, more than partly responsible for the systems of injustice that continue to plague our material and experiential lives.

The Next Generation seems convinced that there is a direct link between intelligence and evolution, as can be seen in the case of the Pakleds, a not-so-bright alien race first introduced in "Samaritan Snare" (1989). In this episode, Riker, in temporary charge of the *Enterprise*, allows La Forge to transport to a Pakled ship to render assistance. The commander concludes that the risk is minimal, calling the aliens

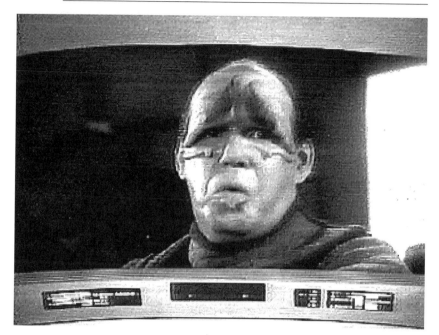

48. A Pakled

"some curious throwbacks." "How they ever mastered the rudiments of space travel," Data confirms, "is a genuine curiosity." What is strikingly intertextual about these "curious throwbacks" is that they are all made up to look fat with protruding brows and balding scalps (figure 48). They even walk and talk extremely slowly. Embodying stereotypes of bodily comportment, speech, and intelligence, the Pakleds become less evolved humanoids.

Everything is as it appears. The Pakleds detain Geordi by force in hopes he will make them "strong." "You think we are not smart," the leader (Christopher Collins) tells Riker. "I think you need to continue to develop," Riker responds. Later, Troi explains their actions: "They're unwilling to wait for the timely evolution of their species' intellectual capacity." In the end, Geordi is rescued and the Pakleds' ability to travel through space is restricted. Though they are crafty enough to acquire a starship and "make it go fast," and even to trick the *Enterprise* and its crew (absent Picard, of course), they are forced by the Federation, a Q to the Pakleds, to evolve into a more intelligent race more slowly than they might wish. Like the black-aliens of Ligon II, the trek continues without them.

49. Transfiguration man

The pinnacle of evolution in Trek is a creature who looks white and becomes god-like. This has been the case throughout the mega-text. In classical Trek, it is the omnipotent Organians of "Errand of Mercy" who, having chosen to take humanoid form, represent our divine destiny. As Spock comments: "I should say the Organians are as far above us on the evolutionary scale as we are above the amoeba." In *The Motion Picture*, Decker, a blond human, synthesizes with the omniscient V'ger in blinding white light. In *The Next Generation*, the evolution of the humanoid life form also takes the figure of a white-humanoid with divine powers. This is clearly the case with "Transfigurations" (1990), in which an alien (Mark LaMura) demonstrates remarkable abilities, including healing an entire ship, transporting objects through matter, and, most specific to the hierarchical discourse of evolution, transforming into glowing white light (figure 49). Finally, Q almost always takes the form of a white male; indeed, all members of the Q Continuum represented in *The Next Generation*, whether male or female, have chosen the white way. According to the neoconservative project of *The Next Generation*, God is not colored, therefore we should all aspire to be not colored as well.

The discourse on evolution extends to the very basis of human and alien taxonomy, making most bipedal Trek aliens members of the same species and, thus, different "races" or subspecies. In real-world science, the term "species" generally refers to a group of living creatures that can produce offspring. Within this standardized taxonomy, species are subdivided into subspecies on the basis of origin and physiognomy. The difference between subspecies can be either minor, such as skin pigmentation, or significant, such as bodily stature (a Great Dane can breed with a poodle, for instances, though the two types of dogs look quite different). This same sense of species frames *The Next Generation*, not only because aliens are called "races" by the characters, but because many different aliens have together produced offspring. There is, for instance, a half-human and half-Betazoid, Troi; a half-human and half-Klingon, K'Ehleyr (Suzie Plakson); a half-human and half-Romulan, Tasha Yar's daughter; a half-Romulan and half-Klingon, Ba'el (Jennifer Gatti); and perhaps the most famous half-breed, a half-human and half-Vulcan, Spock. Moreover, the species intertext not only helps explain the similarity between aliens from different worlds (being bipedal, upright, etc.), but also frames the conflict between them as a question of racism—i.e., of living beings who discriminate and erect sociopolitical hierarchies based on physiognomic difference.

In chapter 2, I noted how the diegetic logic of parallel evolution, Gene Roddenberry's "similar worlds concept," explained all the morphological, physiognomic, and social similarity in the vast and densely populated Trek galaxy. In *The Next Generation*, the striking similarity among aliens is further explained by genetic commonality. This is made explicit in "The Chase," which has Captain Picard, a Klingon captain (John Cothran Jr.), a Romulan captain (Maurice Roëves), and a Cardassian captain (Linda Thorson) competing to decipher a puzzle hidden in the DNA of various worlds. Although the captains and their various starships, or "races," play a game of cat and mouse, some (like the Klingons and Cardassians) thinking the puzzle might be a secret weapon, the end of the story reveals that an ancient civilization, having found itself alone in the galaxy, "seeded" the primal oceans of many worlds with its own DNA. In what amounts to Trek's "Lucy," and in a way slightly reminiscent of the idea in "The Paradise Syndrome" (discussed in chapter 2), a holographic image of the ancient beings informs us that "the seed codes directed your evolution toward a physical form resembling ours." In this instance, the project-in-the-text takes the op-

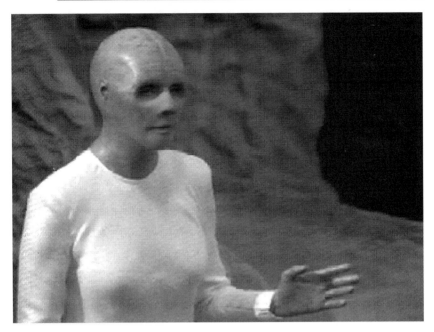

50. "Lucy"

portunity to preach a humanistic ideal. The being continues: "There is something of us in each of you, and so, something of you in each other." What is striking about "Lucy" is that the common ancestor to the bipeds of the universe is brown (figure 50). Like the origins of humankind, Trek races evolved from nonwhite beings. Though dark or even colored is not where we're going, according to the history and evolution intertexts, it is apparently where we come from.

Miscegenation: To Be or Not to Be

If scientific conceptions of species and subspecies are discursive intertexts grounding the meaning of race in *The Next Generation*, then miscegenation (the mixing of people from different "races") becomes yet another discourse involved in the play of Trek signification. And while this is clearly the case with the offspring of otherwise different alien peoples mentioned earlier, it is also the case with the "races" of humans. That is, race is not uniformly displaced onto species in the spinoff, as the ideology of miscegenation makes clear: most of the white-humans stick to their own kind. For example, though Picard becomes involved in several romantic encounters, they are all with white-human females.[18] A relationship between Picard and Guinan is discretely hinted at, specifically when Guinan says to Riker in "Best of Both Worlds, Part II" that her relationship with the Captain "is beyond friendship, beyond family." However, this potential mixing of a white-human and a black-alien, or a British and an African-American star, is never developed. Even in *First Contact*, a feature film in whose genre the norms of production and reception are generally more liberal and provocative, they are only friends. Similarly, Commander Riker, the Kirk-like Casanova of *The Next Generation*, is never with a woman of color, human or alien. Apparently he even prefers white holodeck characters to real black, brown, red, or yellow women. Like Riker, Dr. Crusher has affairs and romantic interests, though all of them are with white-alien and white-human males. Even when the doctor's son, Wesley Crusher, pursues romance, it is with either a white girl or a shape-shifting alien who chooses to present itself as a white girl.[19] Finally, Counselor Troi, who is half-Betazoid and half-human, gets involved in a number of romantic relationships, including one with a genetically enhanced white-human, Aaron (John Synder), in "Masterpiece Society" (1992). Yet only one, Lieutenant Worf, is nonwhite (discussed later). Of the main crew members, it is the colored males—Geordi and Worf—who desire and experience interracial relationships.

There is a thick tension in *The Next Generation*'s discourse on the mixing of the "races." This is especially the case with Geordi, Trek's "model minority," who for the first five years of the series is less than successful in his pursuit of the opposite sex. What is striking about this fact is that all the women he pursues during this period are white; one of them is even a holographic character. Geordi only manages a successful liaison with a white woman once, and in that instance it is due to a boost in his confidence provided by the god-like creature in "Transfigurations." Even in this episode, however, we never actually see the couple engage in intimate activity. They don't kiss. When, in the sixth season, in "Aquiel" (1993), Geordi is successful with a woman—that is to say, he kisses one—she is a black-alien (Renee Jones), and the two are allowed to express physical affection (figure 51). In "All Good Things . . . ," the opening scene hints at Geordi being married to the non-holographic Leah Brahms, with three children, but we never actually see the woman or the children. In other words, we don't know for sure if it's the white-human of earlier episodes, and if we assume that it is, we never actually see any expression of intimacy. *The Next Genera-*

51. Geordi and Aquiel

tion doesn't want to go there. Like so much of the humanism in the series, this interracial relationship is left to our imagination.

The problem of interracial relationships is also displaced onto species, suggesting a fear of miscegenation that is also manifest in the most
metaphoric articulations of imaginary time. And when these relationships involve a black-alien, Trek seems less willing to explore and develop the partnership than it otherwise might be. This is the case with
the relationship between Worf and Troi, which was subtly developed in
the seventh season in such episodes as "Parallels" (1993), "Eye of the
Beholder" (1994), "Genesis," and "All Good Things . . ." (1994). In
"Parallels," Worf and Troi are married in a parallel universe, and this
relationship between their alternates is a sort of foreshadowing of what
is to come. In the other episodes, the pairing of the two is a Trek reality, although it is either represented as deviant or played down. In
"Genesis," for instance, Worf, having "de-evolved" into the venomous
Klingon-creature, bites Troi on the face in order to mark her as his own.
And in "All Good Things . . . ," the couple, having re-evolved, openly
discuss their relationship; but when they are close to kissing, they are

interrupted by Picard. Uhura and Kirk actually came closer to kissing in "Plato's Stepchildren" than Worf and Troi in "All Good Things . . . ."

Chief O'Brien is married to Keiko Ishikawa (Rosalind Chao), an occasionally recurring character. This is actually the first interracial human relationship consistently represented in the Trek mega-text. And while interracial relationships are generally absent among the regular crew and in the original series and feature films, this one is fully realized. In many episodes, O'Brien and Keiko's differences—and how they overcome those differences—are explored and narrativized.[20] Their relationship is depicted as both conflicted and loving. Moreover, the couple has produced a child, Molly, who is played by a child actress who appears to have been cast because of her seemingly Asian and European features. In a few shots in both "Power Play" (1992) and "Disaster" (1992), the camera lingers on the girl's face long enough to allow the spectator to see a multiracial human. Though relegated to subplots, O'Brien, Keiko, and Molly reveal that Trek's miscegenation intertext is not completely hegemonic.

Assimilation: From Worf to Picard?

Assimilation, or the attempt to create a sociocultural melting pot with an all-encompassing ethos, is yet another discourse interwoven into *The Next Generation*'s racial play. In particular, the United Federation of Planets—the galactic institution built on such humanist ideals as democracy, free enterprise, and individual rights—is represented in the series as a great melting pot where all human races and numerous alien societies participate in a unified and unifying mission. Yet, hidden within these ideals, much like the code words of the neoconservative movement, is a Western and white standard. At stake in the modern notion of assimilation is "whitewashing," as David Goldberg notes, where race becomes "a morally irrelevant category."[21] As with the feature films, white—Western and conservative—is the model by which all Others are judged as serviceable and adequate to the ideals of the Federation. If an alien race doesn't quite fit (e.g.,the Ligonians or Pakleds), the mega-text takes its time in assimilating them. If an alien species does fit the assimilationist ideal, its members are either phenotypically white or, if colored, model minorities who are paradoxically kept away from the full privileges of whiteness.

Perhaps the clearest site of a neoconservative spin on the assimilation discourse centers on the Klingons in general and Worf in particular

52. Worf. © 1994 Paramount Pictures Corporation

(figure 52). In classic *Star Trek*, Klingons are the mortal enemy of the Federation. As I argued in chapter 2, for the most part they represent Communists in general and Soviets in particular. Yet, even as Communists and Soviets, they are an amalgam of signifiers, a condensation of Othering intertexts, including darkened skin and sinister Fu Manchu goatees. In the films, particularly *The Undiscovered Country*, the Klingons are still a mortal enemy, albeit one that loses much of its power due to the burden of its military budget. As I argued in chapter 3, the Klingons' eventual treaty with the Federation is the undiscovered country that so clearly parallels the real space-time fall of the Soviet bloc and their subsequent desire to be more like the United States. In *The Next Generation*, the Klingons are no longer a mortal enemy; they have become something quite different from their previous appearances in original Trek and the feature films. In the spinoff, they become a metaphor for a disenfranchised culture very much in the assimilationist purview of the Federation. Of course, the struggle to assimilate the

Klingons is not easy and is never complete; they are innately wild and predatory, as Data confirmed in "The Icarus Factor." Nowhere is this paradox of assimilation more clear than in the representation of Worf, the only Klingon serving aboard the U.S.S. *Enterprise.*

Worf's assimilation began when he was an infant. As a child, the back story tells us, Worf survived a Romulan attack on a Klingon outpost. After being rescued and then adopted by white-humans, he was brought to Earth and raised with Terran values. Hence, he is cultured from birth to be human. Yet, as an adult, Worf is constantly shown struggling with the conflict between his "genetic predisposition toward hostility" and the civility and politeness of humanity. As Leah R. Vande Berg notes, Worf is "always being betwixt and between human and Klingon culture."[22] He even wears a Klingon sash as a symbol of his attachment to his nature. He also often speaks of an innate desire to "wage battle" and "taste blood." Despite never knowing his Klingon side until well into adulthood, Worf is genetically Klingon, an intertext clearly derivative of biological determinism. Yet he chooses to reside among civilized humans, an intertext very much entangled with an assimilationist discourse.

In "Heart of Glory" (1988), the conflict between Worf's nature and his environment is elaborated upon, making visible the intertexts of biological determinism and assimilation that frame the series. The story begins with the *Enterprise* coming across three Klingon refugees. Picard and Riker are suspicious of the reptilian-like trio, but, ever the polite and sophisticated humans, they nonetheless provide the refugees living quarters on the *Enterprise.* We soon find out, however, that the Klingons are renegades seeking to break the alliance between the Federation and the Klingon Empire. Like General Chang in *The Undiscovered Country*, they want to return to the days of glorious battle with the Federation. Upon finding Worf, they attempt to elicit his help: "We are, after all, brothers lost among infidels," Korris (Vaughn Armstrong), the leader of the group, says to the Lieutenant. Worf is thus faced with the option of maintaining his allegiance to the Federation or pursuing his primal instinct with his Klingon "brothers."

As the episode unfolds, we witness just how uncivilized and ritualistic the Klingons are. After one of the three refugees dies, Worf and the other two perform the "Death Ritual." Moments before a Klingon's demise, his comrades look into his eyes and, after the last breath, howl like wolves toward the sky. In a high angle shot, we actually see the

53. Klingon death ritual

three Klingons howling to the sky—their ridged foreheads, dark skin, and dirty teeth visible intertexts of a bestial race (figure 53). Later, the Klingons pressure Worf to wage battle. In a tight medium shot, the second Klingon, Konmel (Charles H. Hyman), speaks of Worf's life among humans: "Those around you did not understand. You frightened them." "They shunned you," the leader adds, "Cursed you. Called you vile names." Finally, they acknowledge Worf's genetic inability to assimilate: "To fit in, the humans demand that you change the one thing that you cannot change." Here, it seems clear, a biological notion of blackness is displaced onto the Klingons while a civilized notion of whiteness is ascribed to the Federation.

In a later cross-cutting sequence that juxtaposes the Klingons discussing their innate desire for battle with Picard showing concern about Worf's intent, the tension—and thus the paradox of assimilation—is affirmed. In the first shot of the sequence, the Klingon leader tells Worf: "Our instincts will lead us." Konmel chimes in: "Instincts that haven't been dulled by living among civilized men." In the next shot, Picard questions Worf's nature: "As I watched Worf, it was like looking at a man I had never known." Later, the captain comments: "I can understand them looking into a dead man's eyes, but the howling?" Finally, after the cross-cuts, the renegades attempt to take over the *Enterprise*. One is killed, and the other points his phaser at the warp drives and threatens to blow up the entire ship. He calls for his "brother" Worf, forcing the Federation Klingon to make a difficult choice: battle or assimilate. Worf chooses the latter and kills his fellow Klingon. This proves his loyalty to Picard and the Federation, and demonstrates his commitment to assimilate despite his genetic predisposition.

After Worf chooses to assimilate, the Trek spinoff takes a closer look at Klingon culture. In "The Icarus Factor," the Klingon "pain ritual" is explained—it is a primitive custom whereby a Klingon must endure a gantlet of electrified pain sticks. In "The Emissary" (1989), we witness the Klingon sex ritual, a violent act where a broken bone is a sign of good luck. "Redemption" (1991) and "Redemption II" (1991) address the Klingon civil war and the notion of "discommendation." "Birthright, Part I" (1993) and "Birthright, Part II" (1993) reveal the Klingons' devotion to paternal heritage. "Rightful Heir" (1993) deals with Klingon religion. Indeed, in later episodes, Worf's loyalty is no longer questioned, and his assimilation becomes almost complete. He is trained and domesticated, becoming a father and a trusted officer who faithfully protects the *Enterprise* and its white captain. Yet, as suggested earlier, his assimilation can only go so far. This seems especially the case in "In All Good Things . . . ," which, as I discussed previously, leaves Worf just outside the love of a white woman (a half-alien at that). He is whitewashed, but like the reality contextualizing today's neoconservative rhetoric, he is nevertheless kept at the periphery of civilized standards.

A Brave Old World

Like the particle discussed in Stephen Hawking's epigraph to this chapter, intertexts impact texts "by every possible path."[23] Intertexts are the stuff of text, creating anything but a "single history" or, for that matter, a predetermined meaning. Hawking himself is an intertext, telling the fictional Albert Einstein "Wrong again, Albert," in "Descent, Part I"—a reference to Einstein's rejection of the notion that God would play dice with the universe (figure 54). To keep with the Hawking analogy, the determination of the particle's trajectory is one of "probability"—of imaginary time—juxtaposed against the curvature

54. Cosmologist Stephen Hawking. © 1994 Paramount Pictures
Corporation

of space-time if your subject is quantum mechanics, or against the shifting and reforming historical context if your subject is popular culture.

In this chapter I have tried to add up some of the waves of intertexts
and their paths as they relate to the specific ways in which *The Next
Generation* articulates race. These intertexts include history, evolution,
miscegenation, and assimilation. Borrowed from the discourses com-
prising the real world, they inform the very textualization of the science

fiction spinoff. And for all its rhetoric of humanism, diversity, and plurality, *The Next Generation* presents us with a future where everything from the multicultural past to the assimilation of dark aliens smacks of a neoconservative project. Perhaps this is most visible in the representation of human evolution as white, particularly with gods like Q, even though the beginning of life is brown as represented in "The Chase." The point: wherever we come from, the course of evolution, of advancement and sophistication, is literally and metaphorically, physically and socially, white. Humans and aliens of color might not get there, or if they do, they might have to "assimilate" and ultimately mind their place, but that's nonetheless *The Next Generation*'s version of the promised land.

5 Reading Race

Trekking through Cyberspace on STREK-L

I have been watching *Star Trek* since its conception because I like it, because it is well done, because it is exciting, because it says things (subtly and neatly) that are difficult to say in "straight" drama, and because science fiction, properly presented, is the type of literature most appropriate to our generation.
—*Isaac Asimov*

Picard: My culture is based on freedom and self-determination.
The Borg: Freedom is irrelevant. Self-determination is irrelevant.

In 1968 NBC threatened to cancel *Star Trek*, then in its second season, because of low ratings. Launching a "Save *Star Trek*" campaign, devout fans lobbied the network to give the science fiction series another chance.[1] After receiving thousands of letters and phone calls, the network made an unprecedented on-air announcement: "And now an announcement of interest to all viewers of *Star Trek*. We are pleased to tell you that *Star Trek* will continue to be seen on NBC television. We know you will be looking forward to seeing the weekly adventure in space on *Star Trek*."[2] Clearly not in tune with the loyalty and buying power of its persistent audience, NBC canceled the series after its third season. Never deterred, the fans kept the nascent mega-text alive in the 1970s by both attending conventions in the thousands and watching the program over and over again in syndication. This loyalty eventually paid off—Paramount brought the Trek universe back to prime time in the 1980s and 1990s in the form of *The Next Generation, Deep Space Nine*, and, as the flagship of its own network (UPN), *Voyager*. George Takei, speaking on the *Star Trek: 25th Anniversary Special* about the enthusiasm and commitment of the fans, succinctly summed up their role in the evolution of the series: "It's their belief. It's their faith. It's their tenacity. It's their energy reserve. It's their endlessly creative, inventive ways of lobbying that gave *Star Trek* this life."[3]

Not long after I chose to write a book on the shifting meaning of race in *Star Trek*, I realized that I had to come to terms with this activist-minded community. These were the people who kept the science fiction series on the air, who faithfully fed Paramount's insatiable bottom line, who wrote creative and bizarre fanzines, who wore funny little ears and greeted each other with odd phrases like "Live long and prosper." In 1992, during the initial stages of my research, I saw an advertisement for a *Star Trek* convention to be held at the famous Bonaventure Hotel in downtown Los Angeles. Since downtown isn't too far from Palms, where I was living at the time, I figured the convention would be a convenient foray into the world of Trek fandom.

I had my fair share of preconceptions about the convention and the likely attendees. Having recently completed preparations for my doctoral exams, where, among other things, I was doing my best to brush up on critical and cultural theory, I figured the event would likely be a depressing illustration of Fredric Jameson's critique of postmodern society. The renowned theorist argues that we are in "a prodigious expansion of culture throughout the social realm, to the point at which everything in our social life—from economic value and state power to practices and to the very structure of the psyche itself—can be said to have become 'cultural' in some original and as yet untheorized sense." [4] For Jameson, the Bonaventure itself, with its "constant busyness" and "distracting space," designed to be almost hermetically cut off from the material life of downtown Los Angeles, is a sort of synecdoche for this "prodigious expanse of culture"—a dangerous phase of history he calls "late capitalism." [5] At stake in such late capitalist monoliths as the Bonaventure is a "weakening of historicity," a decrease in critical consciousness, and an increase in the "political unconscious." Will the fans attending this convention, I asked myself, be aware of the fact that, not too far from the hotel, maybe six blocks away, thousands of Latinos and African-Americans are struggling to survive in a capitalist phase not at all concerned with their history? Will the fans be more interested in utopian illusions than oppressive realities? Will their politics be unconscious? With the stereotype of Trekkers as dweebs interested only in technobabble and nostalgic visions of the future, I figured Jameson would hit too close to home.

The convention was indeed a late capitalist's dream, a postmodern forum for the exchange of everything from phasers to medical tricorders—things that don't exist in real space-time except as simulations of simulations. The convention itself cost sixteen dollars to attend, and that was for a less expensive ticket. A prime ticket, which allowed the buyer special seating, cost thirty dollars. If you drove your car, which is the cultural logic of Los Angeles, parking was an additional twelve dollars; the luxurious hotel chose not to validate for Trekkers. Of course, the commoditization of Trek didn't end with admission fees and parking. Once you got into the convention center there were two large doors you could enter: behind the first was consumer heaven, a bright auditorium stacked wall to wall with *Star Trek* toys, *Star Trek* models, and *Star Trek* memorabilia; behind the second door was film scholar purgatory, a dark and musty auditorium that featured hours and hours of videotaped interviews with faithful *Star Trek* decision makers. The major draw of the convention, the keynote speaker, was Michael Dorn, the actor who plays Worf. Dorn gave an amusing talk that ranged from his favorite episode to his desire to have his character get into a romantic relationship with Marina Sirtis's character, Counselor Troi. He then made himself available in the dealer's room for autographs. Fans stood in long lines and paid a ten-dollar fee for a signed picture of the actor in full Klingon regalia. A Ferengi might have scoffed at the price, but the fans bought up the autographed simulation of a simulated "alien" with rich enthusiasm.

Yet, some elements of what I experienced at the convention cannot be explained by Jameson's theories of either late capitalism or the political unconscious. There's actually much more to what Trek fans do than buying either autographed pictures or the dull propaganda of the decision makers. The real or realizing stuff of the convention occurred in the private rooms, in the halls, and at the hotel's restaurants—away from the centers of exchange. It was the vigorous conversations attendees engaged in, not to mention the trading and free or at-cost distribution of fanzines and original art, that spoke to a political consciousness. One fan, for example, discussed with me the sexual politics of the mega-text, explaining how much she was bothered by the fact that the series had yet to represent a homosexual lifestyle. "The producers are clearly homophobic," she asserted. Another fan, a man, claimed the original series and *The Next Generation* were utterly sexist, keeping the female characters in subservient roles and revealing costuming. I also overheard a group of fans in a heated discussion about whether Cardassians, a warlike species who appear in *The Next Generation* and *Deep Space Nine*, were stereotypes of Arabs. One of the

Trekkers insisted the group write letters to the producers asking them to stop these "anti-Trek" practices. Debates like these, as I will show later, are at the core of what fans traveling the information superhighway write about.

The political consciousness of fans at the convention was not without its hegemonic tendencies. I remember getting into a conversation with a man, about thirty years old, dressed like a Vulcan with pointy ears and raised eyebrows. He argued that the "logical" Vulcans were like the Chinese, both cultures being "essentially mystical." His remark (albeit off-the-cuff) about the "essence" of the Chinese, a profoundly heterogeneous people, reminded me of the implicit racism Edward Said spoke about in *Orientalism*.[6] I remember a number of other fans who were supposed to be dressed like Klingons but to me looked like blackface performers of early cinema. When I asked one of the Trekker Klingons why she chose to make herself up so darkly, all she said was that she identified with their "animal instincts." She then smiled at me in a way that reminded me of how a lustful Klingon female looked at Riker in "A Matter of Honor" (figure 55); like the commander, I quickly moved on to other things.

The only other time I attended a Trek-related public event was to hear Leonard Nimoy give a talk on "Spock and the Jewish Question" at UCLA's Hillel Jewish Center. The audience consisted of students and guests who met every Friday for Shabbat. These were not fans of Trek per se, though there were Trekkers among the group. Rather, they were people interested in the relationship between Jewish actors, fictional characters, and Jewish identity. Nimoy's talk was both moving and amusing. He spoke of how his parents fled the persecution of Jews in the former Soviet Union. He reminisced about his childhood involvement in Yiddish theater. He defended his first book, *I Am Not Spock*, while promoting his new book, *I Am Spock*. The most memorable point of Nimoy's talk, however, came when the actor explained how he came up with the famous hand gesture that accompanies the Vulcan salutation, "Live long and prosper." Nimoy put a sheet over his head, mimicking how the Kohanim of his childhood synagogue, acting as conduits for God's presence, covered themselves with prayer shawls so as not to look upon the Mighty One. He then told the audience about how, instead of covering his eyes as is the custom in such a ceremony, he looked up and saw the Kohanim bent over, holding out their arms in front of them and spreading their fingers apart to form the Hebrew

55. Smiling Klingon female

letter "shin," the first letter in the word "Shaddai." With his pinkie and ring fingers firmly separated from his middle and index fingers, his thumb outstretched, Nimoy simultaneously revealed the Hebrew letter for a word that is God's name and the famous Vulcan hand gesture (figure 56). The Hillel audience laughed and cheered, and somehow I felt closer to Spock, *Star Trek*, and the fan experience.

I relate these personal experiences to the reader because they suggest a number of larger points and methodological concerns I want to tackle in this chapter. First, I want to admit up front that I am also a fan.[7] I enjoy most of the films and all four television series, even *Voyager*, although I'm quite critical of certain episodes and aspects of the megatext. My fan identity notwithstanding, however, I hope that I have balanced my proximity to the science fiction series—the pleasure I get from watching, discussing, and critiquing Trek—with an ethnographic distance that, while certainly not objective, is fair and honest. Like Henry Jenkins, whose insightful work on *Star Trek* fandom directly informs this chapter, "My account exists in a constant movement between these two levels of understanding which are not necessarily in

56. Vulcan salutation

conflict but are also not necessarily in perfect alignment."[8] Of course, the reader will end up judging whether or not I successfully walk this line.

Second, while there are considerable differences between the fan activity I analyze and the fan activity analyzed by Jenkins, like Jenkins's fans, most of the Trekkers I have come in contact with are more than just politically unconscious dweebs who need to, as Jameson might urge, "get a life." While there might be a few consumers in the community who care about nothing more than the trivia of Tribbles, the majority of fans I studied are constantly relating the series to their experiences and sense of the world. Many fans are members of civic groups and fan clubs, often named after simulated starships, that donate their time to community causes and the less privileged. Some lobby the network for change; others lobby each other for the "correct" interpretations. For the most part, these are conscientious people who are conscious of their personal, social, and mediated lives.

Finally and most importantly, the meanings of difference and diversity—and race itself—are central concerns of the fan community, as witnessed in both of my experiences. Trekkers often engage in heated debates about the racial politics of everything from casting to the representations of alien civilizations. In such instances, historicity is not weakened, but elaborated upon, contextualized—made meaningful—in the everyday lives of real people. This is not to suggest that fan activity is politically progressive or without contradictions, as I will also show; but the fans are constantly and consciously reading race into and out of the mega-text. Trekkers might not agree with the notion of a racial order or, if they do, choose to fight it in the same way that Jameson or I might, but they are not necessarily politically unconscious consumers who can't tell the difference between the culture of fiction and the culture of the real world.

Reading, Writing, and Fandom

Since I want to avoid the self-contradictory move of essentializing a group of diverse people, it is perhaps important to explain what I mean by "reader" and "reading" before I move on to actually analyzing Trekkers. While both concepts refer in some way to the people who read books and watch films and television programs, they mean different things and involve competing methodologies within the critical and cultural studies community. They also come fully loaded with a number of troubling assumptions. For instance, readers can be either theoretical constructs, hypothetical or implied by the text, or they can be empirically real, the actual person who picks up a book or sits in a theatre. Similarly, reading can be predetermined by the text, in which case the particularities of the book or film are the center of analysis; or it can be predetermined by the interest, knowledge, and identity of the reader, in which case the actual individual or small group is the center of analysis. Readings can be explained either on psychological grounds, resulting from conscious or unconscious processes, or on social grounds, resulting from an individual or group's social status. The assumptions underpinning these approaches are often riddled with problems, at times leaning toward a reductive model of the reader's mental activity (an all-determining unconscious, for instance) and at other times leaning toward an essentialist conception of social formation (the "masses"). Even the term "reader," which derives from literary theory, is contentious; some scholars choose "speculator" and still others prefer "audience." Whatever the case, it is clear that there are many definitions of what I prefer to label the "reader" and the activity of "reading."

Psychoanalysis, Cognitivism, Media Effects, and Uses and Gratifications

In the late 1960s and 1970s critical studies scholars began to challenge their field's tendency to rely on the author's presumed intent or a critic's unique insight when explaining the significance of a text. Instead, they argued that the reader was the ultimate site of signification, of meaning production. For instance, Roland Barthes, in a seminal essay proclaiming the "death of the author," wrote that "the reader is the space on which all the quotations that make up a writing are inscribed without any of them being lost; a text's unity lies not in its origin but in its destination."[9] Mikhail Bakhtin, perhaps less willing to elide completely the author's role in the production of meaning, nevertheless recognized that texts are meaningful only in their dialogical relationship with the space-time of the utterance and the particularity of the reader: "The work and the world represented in it enter the real world and enrich it, and the real world enters the work and its world as part of the processes of its creations, as well as part of its subsequent life, in a continual renewing of the work through the creative perception of listeners and readers."[10] The emphasis on the reader, then, provided these critics with a necessary counter to the distinctly reductive and potentially elitist emphasis on the "power" of the author and the perceptiveness of the critic to determine the meaning of a text. If the author and his companion, the ideal reader, were not silenced by Barthes and other theorists, they certainly lost much of their persuasiveness.

Concern with the role of the reader led film and television scholars in several directions. In the 1970s, film scholars began theorizing the reader as a subject position, an enunciation, found hidden in the text. Through a synthesis of psychoanalysis, notably that which emphasizes the condensations and displacements of the unconscious, and semiology, initiated by such French intellectuals as Christian Metz and Jean-Louis Baudry, the reader became less a real person engaging in an interpretive practice than a manifestation of various textual systems—from editing to "camera-work"—positioned in dominant ideology.[11] Feminist theorists such as Laura Mulvey and Mary Ann Doane, drawing on the implications of a subject-positioned-in-ideology, showed how classical Hollywood cinema privileged masculine positions that were scopophilic, or fetishistic and voyeuristic.[12] Similarly, scholars such as Beverle Ann Houston extended this approach to television studies, arguing that the popular medium was analogous to a mother's breast, a sort of "boob-tube," providing the positioned spectator with a potentially endless "flow" of patriarchal ideology.[13] While it is not within the scope of this chapter to delineate the subtleties of the psychoanalytically-based approach, suffice it to say that the emphasis on the reader centers on an individual spectator, generally masculine or feminine, who is constituted in ideology, either by the text or by the actual viewing environment (darkened theatre, in the case of cinema). In other words, this is a theoretical reader who is less a social person than a psychical subject, the affect of text-based signifying structures.

The emphasis on an individual reader who is more theoretical than experientially real includes David Bordwell's "hypothetical spectator." This "reader" is distinct from the unconscious one, in that Bordwell borrows from cognitive theories rather than psychoanalysis. "In general," he writes, "film theory has underestimated the importance of the spectator's conscious and preconscious work."[14] More to the point, Bordwell argues that comprehending a film, its style, story, or plot, constitutes a psychologically active process dependent primarily on visual and auditory perception. The text takes advantage of certain hard-wired mental processes and a knowledge base, or schema, of interpretive skills and guides the hypothetical reader to certain interpretations. In turn, the cognitive spectator utilizes cues and patterns supplied by the film's "hollow form" to construct meaning (building inferences, testing hypothesis, etc.).[15] Regardless of the differences between Bordwell's spectator and the psychoanalytic one, in particular his apt recognition that the conscious mind has a significant role to play in the meaning-making process, the two share two fundamental principles: readers exist only in theory and the text, or "work" to use Bordwell's preferred term, is the center of analysis.

Another model used by film and television scholars, though most notably in sociology and mass communications studies rather than critical or cultural studies, is media effects. In brief, this approach is concerned less with abstract theories of subject formation or meaning constructivism than with the material relationships between classes of readers (economic, racial, etc.) and types of texts (Hollywood film, children's television, etc.). Psychological factors, whether unconscious or cognitive, are generally less emphasized than social norms and values. Toward this end, texts are analyzed not for their unique or complex characteristics, as is the case in the psychoanalytic and Bordwellian models, but simply for their "content" (what a story is about, how characters behave, etc.). Moreover, texts overwhelm the relationship between readers and texts in the media effects approach, as readers are assumed to have little agency over media content. In practice, the media effects model tends to make larger causal connections between the ideology of "the masses" and the ideology of the media, with scholars who lean toward a leftist politics seeing mass media as the conduit for a "false ideology," making readers dupes interpolated into the dominant ideology, and scholars leaning toward a rightist politics seeing mass media, specifically the violence and sexual explicitness of much network programming, as participating in the so-called breakdown of the family. In both of these critiques, the reader is a passive collective of empirical subjects, a mass whose very values and behavior are significantly "affected" by media content.

Another sociologically-based approach is the Uses and Gratifications model. Not unlike media effects, the concern here is the relationship between the media and real people. However, proponents of this perspective are less interested in making generalizations about masses of readers than they are in exploring the use-value of media in everyday life—whether, for example, people use media for simple entertainment, to catch up on the news of the day, or for other purposes. Thus, the approach assumes that media content, irrespective of its purported leftist or rightist messages, does not affect readers who have no use for it in their daily lives. Uses and Gratifications readers select and apply media in distinct ways, often in ways that differ markedly from the producer's intentions, or even from other audience members's uses. And they do so based on not only their values, but their interests, associations, and identities as well. The approach de-emphasizes the power of the text, focusing instead on small groups of people who share a program and a sociological relationship (class, race, etc.). As such, the reader is not theoretical or a generalized mass, but empirically real. Uses and Gratifications scholars use surveys and interviews to determine what readers do with texts.

The aforementioned approaches, while containing many useful principles and insights, make assumptions about the reader that are problematic for a study of how diverse, active, and historically situated people read race in Trek. First, while approaches to the relationship between texts and readers necessarily require a certain amount of theorizing, as the psychoanalytic and Bordwellian models intend, especially since this relationship is more complex than any one analysis can fully explain, relying solely on a theoretical reader—a subject of or to texts—is no less reductive or potentially elitist than relying on a notion of either an all-determining author or an ideal reader/critic. Both emphasize the writer/critic's perspective over the reader's actual reading. Second, the psychoanalytic, cognitive, and media effects approaches, for all their differences, fail to show how their readers are part of a diverse social world, utilizing and influenced by a variety of discourses when engaging texts. Readings do not take place in a vacuum, even if the viewing takes place in a darkened theatre. For that matter, media effects, but also to a certain degree Bordwell's cognitive approach, fail to recognize the importance of the viewing environment, thus implying that watching a television program or film in your home, cooking dinner in the kitchen with the television on in the living room, or hanging out with a group of like-minded friends in a sports bar or a theatre are identical situations in terms of your reception of the text. In short, readers in these approaches tend to be transhistorical, undifferentiated, and unaffected by competing discourse or levels of attention.

While the Uses and Gratifications approach gives agency to the readers, making them active rather than passive, it perhaps goes too far in emphasizing psycho-individual readings at the expense of dominating sociocultural formations. In other words, the model often emphasizes individual choice at the expense of macro historical processes. Further, unlike the psychoanalytic and cognitive models, but similar to media effects, the Uses and Gratifactions approach fails to tackle the complexity and distinctiveness of texts, despite the varying and often unique textual, narratological, and stylistic properties that make up film and television programming. While assuming a reader that is anything but a predetermined affect, the Uses and Gratifications approach often goes too far in emphasizing choice at the expense of the complexities of the text and sociopolitical systems of dominance.

Admittedly, the model a scholar chooses for a given analysis depends in part on the questions he or she is asking. If, for instance, the scholar is assessing the relationship between cognitive processes and works of art, then a cognitive-based model would be not only appropriate, but necessary. Nevertheless, it seems to me that any study of race, or, more broadly, the struggle over difference and power, must allow readers access to agency, and thus to choice. Otherwise the future is determined, leaving those who are on the opposite side of race privilege little choice but to join the fray, assimilate, or jump ship. Moreover, any study of race must assume diversity and thus difference. Otherwise the reader is essentialized, making the "look" of difference an anomaly, something not normal, and thus something to be improved. Finally, texts must be considered for both their complexity, their own diversity, and their participation in systems of dominance, their own part in the hegemonic struggle. As I try to show throughout this study, texts are more complex than their content might suggest, and they are also very much in dialogue with the systems of dominance and exploitation that define our social word.

Cultural Studies and Ethnography

Like media effects, the British Cultural Studies approach sees the institutions of mass media as having power to set agendas and affect human consciousness; but it also recognizes that readers both have agency to resist mediated ideologies and, like Uses and Gratifications, use media for different and varied reasons. Stuart Hall laid the foundation for this approach, arguing that while the formal and ideological structure of texts elicits "dominant" readings, or readings that match the ideology of the text, there are other reading positions available, including "negotiated" and "resistant." [16] Hall theorized that these positions are dependent on both the level of involvement in the program and the class orientation of the reader. While critics have pointed out the limitations of his work, namely that he overemphasizes class, Hall's model nevertheless provides an accurate, if only general, account of the readings I heard articulated at the Bonaventure Hotel. Some Trek fans, such as the man who charged the mega-text with stereotyping Arabs, took a distinctly oppositional reading. He wanted to initiate a letter-writing campaign to get the producers to alter what he felt were negative representations of race. Other fans provided what seemed like a dominant reading—for instance, the man who dressed like a Vulcan and argued that the Chinese, like the simulated alien he was pretending to be, were "essentially mystical." Still other fans seemed to negotiate their meanings with more ambiguity, making dark-skinned Klingons their heroes, yet at the same time linking their darkness with innate animalism. As these examples might suggest, Hall's model is useful because it calls attention to the processes of hegemony, of coercion and consent, while recognizing that reading positions are varied and not just dominant or resistant. Readers have both the power to choose and the uniqueness of difference in this approach.

David Morley applies and expands the encoding/decoding model, turning it into an ethnographic approach. Like Hall, Morley argues that texts don't determine readers; rather, readers, texts, and the historic context are partners in the meaning-making process. He writes:

> At the moment of textual encounter other discourses are always in play besides those of the particular text in focus—discourses which depend on other discursive formations, brought into play through the subject's placing in other practices—cultural, educational, institutional. And these other discourses will set some of the terms in which any particular text is engaged and evaluated.[17]

Yet, while he gives agency to readers, Morley calls attention to the systems of dominance and power that inform readers and texts. Quoting Hall, he argues:

> While messages can sustain, potentially, more than one reading, and "there can be no law to ensure that the receiver will 'take' the preferred or dominant reading of an episode . . . in precisely the way in which it has been encoded by the producer" yet still the message is "structured in dominance" by the preferred reading. The moment of "encoding" thus exerts, from the production end, an "over-determining" effect (though not a fully determined closure) on the succeeding moments in the communicative chain.[18]

To get at the relationship between an active reader and texts structured in dominance, Morley analyzes readers as they integrate and interpret television in their everyday lives. He stresses the role of social factors beyond class, the particularities of the text (including genre), and the importance of the viewing environment within the context of everyday life. He writes: "I am interested in . . . what television means to different kinds of people, watching different kinds of programs, in different contexts, and at different times."[19]

John Fiske is one of the most prominent scholars extending the British Cultural Studies method to an American context. Like Hall and Morley, Fiske is concerned with how readers use texts within the context of family viewing and social life. Yet he goes further than his colleagues, arguing that readers have almost complete authority over the text. He writes: "we need to note that television is not the dominating monster it is often thought to be; viewers have considerable control, not only over its meanings, but over the role that it plays in their lives."[20] Fiske also argues that the polysemic nature of the television text, its complex intertextuality for example, facilitates empowerment, rather than restricting choice as Hall and Morley would contend:

> To be popular with a diversity of audiences television must both provoke its readers to the production of meanings and pleasures, and must provide the textual space for these meanings and pleasures to be articulated with the social interests of the readers. Readers will only produce meanings from, and find pleasures in, a television program if it allows for this articulation of their interests.[21]

Fiske concludes that the relationship between the polysemic television text and the active reader reinforces "the power to be different" and is therefore ultimately democratic: "There is a pleasure in playing with television's textuality, in exploiting one's ability to submit oneself to, and to distance oneself from its illusion of reality that is finally a democratic one," he writes, "for it allows the viewer both control of reading relations and access to the process of representation."[22]

There are problems with Fiske's approach and arguments. He seems to make the same mistake of many Uses and Gratifications scholars— namely, giving readers individual agency by minimizing the social power of television texts. Such a position fails to recognize the hegemonic relationship between readers and texts, a historically specific struggle that, while acknowledging resistance, necessarily acknowledges clear lines of power and dominance. As Ien Ang argues: "If viewers can decode a text in different ways and sometimes even give oppositional meanings to it, this should not be conceived as an example of 'audience freedom,' but as a moment in that cultural struggle, an ongoing struggle over meaning and pleasure which is central to the fabric(ation) of everyday life."[23] In the process of conflating an active reader with democratic readings, Fiske ends up romanticizing the polysemic nature of television texts. While his work acknowledges history in the abstract, his recent efforts fail to show how it asserts its versatile power over texts and reader. As Hall warns, "Polysemy must not be confused with pluralism. Connotative codes are not equal among themselves. Any society/culture tends, with varying degrees of closure, to impose its segmentations . . . its classifications of the . . . world upon its members. There remains a dominant cultural order, though it is neither univocal or uncontested."[24] While the television text is not a single message, it does not necessarily elicit democratic readings. As I will show shortly, Trekkers, while conscious of themselves and of history, are not necessarily democratic or progressive.

The ethnographic approach also has its share of problems. A major concern relevant to this study is the tendency among some ethnographers to assume that an objective relationship between researcher and subject is both possible and necessary. Subjects are seen as texts to be unmasked or discovered outside the ideology of the ethnographer. Proponents of the objectivity perspective argue that an interpretive study will likely be overly subjective, political, and therefore untrue. I have two fundamental concerns with this position. First, since the influence of poststructuralism on the study of culture, objectivity has been seen as a myth that, in and of itself, make "objective" studies anything but truth. Indeed, claims of objectivity elide the telling inherent in writing and scholarship, in his-story, and thus perpetuate and naturalize the myth of the value-neutral scholar and study. As I suggested in chapter 1, this has been a troubling problem in the history of academic studies of race. Second and related, just because a study is interpretive does not necessarily mean it is either polemical or false. Subjectivity is not synonymous with fiction, lie, or propaganda. However, the point is actually moot, since the goal of the cultural studies ethnographer is not the hunt for truth, but the pursuit of honest and ethical interpretations. As Ang explains, "It is not the search for (objective, scientific) knowledge in which the researcher is engaged, but the construction of interpretations, of certain ways of understanding the world, always historically located, subjective, and relative."[25] Finally, for the cultural studies ethnographer, the reader of scholarly works, like the reader of broadcast texts, is recognized as having the wherewithal to evaluate and adjudicate an interpretive study of texts and readers based on its method, findings, description, and explanations.

Henry Jenkins, a leading ethnographer of reading in general and *Star Trek* fandom in particular, draws on critical theory to balance his subjectivity. In his important book on fandom, *Textual Poachers: Television Fans & Participatory Culture*, he utilizes Michel de Certeau's notions of "poaching" and the "nomadic" reader in order to describe the relationship between fans and texts. The notion of poaching refers to an active and creative process whereby readers take their favorite elements of a program (characters, storylines, etc.) and, based on their personal needs and pleasures, extend their experiences with Trek through such activities as debating with other fans and writing their own Trek stories. More often than not, such extensions of the original text are not completely faithful to the original. Fanzines, for instance, often cause conflicts with the legal owners of the original text, in this case Paramount, which explains Jenkins's choice of the term "poaching"—a word that assumes "the power differential between" owners of texts, or "landowners," and readers of texts, or "poachers."

The notion of the nomadic reader refers to the process of poaching across many texts. As de Certeau explains: "readers are travelers; they move across lands belonging to someone else, like nomads poaching their way across fields they did not write, despoiling the wealth of Egypt to enjoy it themselves."[26] Poaching is a sort of nomadism in which readers read intertextually, drawing on various texts and discourses in constructing and extending the original text. This activity does not necessarily entail the actual writing of fanzines; rather, it suggests the general processes involved in reading, as all readers poach meaning from all sorts of texts in the meaning-making process.

The notion of a nomadic poacher describes Trek fans. Trekkers are constantly relating the fictional universe to the real world in which they live. They also write and distribute convention reports, critical treatises, and fanzines based on the science fiction series. Moreover, Trekkers do not restrict their poaching to one text, say a specific episode or just one of the many series. Rather, their readings are nomadic, in that they construct and debate the canon utilizing the various television programs, the eight films, the plethora of comics, and even the novels and toys. Indeed, fans are constantly relating their poaches to other science fiction films like *Star Wars*, to television programs like *Battlestar Galactica* (1978–1980), and, most significantly, to real space-time phenomena such as the cold war and the politics of Ronald Reagan. In short, fans poach the mega-text in writerly ways, extending the life of the characters and storylines in directions not necessarily intended by the producers. They mine both Trek texts and the text of the real world for pleasure and socially relevant meanings.

The notion of readers as nomads and reading as poaching led Jenkins to study specific fan communities, including women, gays, and students at MIT.[27] For Jenkins, these groups of fans actively engage in debates about the meaning and politics of the science fiction series. They also attempt to get the producers to address their specific concerns through mail and phone calls. Jenkins argues that these activities are evidence of "resistant readings," or readings that politicize the original text's representations and storylines. For instance, the Gaylaxions I mentioned in chapter 4 write letters to the producers to encourage them to include a gay character in the fictional universe. In the case of women fans, Jenkins found that they often write fanzines that take the original text in directions not consciously intended by the producers, for instance representing Kirk and Spock as lovers. Called "slash," this kind of extension of the Trek experience, according to Jenkins, represents "a powerful form of resistant reading, an active appropriation and transformation of dominant media content into forms of cultural production and circulation that speak to the female fan community's needs and interests."[28] The debates fans engage in, not to mention the writing of fanzines and slash, is persuasive evidence of what I called at the beginning of this essay a political consciousness.

Yet this political consciousness, this resistance, is not necessarily progressive or subversive. While Jenkins is apt to point out the resistant readings of many Trek fans, he is also careful to recognize that their readings ultimately fit within the ideology of the overall series. He writes: "The reading practices characteristic of fandom are never purely and rarely openly resistant to the meanings and categories advanced by programme producers. Often . . . the fans' resistant reading occurs within rather than outside the ideological framework provided by the programme and is fought in the name of fidelity to the programme concepts."[29] Like the texts of Trek and the political projects of contemporary United States culture, including the liberal humanism discussed in chapter 2 and the neoconservatism discussed in chapter 4, fans are informed by the ideologies, politics, and events that make up their mediated and social lives. As Jenkins notes: "There is nothing timeless and unchanging about this culture; fandom originates in response to specific historical conditions (not only specific configurations of television programming, but also the development of feminism, the development of new technologies, the atomization and alienation of contemporary American culture, etc.) and remains constantly in flux."[30] In other words, though fans are generally quite conscious of their politics, their politics are in dialogue with the ambiguities and contradictions defining and redefining the social world.

The Trek fans I analyze, the Trekkers surfing the Internet, are quite different from the fans analyzed by Jenkins. First, unlike Jenkins's fans, the Trekkers I studied cannot be defined by a specific social formation, say women or gays. These fans belong to a cyberspace listserver, or a specific collection of Internet e-mail accounts, whose only criterion for joining is an interest in Trek.[31] Yet while they cannot be defined as a specific social group, they nonetheless share a technological literacy (use of computers and e-mail) and, more generally, an association with educational and government institutions (i.e., ".edu" and ".gov" email addresses). And while certain sociological characteristics can be gleaned from their affiliation with such institutions, namely the fact that they are either seeking an education or are college graduates (many are actually graduate students and professionals), they include male and female, working-class and middle-class, gay and straight, European descent and African descent—to name just a few of the demographic categories. Second and related, the fans I analyze, though distributing among themselves the same things as other fans, are less activist-minded. These Trekkers don't petition the producers of the science fiction series with great consistency, at least not as a group, mainly because there is not one cause they all share in common (e.g., a gay politics, an interest in technology, etc.). This is not to say that individual Internet fans are less proactive. If, as Jay Badenhoop notes, one of the series were to be cancelled, the potential loss would be "a galvanizing or uniting force."[32]

Because the fans I focus on differ markedly from those analyzed by Jenkins, and because my interest is the articulation of race by a diverse fan community, my use of the ethnographic model is also somewhat distinct. Like Jenkins's fans, the Trekkers I analyze are real; however, my fans are embodied behind computer screens and networks of networks. As such, I have never actually met any of them. Some are located in different countries, most are in different cities, making interpersonal communication and interaction impractical. For this reason, perhaps the approach I use can best be described as "cyberspace ethnography." The fans I analyze are also quite active and conscientious, although, unlike Jenkins, I've never discussed their politics with them.[33] This is mainly because I have found people generally defensive and guarded when they are asked to confront the meaning of race. Those who assume a racial hierarchy, for instance, will honestly claim and seemingly believe that their ideas or politics are not racist. Conversely, those who are repulsed by racist hierarchies will fail to consider the complexities and, indeed, the sophistication of racist paradigms and belief systems. So, like my experience with the woman who dressed like a Klingon at the Bonaventure Hotel, I have kept some distance from the fan activities I analyze.

Because the fan community in cyberspace is quite large and diverse, I have focused on a group of fans that belonged to an Internet listserver, "STREK-L," from 1992 to 1994.[34] Like other Internet fans, STREK-L subscribers circulate resources such as filmographies and convention reports. They engage in speculative fiction and often have signature files that, like the original art of Jenkins's fans, are Trek-oriented in theme and design. More importantly, however, STREK-L fans engage in debates about everything from the gaps and conflicts in the Trek canon to the ideology of plot-lines and representations of aliens. In fact, open discussions of race dominate the listserver, prompting one fan, who calls himself "Mr. Mysterious," to complain: "I've been on the list for about 3 years and I too have seen the same ethnic debates ad nauseum. I don't comment on them much anymore because after the 5–6th time, the topic gets boring."[35] Whether agreeing that Trek is racial or racist or not, these fans engage in critical examinations of the mega-text by literally writing and then disseminating their opinions and analysis to other members of the listserver. This form of expression, a sort of nomadic poaching, provides me with concrete empirical evidence for at least one fan group's reading of race in Trek.

"Good Grief, Not Another Meaning!": Poaching Race on STREK-L

The poaching of race by STREK-L subscribers revolves around three general topics. The first of these is casting, specifically the function of actors of color. These dialogues are often inflected with discourses ranging from genetics to political correctness, thus indicating the degree to which the articulation of race among the fans is as nomadic as the broadcast texts are intertextual. Second, the poaching of race involves the use of Trek as a way to understand the contemporaneous world stage, from the war in Bosnia to United States intervention in Haiti. In such instances, the fans often demonstrate a cogent, even at times self-conscious sense of United States and international politics and history. Finally and perhaps most obviously, Trekkers on the Internet read race vis-à-vis Trek aliens, including most consistently Cardassians, Klingons, and Ferengi. Like the texts of Trek discussed in chapters 2, 3, and 4, fans' discussions of aliens reveal a clear racial consciousness.

The readings of race on STREK-L show that fans have a conscientious interest in race that is nonetheless hampered by troubling ambiguities. While overt racist slurs are rare, implicitly racist ideologies are common. While fans embrace Trek's humanist vision of a colorblind society, debates about diversity and difference are often constrained by discourses like biological determinism and political correctness. Fans will often take a moral position in favor of a utopian future where we all get along, and at the same time assume that the West and white-Europeans are socially and culturally superior. At times fans excuse Trek's racism as mere fiction. At other times, fans resist the racism in-the-text and by other fans, condemning it as anti-egalitarian and, in the most humanistic vision of the mega-text, "anti-Trek." Whether racist or not, reactionary or progressive, historicity is not weakened by the fans; rather, it is realized and politicized.

Casting Color: Genes or Political Correctness

One of the most common interests among STREK-L fans is the lives of the actors. Many Trekkers will go to great lengths to track the credits and personal appearances of their favorite star, often distributing among themselves an actor's filmography or a report on his or her latest convention appearance. It is not surprising, then, that within this general interest in stars is a concern with how and why actors of color are used. In fact, fans on STREK-L discuss the politics of casting actors of color with great intensity, often in an attempt to understand both the motivations of the producers and the relationship of the actors to the overall Trek vision. Far from collapsing the difference between real performers and fictional characters, fans understand that the stars, especially those of color, have both a material and a symbolic effect on Trek's imagination of the future.

Like the intertexts interwoven in *The Next Generation*, discourses ranging from biology to political correctness inflect fan debates about the relationship between casting and the Trek vision. This is the case whether the fan is lobbying for more diversity or for less. For instance,

Mary submits the following: "I agree with the view put forth that Star Trek could present a more ethinically diversified cast. . . . In the 24th century wouldn't you say that the members would have to come from a wider gene pool than now? With members coming from a wider gene pool, I would guess that there would be a host of different features a person could have." [36] By grounding her call for a more diverse cast in the notion of "gene pools," Mary offers a biological conception of race. This is also the case with Sherri, who is interested in why African-American actors in Trek lack phenotypical diversity:

> With the happy exception of Levar Burton, and Ben Sisko's actor (the name escapes me now) it seems to me that the majority of black actors chosen to play on ST have been those actors who have more "caucasian" features, who do not have distinctly "black" features. Is this just a warped perception on my part? I keep thinking that most of the black actors I have seen on Trek have been predominately (*sigh* once again, to be PC [politically correct], no offense meant to the sensitive) thin lipped, narrow nosed, and even lighter in skin tone. Now I am perfectly aware that there are great varieties of features and skin tone among all races. I am merely wondering why I see such a seemingly narrow band of a particular race on a show which supposedly represents a future in which such differences are not important. [37]

Sherri goes into detail about "Caucasian" and "black" features as they relate to the symbolic currency of Trek actors, thereby revealing the depth of the correlation between biology, phenotypes, race, and the show's utopian vision of the future.

Perhaps the most intense discussion about actors of color among STREK-L subscribers involved the casting of *Voyager*. Many fans used the publicity surrounding what Paramount executives in 1994 were calling the most diverse cast in Trek history as a way to discuss the implications of such a racially conscious practice. Here the concern centered not only on the bio-logic of Trek's vision of the future, but on contemporaneous politics as well. For instance, some fans were against casting a multiracial group of actors on the grounds of submission to the dogma of political correctness, a neoconservative discourse intertwined with the meaning of race in the 1980s and early 1990s. As Dr. Mike explains, "I hope that it is handled in a non-exploitive way. I don't want to watch it if it's done along the lines of 'Oh, what a marvelous show, we have a nice diverse cast of characters so you simply must watch us.' Let the show's focus be good sci-fi and Trek stories instead of PC in space."[38] Other fans, however, felt strongly that a diverse cast would have a positive effect on the science fiction series. Peter, for instance, concluded it would help the show's storylines: "Okay let me get this straight. Some of you would be nauseated by a really diverse cast on the new show? Why? I'd think the diversity could make for a far more interesting show, since with all that diversity, you'd also have a lot of conflicts. And inter-personal conflicts are often some of the more interesting parts of both DS9 and TNG."[39] For both Dr. Mike and Peter, diversity among the cast of *Voyager* was an issue of politics, with Peter thinking it would be fodder for "a more interesting show."

Discussions about casting and race often get volatile, as accusations of political correctness induce some fans to start "flame wars." (A flame in cyperspace is an overly negative response to what is perceived by the "flamer" as a "stupid" or unacceptable post.) Whether a question of biology, political correctness, or both, STREK-L subscribers are quite sensitive about the meaning of race. For instance, after Sean disagreed with the efforts of the producers to cast a multiracial group of actors for *Voyager* on the grounds that "America is not that diverse," Abdullah fired back: "Sean: You small-minded idiot. America is not part of the federation, earth is. Just because America is not that diverse doesn't mean that the rest of the world isn't. You want all whites on the show? For your information, most humans on earth are asian, from either India or China. Star Trek does not at all represent what a total earth government would really be like. Get a Clue before You post Again."[40] Another fan then responded to Abdullah, implicitly invoking the idea of reverse discrimination, another neoconservative intertext informing the meaning of race in the early 1990s: "For the record, I agree that the producers of Voyager may be including a 'racially-diverse' cast on the show simply to be political correct. No one said that we wanted all whites on the show. The fact of the matter is that placing people of different backgrounds on the show simply because they want to have a racially-mixed cast is prejudiced in itself."[41]

Whether fans are for more diversity or against reverse discrimination, their posts reveal a systematic understanding of race that, in their use of such venerable discourses as genetics and political correctness, is both conscious of and tied to the U.S. racial formation.

Geopolitics: Intergalactic Relations and Polemical Posturing

Fans on STREK-L use the Trek diegesis as a platform to speak to the events and politics of the real world. In doing so, they often discuss international conflicts, particularly the war in Bosnia, the genocide in Somalia, and America's military intervention in Haiti—topics that were very much on the minds and television sets of viewers at the time I was monitoring the listserver. In correlating the fictional universe with the real world, fans often take specific and well-argued positions on everything from the "racism" of United States foreign policy to the right of America to "protect" its borders. In these posts to the listserver, the real world is not collapsed into the fictional world, as postmodernists might speculate; rather, it is explored, analyzed, and, in some instances, even questioned.

The United Federation of Planets and the Prime Directive, Starfleet's dictum not to interfere in the natural evolution of alien words, are the two diegetic logics most commonly used by the fans to discuss events in real space-time. These fictional logics form the entry points for debates about the politics of United States foreign policy. As one reader asks:

> So, if we are to follow a real life 90s version of the Prime Directive, where do we start? Are we (the US and UN) going against the Prime Directive by trying to impose a democratic version of political stability on a politically unstable country (Haiti)? Are we going against the Prime Directive by trying to arrest a politically powerful warlord in Somalia? Why aren't we using the same methods in Bosnia?[42]

This post spurred a debate about whether or not United States involvement in Haiti, Somalia, and Bosnia had racist overtones. As Jeff rhetorically asks: "Uh, it wouldn't have anything to do with the people in Bosnia being of the pale coloration and those in Haiti and Somalia being 'people of color?'" Jeff continues by explaining his position, particularly in regard to paternalism: "I think we are allowing them (the Bosnians) to make their 'own mistakes' because they are European, while the other cultures 'obviously' (severe sarcasm in case you don't realize it) need our help. They haven't advanced far enough for us to let them slaughter themselves. That is a right only Europeans or those with European backgrounds have earned."[43] Ever the sophisticated group, fans are apt to point out each aspect of an argument centering on race, as Bruce did in this response to Jeff:

It's funny, last year, when the debate over Somalia (pre-commitment) was raging and it looked more likely that we would send troops to Bosnia, it was said that "It's obvious we're helping the Bosnians because they're white and leaving the Somalis to starve because we don't care about black people dying." Now that we're in Somalia, the same people say, "It's obvious that we're in Somalia because we're paternalistic towards African nations, while we stay out of Bosnia because we respect their ability to take care of themselves." So which is it? What can the U.S. possibly do that won't be called racist? [44]

Bruce goes on to point out a detailed military reason for his position:

The real reason is easy to understand. Somalia = bands of a hundred to a few thousand men, armed with assault rifles and just enough missiles to be dangerous if treated lightly, a recent period of turmoil, open terrain, easy access by sea, no regional power strong enough militarily to do the job. Bosnia = Several hundred thousand soldiers armed with MIG 21's, T-62 tanks, etc. (not top of the line, but deadly enough), a thousand years of complex and deep-seated hatred, mountainous wooded terrain (not favorable to the U.S. doctrines of artillery & air support), difficult access to interior, and numerous European powers who could clean up their own backyard if they had the intestinal fortitude. Good enough? [45]

As this debate over the racial politics of United States foreign policy might suggest, the Trek universe is used by the fans, much as it was by the decision makers involved in the making of the original *Star Trek* discussed in chapter 2, as a platform to articulate a range of ideas about the world stage. For what is essentially electronic mail, an informal and fairly spontaneous form of communication, these discussions are fairly detailed and cogent, revealing a complex racial consciousness.

Still other fans debate whether a contemporaneous "prime directive" would benefit the nations of the real world. Some fans felt such a dictum would not be beneficial; others felt it would. What is interesting about the polemics of these positions is the constant reference to the past, the history of the real word, to validate and support arguments. Fans are as self-conscious about history as both the decision makers and the broadcast texts. For instance, Bruce writes: "First, colonialism and other outside influences have so thoroughly disrupted the cultures of developing nations that it would be ridiculous to back out now and claim we are letting them develop naturally. I can't think of a parallel from TNG, but the situation is similar to the TOS crew trying to reverse the Nazi influence on the Ekosians (sp?) in 'Patterns of Force.'" Not only are arguments supported by history; they are often sophisticated. Bruce goes on to provide a persuasive rationale for his position:

> I think that we have indeed become such a global community that cultures no longer develop individually as do planetary cultures in the Federation. (Almost) all nations are members of the U.N. and the world economy, and developments in any one necessarily influence the others. Similarly, we assume that in the world community, there are certain standards of human rights that all nations must respect, despite sovereignty. (Thus, the Nazis had no right to commit genocide, even if they had left other nations alone.).[46]

By invoking notions like the global community, world economy, human rights, and the history of Nazi atrocities, Bruce reveals a multifaceted understanding and use of world history. Far from weakening historicity, this fan applies it in order to better understand his world and articulate his concerns.

Fans who oppose the implementation of a real-world prime directive are often assumed by other members of the listserver to be embracing a sociocultural hierarchy. For instance, one fan wrote, "Even though I think the world would be a better place if we abided by the Prime Directive, we only live on one small world. The thing one Third World nation might do might have an unwanted profound impact on much of the world. We can't just ignore something like that like it happened on another planet light-years away." Bettina then responded with the following:

> Agreed, again IF you understand THEIR point of view and THEIR past history and allow them to SHARE or even get the CHANCE to EXPRESS THEIR experiences and technologies without claiming YOURS was "first" or "best", rather than *PRESENTING* YOUR culture and YOUR technology and describing the benefits that YOU have received from using that technology. You have seen Picard adapt this approach, developed from his love for the archeology, history, AND RESPECT for the uniqueness of other cultures.[47]

Bettina's use of capitals to lend emphasis to key words and phrases indicates not only her disgust with the previous post, but a political sensitivity rooted in the humanist ideals of the science fiction series.

At times fans erect explicit sociocultural hierarchies, though they are almost always rationalized as anything but racist. Indeed, fans who erect these levels of privilege and elitism often fit their readings squarely in the humanist vision of the mega-text. As Robert, who acknowledges that he is of "European descent," writes:

> Throughout history, there have been several examples that had disastrous impacts that would probably have been avoided if an ethic like the Prime Directive would have been observed. The largest instance I can think of right off the top of my head have been the invasion of Africa by the Christian European imperialists. Of many centuries, the land and people of the African continent have been exploited for the greed of the Europeans. Ideas and technology have been introduced into Africa that have had a dangerous effect on its people. The Europeans have also imposed their social, economic, and religious agenda on the peoples of the Americas. Throughout this entire conquest, millions upon millions of Africans and Native Americans have been decimated over the centuries from acts of brutality by the self-proclaimed leaders of the world. The ones that did survive, lived their lives in slavery. While these events happened in the past when the European power was motivated to global domination by divine right and economic gain, they still affect the world today through cultural relations and wars.[48]

Despite the cogency of his analysis, Robert's racial consciousness becomes ambiguous as he continues to explain his position. In fact, he goes on to establish a series of hierarchies, revealing how fan activities are contradictory, not only in general, but often within individual posts:

> One place where I would like to see nonintervention is in Somalia. . . . Protecting the people so they can get food only lasts a short time, soon they are out of food and are starving again. Say that they do get enough food and are well-fed, the Somali people probably do not have the social maturity to live in a world where they receive a ample amount of sustenance. If the western powers happened to reduce war there too, the Somali population will experience a sudden growth. Peoples who are poor and/or live under conditions where it is likely that some of their offspring will not survive often have many children, just as most other animals do. With the "natural" danger of war and starvation no longer existent, more children will survive. It would be a wasted effort if western forces would do no less than completely revamp the entire Somali society. Anything less proves unsuccessful in the end and turns out to be just another burden on the hardworking

tax-payers of this nation. I say the situation is hopeless for the Somali people, unless they work on it themselves. A situation like this would probably be easily solved in the 24th century with all of the fantastic technology like replicators. Today, we have very limited resources, certainly resources that would be better used someplace else. Like this country.[49]

Robert doesn't stop with Somalia; he goes on to contend that a real-world prime directive ought to be applied to Haiti as well:

Haiti seems like a very poor, backward sort of place. In addition, it seems like Haiti poses no threat to the U.S. I say let them duke it out on their own. Interfering is just throwing cheap shots at it. We could use the money that would be wasted on a Haitian operation on more important things, like stuff in this country. Also, I don't think we should allow these Haitain boat folk to come up here. We certainly don't need anymore poor people. Also, I've heard Haiti has a large AIDS population, we don't need that. Unless you think it would be neet to wipe out are poor population with AIDS, that could be an option. Not something Picard would do in a situation like this.[50]

Robert's use of code words like "hard-working taxpayers," "work on it themselves," and "let them duke it out on their own" suggest a neoconservative reading formation similar to the project-in-the-text critiqued in chapter 4. Moreover, like the rhetoric of the neoconservative movement, Robert denies that his comments are racist: "I do not, in anyway, have a racist or other view of prejudice toward others in the world. It may seem like it if you misinterpreted what I had to say. Honestly, I believe my personal system of morality and judgment is very similar to that of *Star Trek*."[51] What this request to be read in a particular way suggests is the degree to which some fans are critical of the racism of real-world nations while erecting racist hierarchies. This should be construed not as postmodern unconsciousness, but as a consciousness that, while mindful of history, is often less than progressive and seldom without contradiction.

Alien Races: Phenotypes and Stereotypes

Perhaps the most common way race is articulated on STREK-L is through debates about whether or not Trek aliens are metaphors for real-world peoples and cultures. Many fans use the look and experiences of all sorts of cultures as a way to make sense of the mega-text's extraterrestrial cadre; other fans resist this tendency. Not unlike discussions concerning casting, attempts at correlating real peoples with simulated aliens reveal a racial logic often based on biological determinism. Ironically, fans seem as obsessed with race as a biological essence as they are with history. Moreover, like the use of the fictional diegesis to discuss the international world stage, debates about the representation of aliens are often riddled with didactic diatribes and rabid flame wars. The depiction of aliens is not only the most discussed topic on STREK-L, but the most contentious.

Fans often criticize the science fiction mega-text for lack of diversity within alien societies. The premise for much of this fault-finding is that since there are racial subdivisions among humans, there should be racial subdivisions among aliens. As Rick asks: "We know that the human race has three major racial groups—white, black, and oriental (I know there are scientific designations but these work for now). Why haven't any of the alien species we've seen had racial sub-groups?"[52] Rick's question, for all its confusion about the names of the three so-called races, spurs a tangential debate about the very meaning of race. As April, who calls herself a "Single Caucasoid Female," asks:

> I remember seeing in World Book Encyclopedia as a kid the designators as "Caucasoid," "Negroid," and "Mongoloid," so I know you're not just spouting some theory of your own (you sensitive, 90s guy, you), but then how do anthropologists classify Native Americans and Asian Indians and the peoples of Central and South America? There seems to be a difference between anthropological classifications and racial definition and yet I thought that's how "race" was defined—as different "subspecies" of *Homo sapiens sapiens*.[53]

Sherri jumps into the discussion to clarify the definition of race specific to Native Americans: "I had a suspicion so I picked up the Webster's 9th and looked it up. American Indians (including Eskimos) are considered divisions of Mongoloid stock. This makes sense if you think that once North American and Asia were connected by a land bridge—the people would have come from Asia, meaning they were most likely Mongoloid."[54] Here, Sherri tries to remedy a perceived conflict between biological and anthropological definitions of race by synthesizing data (biology and migration across the Bering Strait) she believes is indicative of the two approaches. Her goal seems to be to create a plausible consensus among the fans, one that maintains such troubling and degrading racial categories as caucasoid, mongoloid, and negroid.

The concern with genes and blood causes some fans to address the issue of alien half-breeds. Similar to the issue of diversity among Trek aliens, the underlying discourse here involves biology. As Bill writes, "successful interbreeding between individuals from different planets is unlikely to occur. Granted (according to the hidden DNA message eps ['The Chase']) most of the humanoid life is DNA based and here on Earth all life is DNA based; you don't see too many half human/half gold fish (I am NOT making any lifestyle judgments here) :) :)."[55] The debate gets quite complicated, revealing the problems with using real-world science to justify the mating rituals of fictional aliens. As Scott explains:

> Consider K'Ehleyr (Worf's mate, and I hope I've got the name right). You'll recall that she was said to be half-Klingon, half-human. Now, even assuming that Klingons and humans are close enough relatives to produce a child (which I don't buy, personally), that makes K'Ehleyr a hybrid—the offspring of two different species. Any biologists out there can correct me if I'm wrong, but I've always heard that hybrids tend to be sterile. Just one more way nature keeps the species separate.[56]

Or as Dennis rationalizes in response to Scott: "Normally this is true. However, such hybrids must be formed between creatures with very similar DNA. Scientist are presently working on techniques where they graft DNA strings on to the DNA of a foreign cell. The intention is to transfer certain desirable characteristics without actually changing the species of the original cell."[57] Yet some of the fans believe alien miscegenation should be read only as fiction: "we're supposed to suspend disbelief anyway, right?"[58] Other fans are more prone to use humor to suggest how ludicrous such comparisons can be: "Mate James Kirk with a Ferengi and get: A pimp."[59]

The discussion of "racial" diversity among aliens and alien miscegenation leads fans to debate whether or not certain Trek aliens are metaphors for certain human populations. In these debates the fans are particularly concerned with physiognomy, the identity of decision makers, and the politics of stereotyping. At times the correlation of fictional aliens and real-world peoples serves a rhetorical purpose, as when subscribers wish to use Trek aliens as a way to criticize events and practices in real space-time. As The Plaid Adder comments: "The Borg are a pretty interesting 90s cultural nightmare, I think. Assimilation, which used to be held up as a laudable goal in the 60s, has been re-vealed as the injury that it is. Add that to the ever-increasing fear of technology and whaddaya get? A bunch of cyborgs lookin' to merge your distinctive personal identity into the Machine."[60] Still other fans use aliens as a way to talk about the "look" and politics of race, par-ticularly when it comes to the Cardassians, Klingons, and Ferengi.

THE CARDASSIANS

According to *The Star Trek: The Next Generation Encyclopedia*, Car-dassians are a "harsh and militaristic race."[61] In the Trek universe, they are colonizers and conquerors, prone to using torture and other in-sidious methods to acquire power. Although their technological capa-bilities are less than those of the United Federation of Planets, they are an intimidating force in the region of space they inhabit. In later episodes of *The Next Generation*, they've even colonized a peaceful, cultured, and highly religious world, Bajor. This makes them a partic-ularly treacherous race in the Trek imagination. In terms of their ap-pearance, while they are humanoid, their physiognomy suggests an aquatic-like evolution. They have bluish-gray, scaly skin and jet-black hair. They have large dimples in the middle of their foreheads and ten-dons reaching from the top of their neck to the middle of their shoul-ders (figure 57).

Much like the Trekkers I met at the convention at the Bonaven-ture hotel in downtown Los Angeles, some STREK-L fans consider the Cardassians metaphors for Arabs, particularly the Iraqis. As Robert explains:

> When they were introduced, they reminded me of the Iraqis. This was because of the way they where presented in the episode "The Wounded," and because of the episodes timely arrival around the time of the war in the Persian Gulf. Later episodes still presented Cardas-sians as an Arab aggressor, a lot because of the way in which they have treated the Bajorans, who I view as the Israelis. Futher aspects about the Cardassians which lead me to this connection involves the labor camps, ethnic cleansing, and the torture involving Captain Picard.[62]

57. Typical Cardassian

Following Robert's line of thinking, Ben provides an even more detailed rationale for the comparison between Cardassians and Iraqis:

> Follow if you will: 1) Poverty—Claims that they need to be agressive in order to claim their fair share, claims which usually result in aggression against even weaker groups, and which seem to be nothing more than excuses for grabbing all they can. Inferior Technology compared to Feds [Federation] Not to the point that they are not a threat but weak enough that apparent numerical superiority is often overcome by the qualitative strength of the FEds. . . . Hatred of Federation for being rich The "torture Picard" ep., the torturer actually states

what rich weaklings the Feds are. He is echoing the statements of dozens of 3rd world despots and Saddam in particular. He also states that all the Cardassian archaeological treasures were stolen or sold off. This directly mirrors the Iraqi experience and is a major complaint of many third world powers.[63]

Robert and Ben provide lists of reasons to support their correlation of the Cardassians with real-world Arabs, revealing not only an implicit awareness of the presumed intent of the producers of the science fiction series, but an interest in juxtaposing the Trek diegesis with contemporaneous international events involving real Arabs. Nevertheless, their racial consciousness assumes troubling stereotypes of Arabs (e.g., torture, claims of poverty, etc.).

THE KLINGONS

Klingons have been a Trek race since the original series. Yet as I noted in chapter 4, their physiognomy changes from the original series to the films and *The Next Generation*. In the former, they are morphologically identical to humans, although they are dark and oily in complexion and all seem to wear the same Fu Manchu mustache. In the films and television spinoffs, they are also dark in complexion and wear that same mustache, but they have ridged foreheads, longer hair, and are generally reptilian in appearance (figure 58). Throughout the megatext's history, they are either a literal or a potential threat to the Federation. Even during the short alliance between the two superpowers in *The Next Generation* and the first few seasons of *Deep Space Nine*, there were countless battles and skirmishes. In the world of today's *Deep Space Nine*, the Klingons are again a totalitarian empire bent on destroying the Federation. Indeed, the Federation and the Klingons just can't get along.

Most fans argue that Klingons from *Star Trek* of the 1960s represent Soviets, as the makers of the original series intended. As Adam writes:

I think in some instances at least, the Klingons were obviously intended to be analagous to the Soviets (a stupid term that: it's like calling someone from America a Congress). Take for example this line from "A Private Little War"—Kirk: Bones, do you remember the twentieth century brush wars on the Asian continent (Vietnam—duh)? Two giant powers struggling (USA, USSR), much like the Klingons (hint, hint) and ourselves?[64]

58. Typical Klingon. © 1992 Paramount Pictures Corporation

Yet another fan, Mark, who makes a not-so-cryptic remark about pigmentation, suggests that the Klingons are supposed to represent Communists in general:

> It seems to me that TOS Klingons represented the 1960s American stereotype of Russians, what with Commander Kolov and all. With their baggy pants and boots they resembled Cossaks. Their swarthy skin probably symbolized the Communist threat then eminating from Russia and China. My guess would be that the Klingons were deliberately created to be consistant with American stereotypes so that the audience could easily relate to the conflict between the Klingons and the Feds.[65]

In short, the consensus among fans is that the producers of the original series succeeded in linking a fictional alien race with a real space-time world power, based on textual characteristics (dialogue) and stereotypes ("swarthy skin").

Fan interpretations of the Klingons shift from Soviets and Communists to several real-world peoples when we shift to the television spin-offs, perhaps due to "a new world order." Yet there is no consensus among fans as to which real space-time culture this next generation of militaristic Klingons represents. Some feel they are metaphors for Arabs. Robert, prone to racist talk, explains: "Remember Klingon Ambassador Kell from ST:TNG 4th season's episode entitled 'The Mind's Eye?' Well, he looks just like Mr. Arafat. I can't believe the resemblance! If you just give Ambassador Kell a 'towel' to put on that bumpy head of his, I wouldn't be able to tell the difference! No offense to any Palestinian Trekkers out there."[66] Still others, such as Barry, feel the new Klingons are "very much like the Japanese, in terms of their sense of 'honor' and 'family.'"[67] Yet another fan is unwilling to give up the Asian influence: "they seem to be a savage race like the Mongols, are warlike, and eat like I imagine the Mongols might have."[68] Again, the correlation of fictional aliens (the text) with real-world peoples often reveals a consciousness that is willing to accept stereotypes.

There are debates that correlate the Klingons with African-Americans. In such cases, fans are critical, even deconstructive, of the stereotypes circulating in the real world. As Mike writes, "I'm also not ready to dismiss accusations of racism re: the klingon empire. On a visual and intuitive level they evoke an identification with african-american folks, and there has been a tradition of viewing both as warlike, uninterested in thoughtful contemplation, comic relief, and in general 'primitive.'"[69] Another fan, who reveals her insecurity about race by pointing out her ethnicity, calls attention to the complex, multifaceted, and thus confusing nature of the Klingon:

> That question about Klingons and African-Americans is quite complex; I'm not sure, as a white Canadian, that I'm qualified to comment! But in a general sense, I'd say that there was probably some aspect of the Klingons which we could say is some kind of "internalized Other." The real racism, tensions etc. "tamed" within these characters who don't *quite* look African-American (in TOS). Does that mean that with Worf, the Afican-American Other has been not only tamed, but co-opted? I'm not really sure how I feel about that.[70]

Yet another fan, who feels his identity as an African-American provides him with a unique perspective, rejects any attempt to associate the Klingons with African-Americans:

I think that people might misinterpeted the African-American actors protraying Klingons as some kind of "between the lines, 'INSULT'"!! Being an African-American man myself. . . . I DON'T THINK SO!! If you look at the old series ST, African-Americans was being protrayed as people with equal intelligence as Caucassions and any other race of people during a very "racist" era in American history.[71]

Finally, Juan, whose tag reads, "It is better to remain silent and be thought a fool, than to speak up and remove all doubt," concurs with Mike: "The Klingons, I think, have shown at least 2 races (albeit they are black and white) because they have Black and White actors playing the roles. If you look, you can tell the difference."[72]

FERENGI

Like the Cardassians, the Ferengi were introduced in *The Next Generation*. Made famous by Armin Shimerman's portrayal of Quark in *Deep Space Nine* (figure 59), they quickly became one of the most talked-about alien species among the fans. This is because they are one of the most unique alien races introduced to date, in terms of both their culture and their appearance. For example, unlike other Trek aliens, the Ferengi are interested not in galactic power or universal democracy, but purely profit. Greedy humanoids, they horde and fetishize gold pressed latinum—the rarest commodity in the galaxy. They are also quite odd-looking, suggesting to me a sort of insect evolution. They are short in stature and have very large ears that, doubling as erogenous zones, extend around the top of their carapace-like heads. They all have big noses, bad teeth, and yellowish-orange skin. They have an almost insatiable desire for alien females, particularly white women, and they treat their own females as possessions; Ferengi women are not allowed to wear clothes. For these reasons, the Federation, Klingons, and Cardassians—actually, almost all Trek races—detest the Ferengi.

With such characteristics, it is no wonder the Ferengi are the most talked-about aliens in relation to race on STREK-L. In fact, debates about these bug-like aliens get quite heated, as fans accuse Trek and each other of everything from racism to Republican bashing and outright stupidity. As Bill facilitated with this comment: "I get the feeling that the Ferenghi might be unconsciously modelled after the common stereotype of Jewish people(?)—please don't flame me—my best friend is Jewish. Something about the obsession with money, cringing,

59. Typical Ferengi. © 1994 Paramount Pictures Corporation

rubbing of hands etc."[73] Comments like these lead fans to accuse each other of anti-Semitism. As Robyn responds: "the connections you establish between Jews and Ferengi are amazingly Anti-semitic. 'Something about the obsession with money', indeed! If your intention was to somehow unmask Anti-Semitism . . . in 'Star Trek', maybe you should've made your argument more clear. As it is, your post strikes me as very racist; the 'but all my friends are Jewish' clause doesn't help much, either."[74] Robyn goes on to suggest a more sensitive, historically specific, and critical approach to discussing the relationship between the Ferengi and Jews:

> As for the Jewish-Ferenghi connection, I just don't feel that it's fruitful to discuss these (racist) connections—for example, the idea that both "races" cringe, hoard money, etc—unless we are going to condemn or question them. I wouldn't bring up a Jewish-Ferengi connection, for example, without mentioning that this kind of thinking and stereotyping has been the basis of countless acts of Anti-Semitism, including the Holocaust.[75]

Other fans resist any attempts at correlating Jews and Ferengi, at times relativising the relationship between fiction and reality. "IMHO," Scotty writes, "this is another example of trying to read more into Trek than the writers put in. Those sensitive to stereotypes can always find an insulting reference somewhere, whether intended or not."[76]

A few fans argue that the Ferengi cannot be based on a stereotype of Jews because of the many characteristics the Ferengi and Jews do not share. As one fan comments:

> Everybody seems to forget that Ferengi (as far as I know) are not a religious type. When you want to compare types (in this case), you cannot circumvent the fact that being a Jew is all about religion, no? The Ferengi as far as I can tell, have not yet displayed any religious tendencies. What the Ferengi display is the kind of savvy that a Jew might have, if we carry the stereotype that the Jewish are rather shrewd people (which you'd need to be to survive this long).[77]

"I do know stereotypes, and I find myself too often for my own desires stereotyping people," another fan advises. "The stereotypes I have applied to Jews dont match the Ferengi at all. (Quark doesnt have a New York accent!)."[78] Posts like these reveal a self-conscious criticism of stereotypes while still errecting stereotypes.

Other fans point out that a few of the producers of Trek are Jewish as evidence that there is no relationship between Jewish stereotypes and the Ferengi. As Ann states: "Basically, since the executive producer is Jewish, I think charges of anti-Semitism are questionable."[79] Robert chimed into the debate with a similar comment:

> This would be a very unwise decision by the Star Trek people to possess such a view toward a integral segment of the population. I am not trying to bring any stereotypes of my own into this, but isn't the head of Star Trek Rick Berman? Well, I would suspect, with a name like Berman, that he is Jewish. Why would he ever want to portray Jews in an unfavorable light? I bet Armin Shimmerman and Wallace Shawn, Quark and Grand Nagus Zek, are Jewish, too. Why would they want to submit to humiliation and betray themselves? Who knows who else at Star Trek are Jewish? Would they allow this outrage of bigotry?[80]

Or, as another fan writes, "I don't believe that Gene Roddenberry (who was around for the 'birth' of the Ferenghi) would have allowed something so tasteless to occur. He especially would not have entertained such a thought. Not that I view him as some moral god-like creature but my gosh, the man was Jewish, wasn't he?"[81] The point these fans invoke is that people don't stereotype their own group identity, and thus Trek can't be anti-Semitic when it comes to the Ferengi. In this regard, another fan suggests: "I think that whether Gene Roddenberry or the writers are/were Jewish is a moot point. Oppressed populations are just as capable of perpetuating stereotypes as anyone else."[82]

Still other fans feel the Ferengi represent capitalists. "I believe that it was reported that the Ferengi were inspired by the Yankee traders of the 19th century," Mark comments, "whatever that stereotype represents."[83] For Rick, they represent the robber barons of the late nineteenth century. "These men included John D. Rockefeller, Cornelius Vanderbilt, J. Pierpont Morgan, and the DuPonts of Delaware," he writes, "who became obscenely wealthy at the expense of the women, men and children of their era. They too pursued profit ruthlessly and again the vast majority of these folks were WASPs."[84] Robert takes the discussion a step further, and suggests that "the Ferengi could be considered as the freeloading capitalist Republicans in this country. To make a comparison to a non-U.S. entity, the Ferengi most resemble the Japanese, due to the same economical characteristics."[85] The attack on Republicans—but not the Japanese—promotes a defensive tirade from another fan:

> Freeloading? If anything, Republicans stand for success through hard work without expectation of handouts, freebies, and dependency on government help. It is the liberals of this country (being liberal doesn't neccessarily include being democrat) who are going to ruin us economically, morally, and socially. The freeloaders of our society have always looked to liberals for continued support of their ways, namely unaccountability and no desire to work for success. I hope that by the 24th century, we have not only cured aids, poverty, hunger, and serious crime, but we will have also demanded all citizens work for a living, contribute to society, and that everyone is accountable fully for their actions and the consequences of those action.[86]

"Personally, I STILL think that the Ferengi are ugly American tourists (Yankee traders?)," Katherine responds. "I'm surprised that no one has mentioned the Ferengis' amazing physical resemblence to Ross Perot."[87] And Holly follows suit: "My husband has always thought that the Ferengi represented Paramount executives—their greed, rules of acquisition, (i.e. copyright laws)."[88]

The question of the representation of the Ferengi prompted subscribers to the list to speculate about where the producers got the name. As with most topics concerning these greedy aliens, there was not a consensus among the fans. Martin suggests: "As for Ferengi, a *real* interesting tidbit: The term is Indian (Hindi I think) for 'outsider'/'foreigner'. It became popular under imperial British rule, as a term of derision for the 'intruders'. Curiouser and curiouser!"[89] But Adam retorts: "Good grief, not another meaning! When I worked with Richard Arnold at the Star Trek Air and Space Museum exhibit, he told me that 'ferengi' was chosen because it means 'trader' in Portuguese. To top that off, my freind's father, who is a translator, also told me that in Arabic or Turk it is a derogatory term for Frenchmen, and translates roughly as siphilyis (sp)."[90] Sinya offered this theory. "I can confirm that the word FARANG means 'White People' in Thai, and it probably came from the Arabic word FERENGI."[91] Finally, another fan sums up both debates: "I never thought of the Ferengi as Jewish stereotypes. I thought they were named after their characteristic ears. Ferengils are parts of the ears."[92]

The Joy of Trek

The quote from Isaac Asimov that opens this chapter spells out his passion for *Star Trek*, his belief that it is "well-done," that it says "something (subtly and neatly) that is difficult to say in 'straight' drama," and that the science fiction genre "is the type of literature most appropriate to our generation."[93] It seems to me that Asimov's reading of Trek characterizes the enduring interest in the series among the fans I've analyzed in this chapter. The science fiction series "says something" to these readers. They engage in debates about Trek, sending comments, suggestions, and critiques to the producers, to each other, and, more abstractly, to other texts and to history. Trek fans show a keen interest in history and a self-conscious ability to read *Star Trek* intertextually. This is especially evident in their humor, as the following sample of "Borg quotes" distributed on the listserver might suggest:

> I am George Bush of Borg. Read my lips: you will be assimilated.
> I am Dan Quayle of Borg. You're speeling is irrellevant.
> I am Bob Dole of Borg. You will be assimilated as soon as we have hearings.

Borg meets Hitler:
    Borg: You will be assimilated. Resistance is futile.
    Hitler: That's what I was going to say.
I am Geraldo of Borg. Next: brothers who assimilate sisters.
I am Ed McMahon of Borg. You may have already been assimilated.
I am Yoda of Borg. Assimilated you will be and resist you will not.
I am Pee Wee Herman of Borg. Let me show you my collective.
I am William Shatner of Borg. Get a life or be assimilated.[94]

Or my own: "I am Fredric Jameson of Borg. Get history or be assimilated." While these poaches are obviously intended to be playful, they nonetheless suggest the self-consciousness of the fans (especially the Shatner line), the intertextuality of fan readings (from George Bush to Pee Wee Herman), and the fans' interest in the sociopolitical world (from Adolf Hitler to George Bush).

Many STREK-L participants embrace Trek as a liberal-humanist text, specifically its utopian vision of the future. These fans see the mega-text as a guide to the way things ought to be: open, expansive, and utopian. True, there is a contingent of fans that couldn't care less about the ideological and political aspects of the science fiction series, preferring the show's technological and scientific narratives. These fans discuss such things as the possibility of warp speed or the improbability of time travel. Most of the Trekkers on the list, however, are interested in both the ideological and the techno-possible. This is a politically conscious group, whose critiques and discussions often call attention to their political and moral concerns. Fans are anything but passive or unconscious dweebs uncritically ensconced in consumer culture.

While there are fans whose utopian vision seems to match their ideas about race, STREK-L demonstrates an ambiguous racial consciousness. Race is almost always defined in biological and pseudoscientific terms, a common-sense articulation that implicitly maintains essentialist and fatalist notions about who we are and where we can go. Moreover, fan interpretations of race, though often articulating a humanist morality, show signs of neoconservatism by invoking such discourses as political correctness and reverse discrimination. As the listserver's subscribers debate the relationship between aliens and real-world people, members choose to engage in racist talk about "towel heads" or to excuse race-in-the-text by capitulating to the ethnicity of the producers. Race is often denied or displaced in favor of a utopian rhetoric. Like the Picard and Borg quotes that also open this chapter,[95] the ideals of freedom and diversity are fundamental elements of fan culture, but so too is the determining pursuit of assimilating all into a white future-time. There is nothing unconscious or ahistorical about these fans. They are simply not uniformly progressive or completely open to the infinite combinations of diversity, at least when their contradictions and ambiguities are considered as fundamental parts of their nomadic poaching. This is not to say that positive dialogue isn't occurring—it is, and that is potentially the most counterhegemonic aspect of STREK-L fandom—but, like the Trek texts themselves, utopian consciousness has a long way to go.

6 Epilogue

Resisting the Race Toward a White Future

Dr. Beverly Crusher: If there's nothing wrong with me, there must be something wrong with the universe.

No one today is purely one thing. Labels like Indian, or woman, or Muslim, or American are not more than starting-points, which if followed into actual experience for only a moment are quickly left behind. Imperialism consolidated the mixture of cultures and identities on a global scale. But its worst and most paradoxical gift was to allow people to believe that they were only, mainly, exclusively, white, or Black, or Western, or Oriental. Yet just as human beings make their own history, they also make their cultures and ethnic identities.
—*Edward Said*

In "The Measure of a Man," Lieutenant Commander Data, the silver-white android of *The Next Generation* who aspires to be human, is the subject of a Judge Advocate General proceeding that will determine his future. With Captain Picard as his defender and Commander Riker as his prosecutor, the military court is to judge if he—or it—is either sentient, and thus due the same rights accorded all members of the United Federation of Planets, or property, and thus a possession of the intergalactic body. Like that of the blonde-haired and blue-eyed androids in *Blade Runner*, Data's plight is an ironic allegory for the real space-time history of racism in which "black" people were considered possessions of "white" masters. And like "Let That Be Your Last Battlefield," discussed in chapter 2, this episode of Trek takes a didactic stand against racial discrimination. The edifying moment is especially clear in the scene in which Guinan, the black-alien bartender whose unique wisdom is known throughout the galaxy, offers a confused Captain Picard a universal perspective: "Consider that in the history of many worlds, there have always been disposable creatures. They do the dirty work. They do the work no one else wants to do because it's too difficult or too hazardous. And an army of Datas all disposable, you don't have to think about their welfare. You don't worry about how they feel."

"What you're talking about," the captain responds with poignant indignation, "is slavery." Realizing that the legal question of whether or not Data is property is nothing more than a "comfortable euphemism," Picard eventually puts up a brilliant defense of the silver-white android. He wins the trial, Data is granted the right to choose his destiny, and the lesson that we should respect the civil rights of all individuals has been told.

Although defending civil rights while criticizing the history of racism, "The Measure of a Man" nonetheless embraces a white ideal. And, like the code words of the neoconservative movement that contextualized its production and initial reception, this embrace is hidden in the details—away from the boisterous rhetoric of humanism. First, Data's victory is not due to his own efforts, but the righteous brilliance of a French-human military officer with a British accent. Like such mainstream Hollywood films as *Mississippi Burning* (1988), in which two European-American FBI agents kick-start the civil rights movement, the white hero who works for the government saves the day for the oppressed Other. Moreover, whiteness is the standard by which Data is judged—and by which he judges himself. His victory at the trial simply means he can continue to pursue his goal of becoming more human/white. This is especially evident in the final lines of the episode. "You're a wise man, my friend," Commander Riker says to Data with a touch of guilt. Riker almost proved in court that Data was merely a machine. "Not yet, sir," Data responds forgivingly, "but with your help, I am learning." Though Data is judged not an "it," the assimilationist tone of his goal to be more human, emphasized at the end of the story like an exclamation mark, ends up undermining the episode's defense of diversity and civil rights.

Yet there is more to "The Measure of a Man" than its camouflaged embrace of a white ideal. In particular, Brent Spiner's performance of Data is touching in its subtlety and moving in its candor. When Data barely tilts his head in response to a racist remark, you can almost hear his positronic brain diligently searching for a logical explanation. When he reacts to a discriminatory remark with silence, you can almost feel his disgust for what is wrong. Data's expressions, or lack thereof, seem more humane than the humanity of his non-android colleagues. He is unaffected yet confident, unassuming yet proud, rational and determined to do what is right despite all the wrong that surrounds him. At least for me, Spiner's Data is an opportunity to see beyond the plea for a neoconservative world toward something quite different: something in the hegemony of whiteness that is anything but hegemonic. The performance is a starting point on a map to resistance.

I am not suggesting that Spiner's Data somehow or in any way excuses the episode's underlying embrace of whiteness. Because I enjoy watching the actor—finding space in his performance for a nonwhite reading—does not mean the episode itself is somehow subversive or democratic. "The Measure of a Man," like the Trek mega-text in general, is structured in dominance. As I argue throughout this book, despite Trek's didactic call for civil rights and multiculturalism, despite its moments of beauty and resistance, the mega-text's imagination has been and continues to be depressingly Western and painfully white. Indeed, whiteness is everywhere in Trek, spread out in all directions like the background noise of the Big Bang. Like the Cardassians, it is polite but insidious. Like the Klingons, it is tenacious in its effort to remain viable. Like the Vulcans, it consistently pretends to be logical in an effort to suppress its emotions. Like the Ferengi, whiteness is never far from profit. And like the humans, it undermines an otherwise beautiful call for a more humane universe. Whiteness dominates the mega-text's common sense, and must be rigorously challenged if the popular series is to push its imagination of the future toward the reality of "infinite diversity in infinite combinations."

Perhaps the chapter on the fans speaks the most poignantly to the meaning of race in Trek specifically and society in general. For the Trekkers surfing the Internet on STREK-L, race is not an illusion or an unconscious formation. For the most part, it is also not simply a thing of the past or something that should be excused in the present. Like Trek, the fans see and talk about race at almost every opportunity—often demonstrating a willingness to challenge its shifting status quo. Yet, because these same fans define race in biologically reductive terms, imbue it with discourses ranging from assimilation to reverse discrimination—and ultimately accept its white ideal—the strategy for challenging Trek's racial play is at best ambiguous and at worst paradoxical. The racial formation cannot be challenged, subverted, and rearticulated if the meaning of whiteness is either accepted as natural or loved.

The most common factor informing the mega-text's continued embrace of whiteness is history itself: in terms of both the representation of the past/future and the impact of the sociopolitical present on its production and reception. Sometimes this history takes the form of explicit historiography. Each series of the mega-text—from the original to the films to the spinoffs to the fans—has represented and spoken to the past and present of the real world: from the cold war to a United Federation of Planets; from the Prime Directive to U.S. intervention in Haiti. Our past and present are fodder for Trek's vision of the future. Yet, history is also of automatic quotations, as Barthes might say, not necessarily explicit representations but no less a fundamental part of the text. This form of history, the influence of the civil rights and neoconservative movements, for example, makes its presence known in Trek's diegetic logics, chronotopes, intertexts, and reading formations: interconnected and interdependent elements that enable the science fiction series to be coherent, relevant—significant. While deep space might be a vacuum, Trek exists in the space-time of history.

Looking closely at both types of history—explicit and contextual—allows us to see what histories are being told, and how. It enables us to examine the contradictions and paradoxes that work under the blinding cover of bright lights to dominate our universe. Indeed, the history of race—or, more specifically, the meaning of whiteness—is everywhere in front of our eyes. We can see it if we look in the right space-times. Yet it is hard if not impossible to do anything about if we think it is either predetermined or the best thing going. If, however, we see whiteness as a sociocultural formation, a historical system of meaning production, that works to privilege some of us at the expense of Others—that steers the racial formation—then we have a chance to challenge its intense veracity and dogged versatility. Like the shape-shifting Changelings of the anal-retentive Dominion who seek to bring a particular order to the galaxy, whiteness is anything but fixed.

There are moments of beauty and resistance in Trek. Contrary to the claim of the undifferentiated Borg collective, resistance is not futile. The white paradox is not always already a given; there are chinks in its armor. The task, it seems to me, is to historicize the history in and of whiteness, with the goal being to create an alternative universe that is more honest about the past and more open to a truly different present. At stake in such an undertaking are our very identities. As Edward Said imagines: "Just as human beings make their own history, they also make their cultures and ethnic identities."[1] For me, Spiner's performance, coupled with my own historical sense of identity and race,

provides an opportunity—complete with its own ironies and contradictions—to realize a different space-time.

Employing a synthesis of sociology, critical theory, and cultural studies, I have tried to uncover the whiteness-in-the-texts of Trek. My intent
was to lay bare the representational and narrative properties of Trek's
racial play, revealing and taking a stand against its myths, ideologies:
histories. Yet, these readings are not "ideal" (or even the best out there).
I am no more right than anyone else. As the uncertainty principle of
quantum physics ultimately suggests, my histories inform the universe
I seek to measure. Nevertheless, like Gene Roddenberry and the fans, I
hope that my readings are at least insightful.

Notes

Chapter 1: The Meaning of Race

1. *The Animated Series* aired on Saturday mornings. A total of 22 episodes were made. Gene Roddenberry reportedly had creative control. Dorothy Fontana, the story editor in the second and third seasons of the original Trek, repeated her function under the title of Associate Producer. All of the original actors, with the exception of Walter Koenig (Chekov), lent their voices to the characters.
2. The Klingon Language Institute (KLI), a federally recognized 501(c)3 nonprofit organization, publishes *HolQeD* (ISSN: 1061–2327), offers a "Klingon Language Seminar," and puts on a "Klingon Language Camp" in order to "facilitate the scholarly exploration of the Klingon language and culture." For information, see the KLI home page on the World Wide Web at http://www.kli.org.
3. Jeffrey Mills, *CCSTSG Enterprises* 45/46 (10 June 1994): 21. As of this writing, subscription information is available from CCSTSG Enterprises, 7 Quarry Street, Ellington, CT, 06029–4147.
4. For a list of the "Rules of Acquisition," see Ira Steven Behre, *The Ferengi Rules of Acquisition* (New York: Pocket Books, 1995). If it's not in your local or college library, it's available at most fine bookstores for about $5.99 (not including tax, of course).
5. Raymond Williams, *Television: Technology and Cultural Form* (New York: Schocken Books, 1974).
6. Rick Altman, "Television Sound," in *Television: The Critical View*, 4th ed., ed. Horace Newcomb (New York: Oxford University Press, 1987). Altman's work on sound extends Williams's theory of programming flow by arguing that, because television viewing takes place in the home, where there are a number of distractions (unlike a theatre), the soundtrack also acts as a mediation between programming flow and what he calls "household flow."
7. Fredric Jameson, "Progress Versus Utopia; or, Can We Imagine the Future?" *Science-Fiction Studies* 27 (July 1982): 151.
8. Save those among us who have been abducted by aliens.
9. Richard J. Herrnstein and Charles Murray, *The Bell Curve: Intelligence and Class Structure in American Life* (New York: Free Press, 1994). For a critique of the assumptions and conclusions of *The Bell Curve*, see Russell Jacoby and Naomi Glauderman, eds., *The Bell*

Curve Debate: History, Documents, Opinions (New York: Random House, 1995).

10. For analysis of the shifting meaning of race in U.S. history, see Thomas F. Gossett, *Race: The History of an Idea in America* (New York: Schocken Books, 1965); Peter Isaac Rose, *The Subject Is Race* (New York: Oxford University Press, 1968); David Theo Goldberg, ed., *Anatomy of Racism* (Minneapolis: University of Minnesota Press, 1990); Michael Omi and Howard Winant, *Racial Formations in the United States* 2d ed. (New York: Routledge, 1994); and Stuart Hall, "New Ethnicity," *ICA Documents* (1988): 27–31.

11. Henry Louis Gates Jr., "Writing 'Race' and the Difference It Makes," in *"Race," Writing, and Difference*, ed. Henry Louis Gates Jr. (Chicago: University of Chicago Press, 1985), 5.

12. Several scholars in the physical sciences have refuted the science of race. See Stephen Jay Gould, *The Mismeasure of Man* (New York: W. W. Norton and Company, 1981); Daniel J. Kevles, *In The Name of Eugenics* (Berkeley: University of California Press, 1985); and Sandra Harding, ed., *The "Racial" Economy of Science* (Bloomington: Indiana University Press, 1993).

13. Luigi Luca Cavalli-Sforza and Francesco Cavalli-Sforza, *The Great Human Diasporas: The History of Diversity and Evolution* (New York: Helix Books, 1995), 229–230. For the methodological underpinning of Cavalli-Sforza's work, see Luigi Luca Cavalli-Sforza et al., *The History and Geography of Human Genes* (Princeton, N.J.: Princeton University Press, 1994).

14. The appearance of circularity here is necessary because not recognizing individual conceptions of race takes real people out of the equation, a reduction that seems to me too abstract and highly hypocritical in light of the history of racism.

15. Omi and Winant, *Racial Formations*, 55.

16. Ibid., 2.

17. Ibid., 1.

18. Ibid., 55.

19. For edited compilations of Gramsci's writings, see Quintin Hoare and Geoffrey Nowell Smith, eds., *Selections from the Prison Notebooks of Antonio Gramsci* (New York: International Publishers, 1971); Lynne Lawner, ed., *Letters from Prison* (New York: Farrar, Straus and Giroux, 1973); and David Forgacs and Geoffrey Nowell-Smith, eds., *Selections from Cultural Writings* (Cambridge: Harvard University Press, 1985).

20. Stuart Hall, "Gramsci's Relevance for the Study of Race and Ethnicity," *Journal of Communication Inquiry* 10, no. 2 (summer 1986): 15.

21. Ibid., 14, italics in original.
22. Gramsci, *Selections from Cultural Writings*, 130.
23. Hall, "Gramsci's Relevance," 20.
24. Stuart Hall, "Race, Articulation and Societies Structured in Dominance," in *Sociological Theories: Race and Colonialism* (Paris: UNESCO, 1980), 334.
25. Ibid., 342.
26. Omi and Winant, *Racial Formations*, 60.
27. Ibid., emphasis removed, 56.
28. Ibid.
29. Daniel Bernardi, ed., *The Birth of Whiteness: Race and the Emergence of U.S. Cinema* (New Brunswick, N.J.: Rutgers University Press, 1996).
30. Herman Gray, "The Endless Slide of Difference: Critical Television Studies, Television and the Question of Race," *Critical Studies of Mass Communication* (June 1993): 191. See also his book-length study, *Watching Race: Television and the Struggle for "Blackness"* (Minneapolis: University of Minnesota Press, 1995).
31. Stephen W. Hawking, *Black Holes and Baby Universes and Other Essays* (New York: Bantam Books, 1993), 92–93.

Chapter 2: The Original *Star Trek*

1. Gene Roddenberry, quoted in Stephen E. Whitfield, *The Making of Star Trek* (New York: Ballentine Books, 1968), 112.
2. Raymond Williams, *Television: Technology and Cultural Form* (New York: Schocken Books, 1975), 121.
3. Tony Bennett and Janet Woollacott, *Bond and Beyond: The Political Career of a Popular Hero* (New York: Methuen, 1987), 202.
4. David Theo Goldberg, *Racist Culture: Philosophy and the Politics of Meaning* (Oxford: Blackwell, 1993), 6–7.
5. Michael Omi and Howard Winant, *Racial Formations in the United States: From the 1960's to the 1990's*, 2d ed. (New York: Routledge, 1994), 95.
6. Roddenberry, quoted in David Alexander, "Gene Roddenberry: Writer, Producer, Philosopher, Humanist," *The Humanist* (March/ April 1991): 30.
7. Ibid., 8.
8. Gene Roddenberry, quoted in Stephen E. Whitfield, *The Making of Star Trek* (New York: Ballentine Books, 1968), 40.
9. Ibid., 112.
10. Ibid., 23.
11. Ibid., 29.

12. Ibid., 126.
13. Almost as if to rub their decision to reject "The Cage" in the faces of NBC's executives, Roddenberry incorporated the footage from the pilot into a two-part episode, "The Menagerie" (1966).
14. "The Star Trek Guide," 3d revision (April 17, 1967), 7.
15. John Meredyth Lucas, quoted in William Shatner with Chris Kreski, *Star Trek Memories* (New York: HarperCollins, 1993), 243.
16. Leonard Nimoy, quoted in Leslie Raddatz, "Product of Two Worlds," *TV Guide*, 4 March 1967, 25.
17. Jean Messerschmidt, Memorandum, 4 September 1968, 2. Documents associated with the making of *Star Trek* are housed in the Gene Roddenberry Papers, Special Collections, Arts Library, University of California-Los Angeles.
18. Nichelle Nichols, quoted in Shatner, *Star Trek Memories*, 285–286.
19. There are several accounts of "the kiss" from the actors involved. In her autobiography, Nichols claims that she and Shatner kissed numerous times. Nonetheless, the shot broadcast doesn't actually show a kiss (as the shots with Spock and Chapel do). See *Beyond Uhura: Star Trek and Other Memories* (New York: G. P. Putnam's Sons, 1994), 193–197.
20. "The Star Trek Guide," 13.
21. Nichols, quoted in *Star Trek Memories*, emphasis in original, 212.
22. "Nichelle Nichols Complains She Hasn't Been Allowed to Leave the Spaceship," *TV Guide*, 15 July 1967, 10.
23. Harlan Ellison, original script for "City on the Edge of Forever" (12 August 1966), 23–24.
24. Ibid., 28.
25. Rick Worland, "Captain Kirk: Cold Warrior," *Journal of Popular Film and Television* 16 (fall 1988), 17.
26. Margaret Armen, "Pale Face" (15 March 1968), 4.
27. Ibid., 8.
28. Hayden White, "The Noble Savage Theme As Fetish," in *Tropics of Discourse* (Baltimore: John Hopkins University Press, 1979), 184.
29. Ibid., 188.
30. White also argues that the noble savage fetish in the eighteenth century shifted to a critique of nobility and the class system rather than a critique of the treatment of the Indians. The referent for the fetish, he writes, "is not the savages of the new or any other world, but humanity in general, in relation to which the very notion of 'nobility' is a contradiction." In the making of "The Paradise Syndrome," there is no trace of a concern with class differences and conflict. Instead, the ref-

erent most commonly articulated is the evolutionary superiority of whiteness en masse (ibid., 191).

31. Gene Roddenberry, memo to Fred Freiberger (31 March 1968), 8.
32. Ibid., 2.
33. Stanley Robertson, letter to Gene Roddenberry (1 April 1968), 1.
34. Roddenberry, memo to Fred Freiberger, 3.
35. Ibid., 7.
36. Richard Dyer, "White," *Screen* 29, no. 4 (autumn 1988): 46.
37. Kellam DeForest Research Report (4 June 1968), 1.
38. Ibid., 3.
39. Bennett and Woollacott, *Bond and Beyond*, 202.
40. Worland, "Captain Kirk: Cold Warrior," 12.
41. Gene Roddenberry, quoted in *The Making of Star Trek*, 207.
42. "Outline to Star Trek," 27, emphasis in original.
43. See Gina Marchetti, *Romance and the "Yellow Peril": Race, Sex, and Discursive Strategies in Hollywood Fiction* (Berkeley: University of California Press, 1993); and Darrell Y. Hamamoto, *Monitored Peril: Asian Americans and the Politics of TV Representation* (Minneapolis: University of Minnesota Press, 1994).
44. Vivian Sobchack, *Screening Space: The American Science Fiction Film*, 2d ed. (New York: Unger Publishing Co., 1991), 297.
45. "The Star Trek Guide," 11.
46. Marchetti, *Romance and the "Yellow Peril,"* 6.
47. This statement is generally attributed to former President Lyndon Johnson.

Chapter 3: Trek on the Silver Screen

1. Paramount used a similar strategy in 1994 with *Voyager* when it launched the United Paramount Network (UPN).
2. The original release length of the film was reportedly edited by the studio, possibly affecting the length of this scene. The version I am referring to is the VHS wide-screen edition, 132 minutes, Paramount Communications Company.
3. Laura Mulvey, "Visual Pleasure and Narrative Cinema," in *Movies and Methods: Volume II*, ed. Bill Nichols (Berkeley: University of California Press, 1985), 309.
4. M. M. Bakhtin, "Forms of Time and of the Chronotope in the Novel," in *The Dialogic Imagination: Four Essays by M. M. Bakhtin* (Austin: University of Texas Press, 1981), 85.
5. Vivian Sobchack, "'Lounge Time': Post-War Crises and the Chronotope of Film Noir," in *Refiguring American Film Genres: History and*

Theory, ed. Nick Browne (Berkeley: University of California Press, forthcoming). See also Michael V. Montgomery, *Carnivals and Commonplaces: Bakhtin's Chronotope, Cultural Studies, and Film* (New York: Peter Lang, 1993).
6. Bakhtin, "Forms of Time," 250.
7. Ibid., 253; emphasis in original.
8. Richard Slotkin, *Gunfighter Nation: The Myth of the Frontier in Twentieth-Century America* (New York: HarperCollins, 1992), 8.
9. Ibid., 10.
10. Ibid., 4.
11. Ibid., 3.
12. Gary Saul Morson and Caryl Emerson, *Mikhail Bakhtin: Creation of a Prosaics* (Stanford, Calif.: Stanford University Press, 1990), 372.
13. Between 1914 and 1949, Microsoft Cinemania '95 (1995) lists a total of 23 science fiction films. From 1950 to 1959, there is a marked increase: 110 science fiction films. From 1960 to 1969 only 68 were made; from 1970 to 1979 only 73. From 1980 to 1989 there is another marked increase: 142 science fiction films. Of course, these numbers reflect to some degree changes in industry organization, including advances in special effects and a Hollywood studio system more willing to produce science fiction films after the box-office success of *Close Encounters of the Third Kind* (1977) and *Star Wars* (1977). Nonetheless, the numbers are pronounced enough to also indicate a correlation between a genre concerned with extraterrestrial difference and a sociopolitical context very much concerned with domestic and national "aliens."
14. See Vivian Sobchack, *Screening Space: The American Science Fiction Film*, 2d ed. (New York: Ungar, 1991), and Patrick Lucanio, *Them or Us: Archetypal Interpretation of Fifties Alien Invasion Films* (Bloomington: Indiana University Press, 1987).
15. Charles Ramírez Berg, "Immigrants, Aliens, and Extraterrestrials: Science Fiction's Alien 'Other' as (Among Other Things) New Hispanic Imagery," *CineAction* 18 (fall 1989): 5.
16. For feminist readings of *Alien, Aliens*, and science fiction films in general, see Annette Kuhn, ed., *Alien Zone: Cultural Theory and Contemporary Science Fiction Cinema* (New York: Verso, 1990), and Constance Penley et al., eds., *Close Encounters: Film, Feminism and Science Fiction* (Minneapolis: University of Minnesota Press, 1991).
17. *The Wrath of Khan* is a sequel to the original Trek episode "Space Seed" (1967).
18. Daniel Bernardi, "The Voice of Whiteness: D. W. Griffith's Biograph Film (1908–1913)," in *The Birth of Whiteness: Race and the Emer-*

gence of *U.S. Cinema*, ed. Daniel Bernardi (New Brunswick, N.J.: Rutgers University Press, 1996), 113–125.

19. To my knowledge, Bakhtin never explicitly states the distinction between master and minor chronotopes. Nonetheless, it seems clear that master chronotopes are larger organizing space-time utterances that contextualize minor chronotopes.

20. This is not universally the case, however. Spock, for instance, dies after saving the *Enterprise* from total destruction in *The Wrath of Khan*, only to be resurrected as more in touch with his emotions—his human side—in the subsequent sequels. Albeit across a series of films, the Vulcan half-breed changes. Yet the change in the character is at best slight, takes place over a series of texts (television and film), and perhaps has as much to do with the actor as with the genre or narrative.

21. Morson and Emerson, *Mikhail Bakhtin*, 379.

22. Bakhtin, "Forms of Time," 243.

23. Ibid., 244.

24. The "look" of the Borg in cinematic Trek changed from their initial appearance in *The Next Generation* TV series. In the films, the Borg are a blotchy mix of muted colors; in the television spinoff, as I will discuss in chapter 4, they are pasty white.

25. This, of course, is not always the case. Saavik, for instance, is played by Kirstie Alley in *The Motion Picture*, but by Robin Curtis in *The Search for Spock* and *The Voyage Home*. In such instances, the needs of the mega-text outweigh the needs of the canon.

26. For an insightful analysis of the relationship between this film and the collapse of the Soviet Union, see Rick Worland, "From the New Frontier to the Final Frontier: *Star Trek* from Kennedy to Gorbachev," *Film & History* 24, nos. 1–2 (1994): 19–35.

27. Stephen W. Hawking, "Space and Time," in *A Brief History of Time* (New York: Bantam Books, 1988), 33.

Chapter 4: *The Next Generation*

1. For biographies of Roddenberry, see David Alexander, *The Authorized Biography of Gene Roddenberry* (New York: Roc, 1994); Joel Engel, *Gene Roddenberry: The Myth and the Man Behind Star Trek* (New York: Hyperion, 1994); and Yvonne Fern, *Gene Roddenberry: The Last Conversation* (Berkeley: University of California Press, 1994).

2. Denise Crosby left the series late in the first season (her character was killed by an evil black sludge-monster—another use of black to suggest evil), but returned periodically playing either Tasha Yar in an

alternative universe or the character's half-Romulan daughter. Gates McFadden left the show for the second season, returning in the third and remaining until the end of the series. During the second season, Diana Muldaur played Dr. Katherine Pulanski. Colm Meaney continues to play the character of Chief O'Brien on *Deep Space Nine*. For a history of the various characters—their job, rank, and background—see William F. B. Vodrey, *The Star Trek: The Next Generation Encyclopedia* (New Philadelphia: Kearsarge Press, 1994).

3. Julia Kristeva, "Word, Language, and Novel," in *Desire in Language: A Semiotic Approach to Literature and Art,* ed. Leon S. Roudiez (New York: Columbia University Press, 1980). The word "intertextuality" comes from Kristeva's translation of Mikhail Bakhtin's notion of dialogism, which Bakhtin used to describe the fundamental relationship of an utterance—from spoken words to novels—to other utterances.

4. Michael Omi and Howard Winant, *Racial Formations in the United States: From the 1960s to the 1990s,* 2d ed. (New York: Routledge, 1994), 136.

5. Building upon Bakhtin's notion of dialogism and Kristeva's notion of intertextuality, Gerard Genette proposes the notion of "transtextuality" as a more expansive yet more specific term to describe the relationship of one text to another. For Genette, there are five categories of transtextuality: (1) intertextuality—the literal quotation, plagiarism, or allusion to one text in another; (2) paratextuality—the relationship between the text and, in the case of film, its titles, dedications, and credits; (3) metatextuality—a critical relationship between texts (e.g., between this book and "Code of Honor"); (4) architextuality—the degree to which a text explicitly or implicitly characterizes itself in its title (e.g., whether a text acknowledges its genre); and (5) hypertextuality—the assimilation of one text (the hypotext) into another (the hypertext), which latter transforms and modifies the former. For my purposes here, I will use the term "intertextuality" in a way similar to Genette's "hypertextuality," opting to use the more well-known term for the sake of clarity. See Gerard Genette, *Palimpsestes: la littérature au second degré* (Paris: Seuil, 1982). For a concise secondary explication of transtextuality, see Robert Stam et al., *New Vocabularies in Film Semiotics* (New York: Routledge, 1992), 206–210.

6. Roland Barthes, "Theory of the Text," in *Untying the Text: A Post-Structuralist Reader*, Robert Young, ed. (Boston: Routledge and Kegan Paul, 1981), 39.

7. Eco's work in this article is concerned with how a text, in this case *Casablanca* (1942), becomes a cult movie. He writes:

> I think that in order to transform a work into a cult object one must be able to break, dislocate, unhinge it so that one can remember only parts of it, irrespective of their original relationship with the whole. . . . Only an unhinged movie survives as a disconnected series of images, of peaks, of visual icebergs. It should display not one central idea but many. It should not reveal a coherent philosophy of composition. It must live on, and because of, its glorious ricketiness.

The "ricketiness" and subsequent cult status of *The Next Generation* in particular and the Trek mega-text more generally seems not unlike Eco's *Casablanca*, though each can clearly be recognized as relying on distinct intertextual frames. Umberto Eco, "*Casablanca*: Cult Movies and Intertextual Collage," in *Travels in Hyper-Reality* (New York: Harcourt Brace Jovanovich, 1986), 198.

8. Kristeva, "Word, Language, and Novel," 65.
9. Omi and Winant, *Racial Formations*, 113.
10. Ibid., 118–135.
11. Ibid., 117.
12. By isolating it here I do not mean to imply that gender is a distinct formation somehow separate from the meaning of race. On the contrary, as I try to show throughout this book, race and gender are part of the same processes of signification. For example, Uhura, Elaan, the white starship, and the feminized lizard-like alien in *Enemy Mine* are figures that reveal the interconnectedness of race and gender ideologies. My goal is to reveal the complexity of Trek play by abstracting gender (and later heterosexism) from race in this section.
13. Lynne Joyrich, "Feminist Enterprise? *Star Trek: The Next Generation* and the Occupation of Femininity," *Cinema Journal* 35, no. 2 (1996): 63–64. See also Amelie Hastie, "A Fabricated Space: Assimilating the Individual on *Star Trek: The Next Generation*," in *Enterprise Zones: Critical Positions on Star Trek*, ed. Taylor Harrison et al. (Boulder, Colo.: Westview Press, 1996), 115–136.
14. Henry Jenkins, "'Out of the Closet and into the Universe': Queers and *Star Trek*," in John Tulloch and Henry Jenkins, *Science Fiction Audiences: Watching Doctor Who and Star Trek* (New York: Routledge, 1995), 245. For a site of fan criticism of the heterosexism of Trek, see The Gay & Lesbian *Star Trek*/Sci Fi Home Page on the World Wide Web, at http://www.gaytrek.com/gaytrek/.
15. The last episode of *The Next Generation*, "All Good Things . . ." (1994), goes back to the original episode of seven years prior, and thus to the multicultural world that is our future. In the story, Picard finds

himself leaping through time—specifically the past, when he was first assigned the *Enterprise*; the present, where he carries out his normal orders; and the future, where he suffers from an incurable disease that is similar to senility. Mocking Picard in each time period is the same motley chorus from "Encounter at Farpoint."

16. Katrina G. Boyd. "Cyborgs in Utopia: The Problem of Radical Difference in *Star Trek: The Next Generation*," in Harrison et al., eds., *Enterprise Zones*, 99.

17. Richard J. Herrnstein and Charles Murray, *The Bell Curve: Intelligence and Class Structure in American Life* (New York: Free Press, 1994).

18. For a list of the romantic relationships of Picard and the other characters, see Vodrey, *The Star Trek: The Next Generation Encyclopedia*, 128–130.

19. See "The Game" (1991) and "The Dauphin" (1989).

20. See, for example, "Data's Day" (1991), "The Wounded" (1991), "Night Terrors" (1991), "The Icarus Factor" (1989), "Disaster" (1991), and "In Theory" (1991).

21. David Theo Goldberg, *Racist Culture: Philosophy and the Politics of Meaning* (Cambridge: Blackwell Publishers, 1993), 7.

22. Leah R. Vande Berg, "Worf as Metonymic Signifier of Racial, Cultural, and National Difference," in *Enterprise Zones*, ed. Harrison et al., 53.

23. Stephen Hawking, "The Uncertainty Principle," *A Brief History of Time* (New York: Bantam Books, 1988), 60.

Chapter 5: Reading Race

1. For a history of the initial campaign to save *Star Trek* from a fan's perspective, see Bjo Trimble, *On The Goodship Enterprise: My 15 Years With Star Trek* (Norfolk: Donning Company, 1982).

2. Quoted in William Shatner with Chris Kreski, *Star Trek Memories* (New York: HarperCollins, 1993), 254.

3. George Takei, quoted in *Star Trek: 25th Anniversary Special* (1991).

4. Fredric Jameson, "Postmodernism, or the Cultural Logic of Late Capitalism," *New Left Review* 146 (1984): 87. For Jameson, postmodernism is a widespread cultural and economic logic representing a phase of capitalism. The theorist argues that this phase, which he identifies as "late capitalism," extends commodification into almost all aspects of both psychical and social life, thereby erasing history and, consequently, a potentially more egalitarian future.

5. Ibid., 82–83.

6. Edward Said, *Orientalism* (New York: Vintage Books, 1979).

7. Though I consider myself a fan, I cannot claim to be a "Trekker." I don't attend conventions. I don't petition Paramount executives to improve shorelines or to pay more attention to the Prime Directive. And I don't write or read fanzines (though the few I have seen were both creative and interesting).

8. Henry Jenkins, *Textual Poachers: Television Fans & Participatory Culture* (New York: Routledge, 1992), 5.

9. Roland Barthes, "The Death of the Author," in *Image-Music-Text* (London: Fontana, 1977), 2.

10. M. M. Bakhtin, "Forms of Time and of the Chronotope in the Novel," in *The Dialogical Imagination: Four Essays by M. M. Bakhtin* (Austin: University of Texas Press, 1981), 254.

11. Christian Metz, *The Imaginary Signifier: Psychoanalysis and the Cinema* (Bloomington: Indian University Press, 1982); Jean-Louis Baudry, "Ideological Effects of the Basic Cinematographic Apparatus" and "The Apparatus: Metapsychological Approaches to the Impression of Reality in Cinema," in *Narrative, Apparatus, Ideology*, ed. Philip Rosen (New York: Columbia University Press, 1986), 286–298, 299–318.

12. Laura Mulvey, "Visual Pleasure and Narrative Cinema" and "Afterthoughts on 'Visual Pleasure and Narrative Cinema' inspired by *Duel in the Sun*," in *Feminism and Film Theory*, ed. Constance Penley (New York: Routledge, 1988), 57–68, 69–79. Mary Ann Doane, *The Desire to Desire: The Woman's Film of the 1940's* (Bloomington: Indiana University Press, 1987).

13. Beverle Houston, "Viewing Television: The Metapsychology of Endless Consumption," *Quarterly Review of Film Studies* 9, no. 3 (1984): 183–195. The crux of Houston's argument is that television spectatorship is one of continual consumption: the flow of television programming is continually interrupted by commercials, thereby creating a lack which, in turn, creates a desire for more consumption.

14. David Bordwell, *Narration in the Fiction Film* (Madison: University of Wisconsin Press, 1985), 30. See also *Making Meaning: Inference and Rhetoric in the Interpretation of Cinema* (Cambridge: Harvard University Press, 1989), esp. chap. 1, "Making Films Mean."

15. Bordwell, *Narration in the Fiction Film*, 31. For Bordwell the process of working the text is much more complex than I've outlined here, but it can be reduced to two functions: either from the bottom up, where inferences are made from perceptual data in an involuntary manner, or from the top down, where inferences are induced or deduced based on expectations, prior experience, etc. See also David Bordwell, "A Case for Cognitivism," *IRIS* 9 (1989): 11–40.

16. Stuart Hall, "Encoding/Decoding in Television Discourse," in *Culture, Media, Language,* ed. Stuart Hall et al. (London: Hutchinson, 1973).

17. David Morley, "Psychoanalytic Theories," in *Television, Audiences & Cultural Studies* (London and New York: Routledge, 1992), 60–61.

18. David Morley, "Theoretical Frameworks," in *Television, Audiences & Cultural Studies,* 52. Morley is quoting Stuart Hall, "Encoding/Decoding in Television Discourse."

19. Ibid., 7.

20. John Fiske, *Television Culture* (New York: Routledge, 1987), 74.

21. Ibid., 83.

22. John Fiske, "Moments of Television: Neither the Text nor the Audience," in *Remote Control: Television, Audiences & Cultural Power,* ed. Ellen Seiter et al. (New York: Routledge, 1989), 71.

23. Ien Ang, "Wanted: Audiences. On the Politics of Empirical Audience Studies," in *Remote Control: Television, Audiences & Cultural Power,* 102.

24. Hall, "Encoding/Decoding in Television Discourse," 13.

25. Ang, "Wanted: Audiences," 105.

26. Michel de Certeau, quoted in Jenkins, *Textual Poachers,* 24. For the original reference, see Michel de Certeau, *The Practice of Everyday Life* (Berkeley: University of California Press, 1984), 174.

27. See John Tulloch and Henry Jenkins, *Science Fiction Audiences: Watching Doctor Who and Star Trek* (New York: Routledge, 1995), esp. chapters 10–12. Constance Penley has also written about gender in the Trek fan community; see her "Feminism, Psychoanalysis and the Study of Popular Culture," in *Cultural Studies,* ed. Lawrence Grossberg et al. (New York: Routledge, 1992).

28. Jenkins and Tulloch, *Science Fiction Audiences,* p. 264.

29. Ibid, 263.

30. Jenkins, *Textual Poachers,* 3.

31. Personal communication, 19 may 1997.

32. To be more specific, a listserver is the administration of an "electronic list" of people interested in a similar topic. When a member sends an e-mail message to the listserver, that message is dispersed to all list members.

33. Their activity on the network enabled me to take a more distant position (though not necessarily less subjective), observing their e-mail without their direct knowledge of me (although most are aware that their posts are public domain).

34. For an overview of *Star Trek* on the Internet during the time I moni-

tored STREK-L, see Michael Wolff, ed., *Nettrek: Your Guide to Trek Life in Cyberspace* (New York: Michael Wolf and Co., 1995).

35. Mr. Mysterious, 15 July 1994. The method I've used to cite fan posts requires some elaboration. First, for the most part I've attributed each post to the name listed after the "From" label attached to all e-mail. Thus, if a person sent a message from another person's account, my citation might not reflect the actual author. Second, in an effort to protect fan identity without losing a sense of their individual identity, I have included either their first name or their nickname. Third, many of the posts are replete with grammatical and spelling errors, so much so that I have chosen not to mark them in the quote (to minimize the chances of misrepresenting the fans, each post was "cut and pasted" from the e-mail to the draft I sent my publisher).

36. "The Mad Hatter," 29 October 1993.

37. Sherri, 24 September 1993. Sherri goes on: "it seems more and more to be that ethnic diversity seems restricted to the main cast, where there is at least a representative or two of several ethnic and racial groups, but that such diversity seems strangely lacking in both guest stars and extras."

38. Dr. Mike, quoted in Katherine, 19 November 1993. In some instances, I downloaded the response to an original post when the original was quoted in the response. This had the benefit of saving space on my then small hard drive.

39. Peter, 18 November 1993.

40. Abdullah, quoted in Terry, 18 November 1993.

41. Terry, 18 November 1993.

42. Anonymous, quoted in Jeff, 20 October 1993.

43. Ibid.

44. Bruce, 21 October 1993.

45. Ibid.

46. Ibid.

47. Bettina, 24 October 1993.

48. Robert, 21 October 1993.

49. Ibid.

50. Ibid.

51. Ibid.

52. Rich, 23 September 1993.

53. April, 23 September 1993.

54. Sherri, 24 September 1993.

55. Bill, 21 July 1994.

56. Scott, 25 July 1994.

57. Dennis, 27 July 1994.
58. Scott, 28 July 1994.
59. Howard, 31 July 1994.
60. The Plaid Adder, 24 September 1993.
61. William F. B. Vodrey, *The* Star Trek: The Next Generation *Encyclopedia* (New Philadelphia: Kearsarge Press, 1994), 30.
62. Robert, 19 October 1993.
63. Ben, 29 September 1993.
64. Adam, 25 October 1993.
65. Mark, 25 October 1993.
66. Robert, 16 September 1993.
67. Barry, 4 June 1994.
68. Stephanie, 27 June 1994.
69. Mike, 27 June 1994.
70. Amanda, 13 October 1993. This was the only post directed to me, not the entire list, in response to the only time I sent a message to a fan.
71. Big Mike "Tank," 12 July 1994.
72. Juan, 25 September 1993.
73. Bill, 8 July 1994.
74. Robyn, 8 July 1994.
75. Ibid.
76. Scotty, 27 June 1994.
77. Ignace, 11 August 1994.
78. Keven, 13 August 1994.
79. Ann, 22 November 1993.
80. Robert, 16 November 1993.
81. Anonymous, quoted in Holly, 28 June 1994.
82. Mike, 28 June 1994. The character of Data actually makes this comparison in "The Last Outpost," which is the first episode the Ferengi appear in. I thank Jay Badenhoop for reminding me of this.
83. Mark, 25 October 1993.
84. Rick, 19 August 1994.
85. Robert, 19 October 1993.
86. Mike, 20 October 1993.
87. Katherine, 16 November 1993.
88. Holly, 28 June 1994.
89. Martin, 30 September 1993.
90. Adam, 30 September 1993.
91. Sinya, 25 April 1994.
92. Holly, 27 June 1994.
93. Isaac Asimov, "Mr. Spock is Dreamy!" *TV Guide*, 29 April 1967, 11.

94. God Empress of Dune, 28 April 1994.

95. *The Next Generation*, "The Best of Both Worlds, Part I" (1990).

Epilogue

1. Edward Said, *Culture and Imperialism* (New York: Vintage Books, 1993), 336.

Select Bibliography

Critical, Cultural, Science Fiction, Film, and Television Studies

Altman, Rick. "Television Sound." In *Television: The Critical View*. 4th ed. Edited by Horace Newcomb. New York: Oxford University Press, 1987.

Ang, Ien. "Wanted: Audiences. On the Politics of Empirical Audience Studies." In *Remote Control: Television, Audiences & Cultural Power*. Edited by Ellen Seiter et al. London and New York: Routledge, 1989.

Bakhtin, M. M. "Forms of Time and of the Chronotope in the Novel." In *The Dialogical Imagination: Four Essays by M. M. Bakhtin*. Austin: University of Texas Press, 1981.

———. "The Bildungsroman and Its Significance in the History of Realism (Toward a Historical Typology of the Novel)." In *Speech Genres and Other Late Essays*. Translated by Vern W. McGee. Austin: University of Texas Press, 1986.

Barthes, Roland. *Elements of Semiology*. New York: Hill and Wang, 1977.

———. "The Death of the Author." In *Image-Music-Text*. London: Fontana, 1977.

———. "Theory of the Text." In *Untying the Text: A Post-Structuralist Reader*. Edited by Robert Young. Boston: Routledge & Kegan Paul, 1981.

Bennett, Tony, and Janet Woollacott. *Bond and Beyond: The Political Career of a Popular Hero*. New York: Methuen, 1987.

Bordwell, David. *Narration in the Fiction Film*. Madison: University of Wisconsin Press, 1985.

———. "A Case for Cognitivism." *IRIS* 9 (spring 1989): 11–40.

———. *Making Meaning: Inference and Rhetoric in the Interpretation of Cinema*. Cambridge: Harvard University Press, 1989.

Browne, Nick, ed. *American Television: New Directions in History and Theory*. Langhorne: Harwood Academic Publishers, 1994.

Doane, Mary Ann. *The Desire to Desire: The Woman's Film of the 1940's*. Bloomington: Indiana University Press, 1987.

Caldwell, John Thornton. *Televisuality: Style, Crisis, and Authority in American Television*. New Brunswick, N.J.: Rutgers University Press, 1985.

Eco, Umberto. *A Theory of Semiotics*. Bloomington: Indiana University Press, 1979.

Fiske, John. *Television Culture*. New York: Routledge, 1987.

———. "Moments of Television: Neither the Text nor the Audience." In *Remote Control: Television, Audiences & Cultural Power*. Edited by Ellen Seiter et al. London and New York: Routledge, 1989.

Genette, Gerard. *Palimpsestes: la littérature au second degré.* Paris: Seuil, 1982.

Germino, Dante. *Antonio Gramsci: Architect of a New Politics.* Baton Rouge: Louisiana State University Press, 1990.

Gramsci, Antonio. *Selections From the Prison Notebooks of Antonio Gramsci.* Edited by Quintin Hoare and Geoffrey Nowell Smith. New York: International Publishers, 1971.

———. *Letters from Prison.* Edited by Lynne Lawner. New York: Harper & Row, 1973.

———. *Selections from Cultural Writings.* Edited by David Forgacs and Geoffrey Nowell-Smith. Cambridge: Harvard University Press, 1985.

Grossberg, Lawrence, Cary Nelson, and Paula Treichler, eds. *Cultural Studies.* New York: Routledge, Chapman and Hall, 1991.

Hall, Stuart. "Encoding/Decoding in Television Discourse." In *Culture, Media, Langauge.* Edited by Stuart Hall et al. London: Hutchinson, 1973.

———. "Race, Articulation and Societies Structured in Dominance." In *Sociological Theories: Race and Colonialism.* Paris: UNESCO, 1980.

Hawking, Stephen W. *A Brief History of Time.* New York: Bantam Books, 1988.

———. *Black Holes and Baby Universes and Other Essays.* New York: Bantam Books, 1993.

Houston, Beverle. "Viewing Television: The Metapsychology of Endless Consumption." *Quarterly Review of Film Studies* 9, no. 3 (summer 1984): 183–195.

Jameson, Fredric. *The Political Unconscious: Narrative as a Socially Symbolic Act.* New York: Cornell University Press, 1981.

———. "Progress vs. Utopia; or, Can We Imagine the Future?" *Science Fiction Studies,* 27 September 1982, 147–158.

———. "Postmodernism, or the Cultural Logic of Late Capitalism." *New Left Review* 146 (July-August 1984): 53–94.

———. "Nostalgia for the Present." *The South Atlantic Quarterly* 88 (spring 1989): 517–537.

Jenkins, Henry. *Textual Poachers: Television Fans & Participatory Culture.* New York: Routledge, 1992.

Kristeva, Julia. "Word, Language, and Novel." In *Desire in Language: A Semiotic Approach to Literature and Art.* Edited by Leon S. Roudiez. New York: Columbia University Press, 1980.

Kuhn, Annette, ed. *Alien Zone: Cultural Theory and Contemporary Science Fiction Cinema.* New York: Verso, 1990.

Landon, Brooks. *The Aesthetics of Ambivalence: Rethinking Science Fiction Film in the Age of Electronic (Re)Production.* Westport, Conn.: Greenwood Press, 1992.

Landy, Marcia. *Film, Politics, and Gramsci.* Minneapolis: University of Minnesota Press, 1994.

Lucanio, Patrick. *Them or Us: Archetypal Interpretations of Fifties Alien Invasion Films.* Bloomington: Indiana University Press, 1987.

Metz, Christian. *The Imaginary Signifier: Psychoanalysis and the Cinema.* Bloomington: Indiana University Press, 1982.

Montgomery, Michael V. *Carnivals and Commonplaces: Bakhtin's Chronotope, Cultural Studies, and Film.* New York: Peter Lang, 1993.

Morley, David. *The Nationwide Audience: Structures and Decoding.* London: British Film Institute, 1980.

———. *Family Television.* London: Comedia, 1986.

———. *Television, Audiences & Cultural Studies.* London and New York: Routledge, 1992.

Morson, Gary Saul, and Caryl Emerson. *Mikhail Bakhtin: Creation of a Prosaics.* Stanford, Calif.: Stanford University Press, 1990.

Mulvey, Laura. "Visual Pleasure and Narrative Cinema." In *Movies and Methods: Volume II.* Edited by Bill Nichols. Berkeley: University of California Press, 1985.

Penley, Constance, ed. *Feminism and Film Theory.* New York: Routledge, 1988.

Penley, Constance, et al., eds. *Close Encounters: Film, Feminism and Science Fiction.* Minneapolis: University of Minnesota Press, 1991.

Rosen, Philip, ed. *Narrative, Apparatus, Ideology.* New York: Columbia University Press, 1986.

Seiter, Ellen, et al., eds. *Remote Control: Television, Audiences, and Cultural Power.* London: Routledge, 1989.

Siegel, Mark. "Towards an Aesthetic of Science Fiction Television." *Extrapolations* 25 (spring 1984): 60–75.

Sobchack, Vivian. "Cities on the Edge of Time: The Urban Science Fiction Film." *East-West Film Journal* 3, no. 1 (December 1988): 4–19.

———. *Screening Space: The American Science Fiction Film.* 2d ed. New York: The Unger Publishing Company, 1991.

———. "'Lounge Time': Post-War Crises and the Chronotope of Film Noir." In *Refiguring American Film Genres: History and Theory.* Edited by Nick Browne. Berkeley: University of California Press, forthcoming.

Stam, Robert. *Subversive Pleasures: Bakhtin, Cultural Criticism, and Film.* Baltimore: Johns Hopkins University Press, 1989.

Stam, Robert, Robert Burgoyne, and Sandy Flitterman-Lewis. *New Vocabularies in Film Semiotics: Structuralism, Post-Structuralism and Beyond.* New York: Routledge, 1992.

Williams, Raymond. *Television: Technology and Cultural Form.* New York: Schocken Books, 1975.

Race (Theory, History, and Criticism)

Berg, Charles Ramirez. "Immigrants, Aliens and Extraterrestrials: Science Fiction's Alien 'Other' as (Among Other Things) New Hispanic Imagery." *CineAction!* (Fall 1989): 3–17.

————. "Stereotyping in Films in General and of the Hispanic in Particular." *The Howard Journal of Communications* 2, no. 3 (summer 1990): 286–300.

Bernardi, Daniel, ed. *The Birth of Whiteness: Race and the Emergence of United States Cinema.* New Brunswick, N.J.: Rutgers University Press, 1996.

Berry, Mary Frances. *Black Resistance, White Law: A History of Constitutional Racism in America.* New York: A. Lane, Penguin Press, 1994.

Bogle, Donald. *Blacks in American Films and Television.* New York: Simon & Schuster, 1989.

Cavalli-Sforza, Luigi Luca, and Francesco Cavalli-Sforza. *The Great Human Diasporas: The History of Diversity and Evolution.* New York: Helix Books, 1995.

Cavalli-Sforza, Luigi Luca, Paolo Menozzi, and Alberto Piazza. *The History and Geography of Human Genes.* Princeton, N.J.: Princeton University Press, 1994.

Dyer, Richard. "White." *Screen* 29, no. 4 (autumn 1988): 44–64.

Frankenberg, Ruth. *White Women, Race Matters: The Social Construction of Whiteness.* Minneapolis: University of Minnesota Press, 1993.

Friedman, Lester D., ed. *Unspeakable Images: Ethnicity and the American Cinema.* Urbana: University of Illinois Press, 1991.

Gates, Henry Louis, ed. *"Race," Writing and Difference.* Chicago: University of Chicago Press, 1985.

Goldberg, David. *Racist Culture: Philosophy and the Politics of Meaning.* Oxford: Blackwell, 1994.

————, ed. *Anatomy of Racism.* Minneapolis: University of Minnesota Press, 1990.

Gossett, Thomas F. *Race: The History of an Idea in America.* New York: Schocken Books, 1965.

Gould, Stephen Jay. *The Mismeasure of Man.* New York: W. W. Norton, 1981.

Grey, Herman. "Television, Black Americans, and the American Dream." *Critical Studies in Mass Communication* 4, no. 4 (1989): 376–387.

———. *Watching Race: Television and the Struggle for "Blackness."* Minneapolis: University of Minnesota Press, 1995.

Hall, Stuart. "Race, Articulation and Societies Structured in Dominance." In *Sociological Theories: Race and Colonialism.* Paris: UNESCO, 1980.

———. "The Whites of Their Eyes: Racist Ideologies and the Media." In *Silver Lining: Some Sketches for the Eighties.* Edited by George Bridges and Rosalind Brunt. London: Lawrence and Wishart, 1981.

———. "Gramsci's Relevance for the Study of Race and Ethnicity." *Journal of Communication Inquiry* 10, no. 2 (summer 1986): 5–27.

———. "New Ethnicity." *ICA Documents* (1988): 27–31.

———. "Cultural Identity and Cinematic Representation." *Framework* (1989): 68–81.

Hamamoto, Daryl. *Monitored Peril: Asian Americans and the Politics of TV Representation.* Minneapolis: University of Minnesota Press, 1994.

Harding, Sandra, ed. *The "Racial" Economy of Science: Toward a Democratic Future.* Bloomington: Indiana University Press, 1993.

Herrnstein, Richard J., and Charles Murray. *The Bell Curve: Intelligence and Class Structure in American Life.* New York: Free Press, 1994.

hooks, bell. "Representing Whiteness in the Black Imagination." In *Cultural Studies.* Edited by Lawrence Grossberg et al. New York: Routledge, 1992.

Jacoby, Russell, and Naomi Glauberman, eds. *The Bell Curve Debate: History, Documents, Opinions.* New York: Times Books, 1995.

Jhally, Sut, and Justin Lewis. *Enlightened Racism: The Cosby Show, Audiences, and the Myth of the American Dream.* Boulder, Colo.: Westview Press, 1992.

Kevles, Daniel J. *In The Name of Eugenics: Genetics and the Uses of Human Heredity.* Berkeley: University of California Press, 1985.

MacDonald, J. Fred. *Blacks and White TV: Afro-Americans in Television and Video Criticism.* Chicago: Nelson-Hall, 1983.

Marchetti, Gina. *Romance and the "Yellow Peril": Race, Sex, and Discursive Strategies in Hollywood Fiction.* Berkeley: University of California Press, 1993.

Morrison, Toni. *Playing in the Dark: Whiteness and the Literary Imagination.* Cambridge: Harvard University Press, 1992.

Omi, Michael. "In Living Color: Race and American Culture." In *Cultural Politics in Contemporary America.* Edited by Ian Angus and Sut Jhally. New York: Routledge, 1989.

Omi, Michael, and Howard Winant. *Racial Formations in the United States: From the 1960's to the 1990's.* 2d ed. New York: Routledge, 1994.

Roediger, David R. *The Wages of Whiteness: Race and the Making of the American Working Class.* New York: Verso, 1991.

————. *Towards the Abolition of Whiteness: Essays on Race, Politics, and Working Class History*. New York: Verso, 1994.

Rose, Peter Isaac. *The Subject Is Race: Traditional Ideologies and the Teaching of Race Relations*. New York: Oxford University Press, 1968.

Said, Edward. *Orientalism*. New York: Vintage Books, 1979.

Shohat, Ella, and Robert Stam. *Unthinking Eurocentrism: Multiculturalism and the Media*. New York: Routledge, 1994.

Slotkin, Richard. *Gunfighter Nation: The Myth of the Frontier in Twentieth-Century America*. New York: HarperCollins, 1992.

West, Cornel. *Race Matters*. Boston: Beacon Press, 1993.

White, Hayden. "The Noble Savage Theme as Fetish." In *Tropics of Discourse*. Baltimore and London: Johns Hopkins University Press, 1979.

Woll, Allen L., and Randal M. Miller, eds. *Ethnic and Racial Images in American Film and Television*. New York: Garland Publishing, 1987.

Wong, Eugene Franklin. *On Visual Media Racism: Asians in American Motion Pictures*. New York: Arno Press, 1978.

Star Trek

Alexander, David. "Gene Roddenberry: Writer, Producer, Philosopher, Humanist." *The Humanist* 51 (March/April 1991): 5–30.

————. *Star Trek Creator*. New York: Penguin Books, 1994.

Asherman, Allan. *The Star Trek Interview Book*. New York: Pocket Books, 1988.

————. *The Star Trek Compendium*. New York: Pocket Books, 1989.

Asimov, Isaac. "Mr. Spock Is Dreamy!" *TV Guide*, 29 April 1967, 9–11.

Behre, Ira Steven. *The Ferengi Rules of Acquisition*. New York: Pocket Books, 1995.

Berg, Leah R. Vande. "Worf as Metonymic Signifier of Racial, Cultural, and National Difference." In *Enterprize Zones: Critical Positions on Star Trek*. Edited by Taylor Harrison et al. Boulder, Colo.: Westview Press, 1996.

Bernardi, Daniel. "Infinite Diversity in Infinite Combinations: Diegetic Logics and Racial Articulations in Star Trek." *Film & History* 24, nos. 1 & 2 (February–May 1994).

————. "Star Trek in the 1960s: Liberal-Humanism and the Production of Race." *Science Fiction Studies* 24, no. 72 (July 1997).

Blair, Karin. "The Garden in the Machine: The Why of Star Trek." In *Television: The Critical View*. 3d ed. Edited by Horace Newcomb. New York: Oxford University Press, 1982.

————. "Sex and *Star Trek*." *Science-Fiction Studies* 10 (November 1983): 292–297.

Boyd, Katrina G. "Cyborgs in Utopia: The Problem of Radical Difference in *Star Trek: The Next Generation.*" In *Enterprise Zones.* Edited by Taylor Harrison et al. Boulder, Colo.: Westview Press, 1996.

Buxton, David. *From the Avengers to Miami Vice: Form and Ideology in Television Series.* New York: Manchester University Press, 1990.

Cranny-Francis, Ann. "Sexuality and Sex-Role Stereotypes in *Star Trek.*" *Science-Fiction Studies* 12 (November 1985): 274–284.

Ellington, Jan Elizabeth, and Joseph Critelli. "Analysis of a Modern Myth: The *Star Trek* Series." *Extrapolations* 24 (fall 1983): 241–250.

Engel, Joel. *Gene Roddenberry: The Myth and the Man Behind Star Trek.* New York: Hyperion, 1994.

Farkas, Michael Eugene. "The Final Frontier: Critical Theory and the *Star Trek* Phenomenon." Ph.D. diss., University of Windsor, 1994.

Fern, Yvonne. *Gene Roddenberry: The Last Conversation.* Berkeley: University of California Press, 1994.

Franklin, H. Bruce. "*Star Trek* in the Vietnam Era." *Science-Fiction Studies* 21 (1994): 24–34.

Fulton, Valerie. "An Other Frontier: Voyaging West with Mark Twain and *Star Trek*'s Imperial Subject." *Postmodern Culture* 4, no. 3 (May 1994).

Gene Roddenberry Papers. Special Collections, Arts Library, University of California, Los Angeles.

Gentry, Christine, and Sally Gibson-Downs. *Greenberg's Guide to Star Trek Collectibles.* Sykesville, Md.: Greenberg Publishers, 1991–1992.

Gerrold, David. *The World of Star Trek.* New York: Ballantine Books, 1973.

Gibberman, Susan. *Star Trek: An Annotated Guide to Resources on the Development, the Phenomenon, the People, the Television Series, the Films, the Novels and the Recordings.* Jefferson, N.C.: McFarland and Company, 1991.

Goldsmith, Marlene Herbert. "Video Values Education." Ph.D. diss., University of Minnesota, 1982.

Goulding, J. *Empire, Aliens and Conquest: A Critique of American Ideology in* Star Trek *and other Science Fiction Adventures.* Toronto: Sisyphus, 1995.

Greenberg, Harvey R. "In Search of Spock." *Journal of Popular Film & Television* 12 (summer 1984): 52–65.

Harrison, Taylor, et al., eds. *Enterprise Zones: Critical Positions on Star Trek.* Boulder, Colo.: Westview Press, 1996.

Helford, Elyce Rae. "Reading Space Fictions: Representations of Gender, Race, and Species in Popular Culture." Ph.D. diss., University of Iowa, 1992.

Henderson, Mary. "Professional Women in Star Trek, 1964–1969." *Film & History* 24, nos. 1–2 (February–May 1994): 48–59.

The Internet Movie Database. World Wide Web: http://us.imdb.com/search.

Jackson, Joseph E. F. "Power and Gender Relations in the Television Star Treks: A Social Semiotic Analysis." Ph.D. diss., University of Alberta, 1992.

Jenkins, Henry. *Textual Poachers: Television Fans & Participatory Culture.* New York: Routledge, 1992.

Jewett, Robert, and John Shelton Lawrence. *The American Mono-myth.* Garden City, N.Y.: Anchor Press/Doubleday, 1977.

Joseph, Paul, and Sharon Carton. "The Law of the Federation: Images of Law, Lawyers, and the Legal System in *Star Trek: The Next Generation.*" *The University of Toledo Law Review* 24, no. 1 (fall 1992): 43–85.

Joyrich, Lynne. "Feminist Enterprise? *Star Trek: The Next Generation* and the Occupation of Femininity." *Cinema Journal* 35, no. 2 (winter 1996): 61–84.

Harrison, Taylor et al., eds. *Enterprise Zones: Critical Positions on Star Trek.* Boulder, Colo.: Westview Press, 1996.

Hastie, Amelie. "A Fabricated Space: Assimilating the Individual on *Star Trek: The Next Generation.*" In *Enterprise Zones: Critical Positions on Star Trek.* Edited by Taylor Harrison et al. Boulder, Colo.: Westview Press, 1996.

Klingon Language Institute (KLI). World Wide Web: thttp://www.kli.org.

Mills, Jeffrey. *CCSTSG Enterprises* 45/46, 10 June 1994.

"Nichelle Nichols Complains She Hasn't Been Allowed to Leave the Spaceship." *TV Guide*, 15 July 1967, 10.

Nichols, Nichelle. *Beyond Uhura: Star Trek and Other Memories.* New York: G. P. Putnam's Sons, 1994.

Nimoy, Leonard. *I Am Not Spock.* New York: Ballantine, 1975.

———. *I Am Spock.* New York: Hyperion, 1995.

Oliver, Gwendolyn Maria. "A Critical Examination of the Mythological and Symbolic Elements of the Modern Science Fiction Series: *Star Trek* and *Doctor Who.*" Ph.D. diss., Louisiana State University and Agricultural & Mechanical College, 1987.

Peel, John. *The Trek Encyclopedia.* 2d ed. Las Vegas, Nev.: Pioneer Books, 1992.

Penley, Constance. "Feminism, Psychoanalysis and the Study of Popular Culture." In *Cultural Studies.* Edited by Lawrence Grossberg, Cary Nelson, and Paula Treichler. New York: Routledge, Chapman and Hall, 1991.

Perrine, Toni A. "Beyond Apocalypse: Recent Representations of Nuclear War and Its Aftermath in United States Narrative Film." Ph.D. diss., Northwestern University, 1991.

Puckett, Thomas F. N. "The Phenomenology of Communication and Culture: Michel Foucault's Thematics in the Televised Popular Discourse of *Star Trek*." Ph.D. diss., Southern Illinois University, Carbondale, 1993.

Raddatz, Leslie. "Product of Two Worlds." *TV Guide*, 23 March 1967, 24.

Roth, Lane. "Death and Rebirth in *Star Trek II: The Wrath of Khan*." *Extrapolations* 28 (summer 1987): 159–166.

Said, Edward. *Culture and Imperialism*. New York: Vintage Books, 1993.

Selly, April. "'I Have Been and Ever Shall Be, Your Friend': *Star Trek, The Deerslayer* and the American Romance." *Journal of Popular Culture* 20 (summer 1986): 89–104.

———. "Transcendentalism in *Star Trek: The Next Generation*." *Journal of American Culture* 13 (spring 1990): 31–34.

Shatner, William with Chris Kreski. *Star Trek Memories*. New York: HarperCollins, 1993.

"Star Trek Classic List of Lists." Compiled by Mark Arthur Holtz. Last revised May 1996. ftp://ftp.cc.umanitoba.ca/startrek/quickref.tos

"The *Star Trek* Guide." Third Revision (April 17, 1967). Gene Roddenberry Papers, Arts Library, UCLA.

Star Trek: Omnipedia. CD-ROM. New York: Simon & Schuster Interactive, 1995.

"Star Trek: The Next Generation Quick Reference Guide." ftp://ftp.cc.umanitoba.ca/startrek/quickref.tng

Takei, George. *To The Stars: The Autobiography of George Takei*. New York: Pocket Books, 1994.

Trimble, Bjo. *On The Goodship Enterprise: My 15 Years With Star Trek*. Norfolk, Virginia Beach: Donning Company, 1982.

Tulloch, John, and Henry Jenkins. *Science Fiction Audiences: Watching Doctor Who and* Star Trek. New York: Routledge, 1995.

Tyrrel, William Blake. "Star Trek as Myth and Television as Myth Maker." *Journal of Popular Culture* 10 (spring 1977): 181–197.

Van Hise, James. *Trek: The Making of the Movies*. Las Vegas, Nev.: Pioneer Books, 1992.

Vodrey, William F. B. Star Trek: The Next Generation *Technical Manual*. New Philadelphia: Kearsarge Press, 1994.

Waterman, Amy E. "Collection and Recollection: The Social and Symbolic Function of Motion Picture Memorabilia." Ph.D. diss., New York University, 1991.

Westfahl, Gary. "Where No Market Has Gone Before: 'The Science Fiction Industry' and the Star Trek Industry." *Extrapolation* 37, no. 4 (1996): 291–301.

Whitfield, Stephen E., and Gene Roddenberry. *The Making of Star Trek*. New York: Ballantine Books, 1968.

Wilcox, Rhonda V. "Dating Data: Miscegenation in *Star Trek: The Next Generation*." *Extrapolation* 34, no. 3 (1993): 265–277.

Wolf, Michael, ed. *Nettrek: Your Guide to Trek Life in Cyberspace*. New York: Michael Wolf & Company, 1995.

Worland, Rick. "Captain Kirk: Cold Warrior." *Journal of Popular Film and Television* 6 (fall 1988): 10–17.

———. "From the New Frontier to the Final Frontier: *Star Trek* from Kennedy to Gorbachev." *Film & History* 24, nos. 1–2 (1994): 19–35.

Filmography

Writer: Gene Roddenberry
Director: Marc Daniels

13. "The Conscience of the King" (12/08/66)
Writer: Barry Trivers
Director: Gerd Oswald

14. "Balance of Terror" (12/15/66)
Writer: Paul Schneider
Director: Vincent McEveety

15. "Shore Leave" (12/29/66)
Writer: Theodore Sturgeon
Director: Robert Sparr

16. "The Galileo Seven" (1/05/67)
Writers: Oliver Crawford and S. Bar David
Director: Robert Gist

17. "The Squire of Gothos" (1/12/67)
Writer: Paul Schneider
Director: Don McDougall

18. "Arena" (1/19/67)
Writer: Gene L. Coon
Director: Joseph Pevney

19. "Tomorrow Is Yesterday" (1/26/67)
Writer: D. C. Fontana
Director: Michael O'Herlihy

20. "Court Martial" (2/02/67)
Writers: Don M. Mankiewicz and Stephen Carabatsos
Director: Marc Daniels

21. "The Return of the Archons" (2/09/67)
Writer: Boris Sobelman
Director: Joseph Pevney

22. "Space Seed" (2/16/67)
Writers: Gene L. Coon and Carey Wilbur
Director: Marc Daniels

23. "A Taste of Armageddon" (2/23/67)
Writers: Robert Hamner and Gene L. Coon
Director: Joseph Pevney

24. "This Side of Paradise" (3/02/67)
Writer: D. C. Fontana
Director: Ralph Senensky

25. "The Devil in the Dark" (3/09/67)
Writer: Gene L. Coon
Director: Joseph Pevney

26. "Errand of Mercy" (3/16/67)
    Writer: Gene L. Coon
    Director: John Newland
27. "The Alternative Factor" (3/23/67)
    Writer: Don Ingalls
    Director: Gerd Oswald
28. "The City on the Edge of Forever" (4/06/67)
    Writer: Harlan Ellison
    Director: Joseph Pevney
29. "Operation—Annihilate" (4/13/67)
    Writer: Stephen W. Carabatsos
    Director: Herschel Daugherty

Second Season

30. "Amok Time" (9/15/67)
    Writer: Theodore Sturgeon
    Director: Joseph Pevney
31. "Who Morns for Adonais" (9/22/67)
    Writers: Gilbert Ralston and Gene L. Coon
    Director: Marc Daniels
32. "The Changeling" (9/29/67)
    Writer: John Meredyth Lucas
    Director: Marc Daniels
33. "Mirror, Mirror" (10/06/67)
    Writer: Jerome Bixby
    Director: Marc Daniels
34. "The Apple" (10/13/67)
    Writers: Max Ehrlich and Gene L. Coon
    Director: Joseph Pevney
35. "The Doomsday Machine" (10/20/67)
    Writer: Norman Spinrad
    Director: Marc Daniels
36. "Catspaw" (10/27/67)
    Writers: Robert Bloch and D. C. Fontana
    Director: Joseph Pevney
37. "I, Mudd" (11/03/67)
    Writer: Stephen Kandel
    Director: Marc Daniels
38. "Metamorphosis" (11/10/67)
    Writer: Gene L. Coon
    Director: Ralph Senensky

39. "Journey to Babel" (11/17/67)
    Writer: D. C. Fontana
    Director: Joseph Pevney
40. "Friday's Child" (12/01/67)
    Writer: D. C. Fontana
    Director: Joseph Pevney
41. "The Deadly Years" (12/08/67)
    Writer: David P. Harmon
    Director: Joseph Pevney
42. "Obsession" (12/15/67)
    Writer: Art Wallace
    Director: Ralph Senensky
43. "Wolf in the Fold" (12/22/67)
    Writer: Robert Bloch
    Director: Joseph Pevney
44. "The Trouble with Tribbles" (12/29/67)
    Writer: David Gerrold
    Director: Joseph Pevney
45. "The Gamesters of Triskellion" (1/05/68)
    Writer: Margaret Armen
    Director: Gene Nelson
46. "A Piece of the Action" (1/12/68)
    Writer: David P. Harmon
    Director: James Komack
47. "The Immunity Syndrome" (1/19/68)
    Writer: Robert Sabaroff
    Director: Joseph Pevney
48. "A Private Little War" (2/02/68)
    Writer: Gene Roddenberry
    Director: Marc Daniels
49. "Return to Tomorrow" (2/09/68)
    Writer: John Kingsbridge
    Director: Ralph Senensky
50. "Patterns of Force" (2/16/68)
    Writer: John Meredyth Lucas
    Director: Vincent McEveety
51. "By Any Other Name" (2/23/68)
    Writers: D. C. Fontana and Jerome Bixby
    Director: Marc Daniels
52. "The Omega Glory" (3/01/68)
    Writer: Gene Roddenberry
    Director: Vincent McEveety

53. "The Ultimate Computer" (3/08/68)
    Writer: D. C. Fontana
    Director: John Meredyth Lucas
54. "Bread and Circuses" (3/15/68)
    Writers: Gene Roddenberry and Gene L. Coon
    Director: Ralph Senensky
55. "Assignment: Earth" (3/29/68)
    Writer: Art Wallace
    Director: Marc Daniels

Third Season

56. "Spock's Brain" (9/20/68)
    Writer: Lee Cronin
    Director: Marc Daniels
57. "The *Enterprise* Incident" (9/27/68)
    Writer: D. C. Fontana
    Director: John Meredyth Lucas
58. "The Paradise Syndrome" (10/04/68)
    Writer: Margaret Armen
    Director: Jud Taylor
59. "And the Children Shall Lead" (10/11/68)
    Writer: Edward J. Lasko
    Director: Marvin Chomsky
60. "Is There in Truth No Beauty?" (10/18/68)
    Writer: Jean Lisette Aroeste
    Director: Ralph Senensky
61. "Spectre of the Gun" (10/25/68)
    Writer: Lee Cronin
    Director: Vincent McEveety
62. "Day of the Dove" (11/01/68)
    Writer: Jerome Bixby
    Director: Marvin Chomsky
63. "For the World Is Hollow" (11/08/68)
    Writer: Rik Vollaerts
    Director: Tony Leader
64. "The Tholian Web" (11/15/68)
    Writers: Judy Burns and Chet Richards
    Director: Ralph Senensky
65. "Plato's Stepchildren" (11/22/68)
    Writer: Meyer Dolinsky
    Director: David Alexander
66. "Wink of an Eye" (11/29/68)

Writer: Arthur Heinemann
Director: Jud Taylor
67. "The Empath" (12/06/68)
Writer: Joyce Muskat
Director: John Erman
68. "Elaan of Troyius" (12/20/68)
Writer: John Meredyth Lucas
Director: John Meredyth Lucas
69. "Whom Gods Destroy" (1/03/69)
Writer: Lee Erwin
Director: Herb Wallerstein
70. "Let That Be Your Last Battlefield" (1/10/69)
Writer: Oliver Crawford
Director: Jud Taylor
71. "The Mark of Gideon" (1/17/69)
Writers: George F. Slavin and Stanley Adams
Director: Jud Taylor
72. "That Which Survives" (1/24/69)
Writer: John Meredyth Lucas
Director: Herb Wallerstein
73. "The Lights of Zetar" (1/31/69)
Writers: Jeremy Tarcher and Shari Lewis
Director: Herb Kenwith
74. "Requiem for Methuselah" (2/14/69)
Writer: Jerome Bixby
Director: Murray Golden
75. "The Way to Eden" (2/21/69)
Writer: Arthur Heinemann
Director: David Alexander
76. "The Cloudminders" (2/28/69)
Writer: Margaret Armen
Director: Jud Taylor
77. "The Savage Curtain" (3/07/69)
Writers: Arthur Heinemann and Gene Roddenberry
Director: Herschel Daugherty
78. "All Our Yesterdays" (3/14/69)
Writer: Jean Lisette Aroeste
Director: Marvin Chomsky
79. "Turnabout Intruder" (6/03/69)
Writer: Arthur Singer
Director: Herb Wallerstein

Feature Trek

1. *Star Trek: The Motion Picture* (1979)
   Producer: Gene Roddenberry
   Director: Robert Wise
   Screenplay: Harold Livingston
   Story: Alan Dean Foster
2. *Star Trek II: The Wrath of Khan* (1982)
   Executive Producer: Harve Bennett
   Producer: Robert Sallin
   Director: Nicholas Meyer
   Screenplay: Jack B. Sowards
   Story: Harve Bennett and Jack Sowards
3. *Star Trek III: The Search for Spock* (1984)
   Executive Producer: Gary Nardino
   Producer: Harve Bennett
   Director: Leonard Nimoy
   Screenplay: Harve Bennett
   Story: Harve Bennett
4. *Star Trek IV: The Voyage Home* (1986)
   Executive Producer: Ralph Winter
   Producer: Harve Bennett
   Director: Leonard Nimoy
   Screenplay: Steve Meerson, Peter Krikes, Harve Bennett, and Nicholas
   Meyer
   Story: Leonard Nimoy and Harve Bennett
5. *Star Trek V: The Final Frontier* (1989)
   Executive Producer: Ralph Winter
   Producer: Harve Bennett
   Director: William Shatner
   Screenplay: David Loughery
   Story: William Shatner, Harve Bennett, and David Loughery
6. *Star Trek VI: The Undiscovered Country* (1991)
   Executive Producer: Leonard Nimoy
   Producer: Ralph Winter
   Director: Nicholas Meyer
   Screenplay: Nicholas Meyer and Denny Martin Flinn
   Story: Leonard Nimoy, Lawrence Konner, and Mark Rosenthal
7. *Star Trek: Generations* (1994)
   Executive: Bernie Williams
   Producers: Rick Berman and Peter Lauritson

Director: David Carson
Story: Rick Berman, Brannon Braga, and Ronald D. Moore
8. *First Contact* (1996)
Executive Producer: Rick Berman
Producers: Marty Hornstein and Peter Lauritson
Director: Jonathan Frakes
Story: Rick Berman, Brannon Braga, and Ronald D. Moore

Star Trek: The Next Generation

First Season

1/2. "Encounter at Farpoint" (9/26/87)
Writers: D. C. Fontana and Gene Roddenberry
Director: Corey Allen
3. "The Naked Now" (10/03/87)
Teleplay: J. Michael Bingham
Story: John D. F. Black and J. Michael Bingham
Director: Paul Lynch
4. "Code of Honor" (10/10/87)
Writers: Katharyn Powers and Michael Baron
Director: Russ Mayberry
5. "The Last Outpost" (10/18/87)
Teleplay: Herbert Wright
Story: Richard Krzemien
Director: Richard Colla
6. "Where No One Has Gone Before" (10/24/87)
Writers: Diane Duane and Michael Reaves
Director: Rob Bowman
7. "Lonely Among Us" (10/31/87)
Teleplay: D. C. Fontana
Story: Michael Halperin
Director: Cliff Bole
8. "Justice" (11/07/87)
Teleplay: Worley Thorne
Story: Ralph Wills and Worley Thorne
Director: James L. Conway
9. "The Battle" (11/14/87)
Teleplay: Herbert Wright
Story: Larry Forrester
Director: Rob Bowman
10. "Hide and Q" (11/21/87)
Teleplay: C. J. Holland and Gene Roddenberry

Story: C. J. Holland
Director: Cliff Bole
11. "Haven" (1/28/87)
    Teleplay: Tracy Tormé
    Story: Tracy Tormé and Lan O'Kun
    Director: Richard Compton
12. "The Big Goodbye" (1/09/88)
    Writer: Tracy Tormé
    Director: Joseph L. Scanlan
13. "Datalore" (1/16/88)
    Teleplay: Robert Lewin and Gene Roddenberry
    Story: Robert Lewin and Maurice Hurley
    Director: Rob Bowman
14. "Angel One" (1/23/88)
    Writer: Patrick Barry
    Director: Michael Rhodes
15. "11001001" (1/30/88)
    Writer: Maurice Hurley and Robert Lewin
    Director: Paul Lynch
16. "Too Short a Season" (2/06/88)
    Teleplay: Michael Michaelian and D. C. Fontana
    Story: Michael Michaelian
    Director: Rob Bowman
17. "When the Bough Breaks" (2/13/88)
    Writer: Hannah Louise Shearer
    Director: Kim Manners
18. "Home Soil" (2/20/88)
    Teleplay: Robert Sabaroff
    Story: Karl Geurs, Ralph Sanchez, and Robert Sabaroff
    Director: Corey Allen
19. "Coming of Age" (3/12/88)
    Writer: Sandy Fries
    Director: Mike Vejar
20. "Heart of Glory" (3/19/88)
    Teleplay: Maurice Hurley
    Story: Maurice Hurley, Herbert Wright, and D.C. Fontana
    Director: Rob Bowman
21. "The Arsenal of Freedom" (4/09/88)
    Teleplay: Richard Manning and Hans Beimler
    Story: Maurice Hurley and Robert Lewin
    Director: Les Landau
22. "Symbiosis" (4/16/88)

Teleplay: Robert Lewin, Richard Manning, and Hans Beimler
Story: Robert Lewin
Director: Win Phelps

23. "Skin of Evin" (4/23/88)
Teleplay: Joseph Stefano and Hannah Louise Shearer
Story: Joseph Stefano
Director: Joseph L. Scanlan

24. "We'll Always Have Paris" (4/30/88)
Writers: Deborah Dean Davis and Hannah Louise Shearer
Director: Robert Becker

25. "Conspiracy" (5/07/88)
Teleplay: Tracy Tormé
Story: Robert Sabaroff
Director: Cliff Bole

26. "The Neutral Zone" (5/14/88)
Television Story and Teleplay: Maurice Hurley
Story: Deborah McIntyre and Mona Clee
Director: James L. Conway

Second Season

27. "The Child" (11/19/88)
Writers: Jaron Summers, Jon Povill, and Maurice Hurley
Director: Rob Bowman

28. "Where Silence Has Lease" (11/26/88)
Writer: Jack B. Sowards
Director: Winrich Kolbe

29. "Elementary, Dear Data" (12/03/88)
Writer: Brian Alan Lane
Director: Rob Bowman

30. "The Outrageous Okona" (12/10/88)
Teleplay: Burton Armus
Story: Les Menchen, Lance Dickson, and David Landsberg
Director: Robert Becker

31. "Loud as a Whisper" (1/07/89)
Writer: Jacqueline Zambrano
Director: Larry Shaw

32. "The Schizoid Man" (1/21/89)
Teleplay: Tracy Tormé
Story: Richard Manning and Hans Beimler
Director: Les Landau

33. "Unnatural Selection" (1/28/89)

Writers: John Mason and Mike Gray
Director: Paul Lynch
34. "A Matter of Honor" (2/04/89)
    Teleplay: Burton Armus
    Story: Wanda M. Haight, Gregory Amos, and Burton Armus
    Director: Rob Bowman
35. "The Measure of a Man" (2/11/89)
    Writer: Melinda M. Snodgrass
    Director: Robert Scheerer
36. "The Dauphin" (2/18/89)
    Writers: Scott Rubenstein and Leonard Mlodinow
    Director: Rob Bowman
37. "Contagion" (3/18/89)
    Writers: Steve Gerber and Beth Woods
    Director: Joseph L. Scanlan
38. "The Royale" (3/25/89)
    Writer: Keith Mills
    Director: Cliff Bole
39. "Time Squared" (4/01/89)
    Teleplay: Maurice Hurley
    Story: Kurt Michael Bensmiller
    Director: Joseph L. Scanlan
40. "The Icarus Factor" (4/22/89)
    Teleplay: David Assael and Robert L. McCullough
    Story: David Assael
    Director: Robert Iscove
41. "Pen Pals" (4/29/89)
    Teleplay: Melinda M. Snodgrass
    Story: Hannah Louise Shearer
    Director: Winrich Kolbe
42. "Q Who" (5/06/89)
    Writer: Maurice Hurley
    Director: Rob Bowman
43. "Samaritan Snare" (5/13/89)
    Writer: Robert L. McCullough
    Director: Les Landau
44. "Up the Long Ladder" (5/20/89)
    Writer: Melinda M. Snodgrass
    Director: Winrich Kolbe
45. "Manhunt" (6/17/89)
    Writer: Terry Devereaux

Director: Rob Bowman
46. "The Emissary" (6/24/89)
    Television Story and Teleplay: Richard Manning and Hans Beimler
    Based on an unpublished story by Thomas H. Calder
    Director: Cliff Bole
47. "Peak Performance" (7/08/89)
    Writer: David Kemper
    Director: Robert Scheerer
48. "Shades of Gray" (7/15/89)
    Teleplay: Maurice Hurley, Richard Manning, and Hans Beimler
    Story: Maurice Hurley
    Director: Rob Bowman

Third Season

49. "Evolution" (9/23/89)
    Teleplay: Michael Piller
    Story: Michael Piller and Michael Wagner
    Director: Winrich Kolbe
50. "The Ensigns of Command" (9/30/89)
    Writer: Melinda M. Snodgrass
    Director: Cliff Bole
51. "The Survivors" (10/07/89)
    Writer: Michael Wagner
    Director: Les Landau
52. "Who Watches the Watchers" (10/14/89)
    Writers: Richard Manning and Hans Beimler
    Director: Robert Wiemer
53. "The Bonding" (10/21/89)
    Writer: Ronald D. Moore
    Director: Winrich Kolbe
54. "Booby Trap" (10/28/89)
    Teleplay: Ron Roman, Michael Piller, and Richard Danus
    Story: Michael Wagner and Ron Roman
    Director: Gabrielle Beaumont
55. "The Enemy" (11/04/89)
    Writer: David Kemper
    Story: Michael Piller
    Director: David Carson
56. "The Price" (11/11/89)
    Writer: Hannah Louise Shearer
    Director: Robert Scheerer
57. "The Vengeance Factor" (11/18/89)

Writer: Sam Rolfe
Director: Timothy Bond
58. "The Defector" (12/30/89)
    Writer: Ronald D. Moore
    Director: Robert Scheerer
59. "The Hunted" (1/06/90)
    Writer: Robin Bernheim
    Director: Cliff Bole
60. "The High Ground" (1/27/90)
    Writer: Melinda M. Snodgrass
    Director: Gabrielle Beaumont
61. "Deja Q" (2/03/90)
    Writer: Richard Danus
    Director: Les Landau
62. "A Matter of Perspective" (2/10/90)
    Writer: Ed Zuckerman
    Director: Cliff Bole
63. "Yesterday's *Enterprise*" (2/17/90)
    Teleplay: Ira Behr, Richard Manning, Hans Beimler, and Ronald
    Moore
    Story: Trent Christopher Ganino and Eric A. Stillwell
    Director: David Carson
64. "The Offspring" (3/10/90)
    Writer: René Echevarria
    Director: Jonathan Frakes
65. "Sins of the Father" (3/17/90)
    Teleplay: Ronald D. Moore and W. Reed Moran
    Based on a teleplay by Drew Deighan
    Director: Les Landau
66. "Allegiance" (3/24/90)
    Writers: Richard Manning and Hans Beimler
    Director: Winrich Kolbe
67. "Captain's Holiday" (3/31/90)
    Writer: Ira Steven Behr
    Director: Chip Chalmers
68. "Tin Man" (4/21/90)
    Writers: Dennis Putman Bailey and David Bischoff
    Director: Robert Scheerer
69. "Hollow Pursuits" (4/28/90)
    Writer: Sally Caves
    Director: Cliff Bole
70. "The Most Toys" (5/05/90)

Writer: Shari Goodhartz
Director: Timothy Bond

71. "Sarek" (5/12/90)
    Television Story and Teleplay: Peter S. Beagle
    From an unpublished story by Mark Cushman and Jake Jacobs
    Director: Les Landau

72. "Menage à Troi" (05/26/90)
    Writers: Fred Bronson and Susan Sackett
    Director: Robert Legato

73. "Transfigurations" (06/02/90)
    Writer: René Echevarria
    Director: Tom Benko

74. "The Best of Both Worlds I" (06/16/90)
    Writer: Michael Piller
    Director: Cliff Bole

Fourth Season

75. "Best of Both Worlds II" (9/22/90)
    Writer: Michael Piller
    Director: Cliff Bole

76. "Family" (9/29/90)
    Writer: Ronald D. Moore
    Director: Les Landau

77. "Brothers" (10/06/90)
    Writer: Rick Berman
    Director: Rob Bowman

78. "Suddenly Human" (10/13/90)
    Teleplay: John Whelpley and Jeri Taylor
    Story: Ralph Phillips
    Director: Gabrielle Beaumont

79. "Remember Me" (10/20/90)
    Writer: Lee Sheldon
    Director: Cliff Bole

80. "Legacy" (10/27/90)
    Writer: Joe Menosky
    Director: Robert Scheerer

81. "Reunion" (11/03/90)
    Teleplay: Thomas Perry, Jo Perry, Ronald Moore, and Brannon Braga
    Story: Drew Deighan, Thomas Perry, and Jo Perry
    Director: Jonathan Frakes

82. "Future Imperfect" (11/10/90)
    Writers: J. Larry Carroll and David Bennett Carren

Director: Les Landau
83. "Final Mission" (11/17/90)
    Teleplay: Kasey Arnold-Ince and Jeri Taylor
    Story: Kasey Arnold-Ince
    Director: Corey Allen
84. "The Loss" (12/29/90)
    Teleplay: Hilary J. Bader, Alan J. Adler, and Vanessa Greene
    Story: Hilary J. Bader
    Director: Chip Chalmers
85. "Data's Day" (1/05/91)
    Teleplay: Harold Apter and Ronald D. Moore
    Story: Harold Apter
    Director: Robert Wiemer
86. "The Wounded" (1/26/91)
    Teleplay: Jeri Taylor
    Story: Stuart Charno, Sara Charno, and Cy Chermak
    Director: Chip Chalmers
87. "Devil's Due" (2/02/91)
    Teleplay: Philip Lazebnik
    Story: Philip Lazebnik and William Douglas Lansford
    Director: Tom Benko
88. "Clues" (2/09/91)
    Teleplay: Bruce D. Arthurs and Joe Menosky
    Story: Bruce D. Arthurs
    Director: Les Landau
89. "First Contact" (2/16/91)
    Teleplay: Dennis Russell Bailey, David Bischoff, Joe Menosky, Ronald D. Moore, and Michael Piller
    Story: Marc Scott Zicree
    Director: Cliff Bole
90. "Galaxy's Child" (3/09/91)
    Teleplay: Maurice Hurley
    Story: Thomas Kortozian
    Director: Winrich Kolbe
91. "Night Terrors" (3/16/91)
    Teleplay: Pamela Douglas and Jeri Taylor
    Story: Shari Goodhartz
    Director: Les Landau
92. "Identity Crisis" (3/23/91)
    Teleplay: Brannon Braga
    Based on a story by Timothy de Haas
    Director: Winrich Kolbe

93. "The Nth Degree" (3/30/91)
    Writer: Joe Menosky
    Director: Robert Legato
94. "Qpid" (4/20/91)
    Teleplay: Ira Steven Behr
    Story: Randee Russell and Ira Steven Behr
    Director: Cliff Bole
95. "The Drumhead" (4/27/91)
    Writer: Jeri Taylor
    Director: Jonathan Frakes
96. "Half a Life" (5/04/91)
    Teleplay: Peter Allen Fields
    Story: Ted Roberts and Peter Allen Fields
    Director: Les Landau
97. "The Host" (5/11/91)
    Writer: Michael Horvat
    Director: Marvin V. Rush
98. "The Mind's Eye" (5/25/91)
    Teleplay: René Echevarria
    Story: Ken Schafer and René Echevarria
    Director: David Livingston
99. "In Theory" (6/01/91)
    Teleplay: Ronald D. Moore and Joe Menosky
    Director: Patrick Stewart
100. "Redemption" (6/15/91)
    Writer: Ronald D. Moore
    Director: Cliff Bole

Fifth Season

101. "Redemption II" (9/21/91)
    Writer: Ronald D. Moore
    Director: David Carson
102. "Darmok" (9/28/91)
    Teleplay: Joe Menosky
    Story: Philip Lazebnik and Joe Menosky
    Director: Winrich Kolbe
103. "Ensign Ro" (10/05/91)
    Teleplay: Michael Piller
    Story: Richard Berman and Michael Piller
    Director: Les Landau
104. "Silicon Avatar" (10/12/91)
    Teleplay: Jeri Taylor

Story: Lawrence V. Conley
Director: Cliff Bole
105. "Disaster" (10/19/91)
Teleplay: Ronald D. Moore
Story: Ron Jarvis and Philip A. Scorza
Director: Gabrielle Beaumont
106. "The Game" (10/26/91)
Teleplay: Brannon Braga
Story: Susan Sackett, Fred Bronson, and Brannon Braga
Director: Corey Allen
107. "Unification: Part I" (11/02/91)
Teleplay: Jeri Taylor
Story: Rick Berman and Michael Piller
Director: Les Landau
108. "Unification: Part II" (11/09/91)
Teleplay: Michael Piller
Story: Rick Berman and Michael Piller
Director: Cliff Bole
109. "A Matter of Time" (11/16/91)
Teleplay: Rick Berman
Director: Paul Lynch
110. "New Ground" (1/04/92)
Teleplay: Grant Rosenberg
Story: Sara Charno and Stuart Charno
Director: Robert Scheerer
111. "Hero Worship" (1/25/92)
Teleplay: Joe Menosky
Story: Hilary J. Bader
Director: Patrick Stewart
112. "Violations" (2/01/92)
Teleplay: Pamela Gray and Jeri Taylor
Story: Shari Goodhartz, T. Michael Gray, and Pamela Gray
Director: Robert Wiemer
113. "The Masterpiece Society" (2/08/92)
Teleplay: Adam Belanoff and Michael Piller
Story: James Kahn and Adam Belanoff
Director: Winrich Kolbe
114. "Conundrum" (2/15/92)
Teleplay: Barry Schkolnick
Story: Paul Schiffer
Director: Les Landau
115. "Power Play" (2/22/92)

Teleplay: Rene Balcer, Herbert J. Wright, and Brannon Braga
Story: Paul Ruben and Maurice Hurley
Director: David Livingston

116. "Ethics" (2/29/92)
Teleplay: Ronald D. Moore
Story: Sara Charno and Stuart Charno
Director: Chip Chalmers

117. "The Outcast" (3/14/92)
Writer: Jeri Taylor
Director: Robert Scheerer

118. "Cause and Effect" (3/21/92)
Writer: Brannon Braga
Director: Jonathan Frakes

119. "The First Duty" (3/28/92)
Writers: Ronald D. Moore and Naren Shankar
Director: Paul Lynch

120. "Cost of Living" (4/18/92)
Writer: Peter Allan Fields
Director: Winrich Kolbe

121. "The Perfect Mate" (4/25/92)
Teleplay: Gary Perconte and Michael Piller
Story: René Echevarria and Gary Perconte
Director: Cliff Bole

122. "Imaginary Friend" (5/02/92)
Teleplay: Edithe Swensen and Brannon Braga
Story: Jean Louise Matthias, Ronald Wilderson, and Richard Fliegel
Director: Gabrielle Beaumont

123. "I Borg" (5/09/92)
Writer: René Echevarria
Director: Robert Lederman

124. "The Next Phase" (5/16/92)
Writer: Ronald D. Moore
Director: David Carson

125. "Inner Light" (5/30/92)
Teleplay: Morgan Gendel and Peter Allan Fields
Story: Morgan Gendel
Director: Peter Lauritson

126. "Time's Arrow, Part I" (6/13/92)
Teleplay: Joe Menosky and Michael Piller
Story: Joe Menosky
Director: Les Landau

Sixth Season

127. "Time's Arrow, Part II" (9/19/92)
    Teleplay: Jeri Taylor
    Story: Joe Menosky
    Director: Les Landau
128. "Realm of Fear" (9/26/92)
    Writer: Brannon Braga
    Director: Cliff Bole
129. "Man of the People" (10/03/92)
    Writer: Frank Abatemarco
    Director: Winrich Kolbe
130. "Relics" (10/10/92)
    Writer: Ronald D. Moore
    Director: Alexander Singer
131. "Schisms" (10/17/92)
    Teleplay: Brannon Braga
    Story: Jean Louise Matthias and Ron Wilkerson
    Director: Robert Wiemer
132. "True Q" (10/24/92)
    Writer: René Echevarria
    Director: Robert Scheerer
133. "Rascals" (10/31/92)
    Teleplay: Alison Hock
    Story: Ward Botsford, Diana Dru Botsford, and Michael Piller
    Director: Adam Nimoy
134. "A Fistful of Datas" (11/07/92)
    Teleplay: Robert Hewitt Wolfe and Brannon Braga
    Story: Robert Hewitt Wolfe
    Director: Patrick Stewart
135. "The Quality of Life" (11/14/92)
    Writer: Naren Shankar
    Director: Jonathan Frakes
136. "Chain of Command, Part I" (12/12/92)
    Teleplay: Ronald D. Moore
    Story: Frank Abatemarco
    Director: Robert Scheerer
137. "Chain of Command, Part II" (12/19/92)
    Writer: Frank Abatemarco
    Director: Les Landau
138. "Ship in a Bottle" (1/23/93)

Writer: René Echevarria
Director: Alexander Singer
139. "Aquiel" (1/30/93)
Teleplay: Brannon Braga and Ronald D. Moore
Story: Jeri Taylor
Director: Cliff Bole
140. "Face of the Enemy" (2/06/93)
Teleplay: Naren Shankar
Story: René Echevarria
Director: Gabrielle Beaumont
141. "Tapestry" (2/13/93)
Writer: Ronald D. Moore
Director: Les Landau
142. "Birthright, Part I" (2/20/93)
Writer: Brannon Braga
Director: Winrich Kolbe
143. "Birthright, Part II" (2/27/93)
Writer: René Echevarria
Director: Dan Curry
144. "Starship Mine" (3/27/93)
Writer: Morgan Gendel
Director: Cliff Bole
145. "Lessons" (4/03/93)
Writers: Ronald Wilkerson and Jean Louise Matthias
Director: Robert Wiemer
146. "The Chase" (4/24/93)
Teleplay: Joe Menosky
Story: Joe Menosky and Ronald D. Moore
Director: Jonathan Frakes
147. "Frame of Mind" (5/01/93)
Writer: Brannon Braga
Director: James L. Conway
148. "Suspicions" (5/08/93)
Writers: Joe Menosky and Naren Shankar
Director: Cliff Bole
149. "Rightful Heir" (5/15/93)
Teleplay: Ronald D. Moore
Story: James E. Brooks
Director: Winrich Kolbe
150. "Second Chances" (5/22/93)
Teleplay: René Echevarria
Story: Michael A. Medlock

Director: LeVar Burton
151. "Timescape" (6/12/93)
     Writer: Brannon Braga
     Director: Adam Nimoy
152. "Descent" (6/19/93)
     Teleplay: Ronald D. Moore
     Story: Jeri Taylor
     Director: Alexander Singer

Seventh Season

153. "Descent, Part II" (9/18/93)
     Writer: René Echevarria
     Director: Alexander Singer
154. "Liaisons" (9/25/93)
     Teleplay: Jeanne Carrigan Fauci and Lisa Rich
     Story: Roger Eschbacher and Jaq Greenspon
     Director: Cliff Bole
155. "Interface" (10/02/93)
     Writer: Joe Menosky
     Director: Robert Wiemer
156. "Gambit, Part I" (10/09/93)
     Teleplay: Naren Shankar
     Story: Christopher Hatton and Naren Shankar
     Director: Peter Lauritson
157. "Gambit, Part II" (10/16/93)
     Teleplay: Ronald D. Moore
     Story: Naren Shankar
     Director: Alexander Singer
158. "Phantasms" (10/23/93)
     Writer: Brannon Braga
     Director: Patrick Stewart
159. "Dark Page" (10/30/93)
     Writer: Hilary J. Bader
     Director: Les Landau
160. "Attached" (11/06/93)
     Writer: Nicholas Sagan
     Director: Jonathan Frakes
161. "Force of Nature" (11/13/93)
     Writer: Naren Shankar
     Director: Robert Lederman
162. "Inheritance" (11/20/93)
     Teleplay: Dan Koeppel and René Echevarria

Story: Dan Koeppel
Director: Robert Scheerer

163. "Parallels" (11/27/93)
Writer: Brannon Braga
Director: Robert Wiemer

164. "The Pegasus" (1/08/94)
Writer: Ronald D. Moore
Director: LeVar Burton

165. "Homeward" (1/15/94)
Teleplay: Naren Shankar
Television Story: Spike Steingasser
Director: Alexander Singer

166. "Sub Rosa" (1/29/94)
Teleplay: Brannon Braga
Television Story: Jeri Taylor
Director: Jonathan Frakes

167. "Lower Decks" (2/05/94)
Teleplay: René Echevarria
Director: Gabrielle Beaumont

168. "Thine Own Self" (2/12/94)
Teleplay: Ronald D. Moore
Story: Christopher Hatton
Director: Winrich Kolbe

169. "Masks" (2/19/94)
Writer: Joe Menosky
Director: Robert Wiemer

170. "Eye of the Beholder" (2/26/94)
Teleplay: René Echevarria
Story: Brannon Braga
Director: Cliff Bole

171. "Genesis" (3/19/94)
Writer: Brannon Braga
Director: Gates McFadden

172. "Journey's End" (3/26/94)
Writer: Ronald D. Moore
Director: Corey Allen

173. "Firstborn" (4/23/94)
Teleplay: René Echevarria
Story: Mark Kalbfeld
Director: Jonathan West

174. "Bloodlines" (4/30/94)
Writer: Nicholas Sagan

Director: Les Landau
175. "Emergence" (5/07/94)
Teleplay: Joe Menosky
Story: Brannon Braga
Director: Cliff Bole
176. "Preemptive Strike" (5/14/94)
Teleplay: René Echevarria
Story: Naren Shankar
Director: Patrick Stewart
177. "All Good Things . . ." (5/23/94)
Writers: Ronald D. Moore and Brannon Braga
Director: Winrich Kolbe

Index

fanzines, 7–8, 138–139, 152–153,
193n7; "slash," 153
Farrakhan, Minister Louis, parody of,
1–3
far Right, 114
Federation, The, 3, 51–53, 56–57,
64, 76, 87–88, 95, 97, 100–101,
109, 124; as topic of fan discussion,
166–168
feminism, 144–145, 188n16, 194n27
Ferengi (characters, *Deep Space Nine;
The Next Generation*), 8, 11, 24,
139; as topic of fan discussion, 165–
166, 171–175, 180, 196n82
"Ferengi Awards, The," 8
Ferguson, Jessie Lawrence, 107
fetish, 42, 45, 65, 72, 115–116, 145
Fierstein, Harvey, 90
Fifth Element, The, 80, 88–90
Final Frontier, The, 10, 70, 76
First Contact, 10, 70, 77, 80, 87–88,
95–96, 120, 128
Fisher, Carrie, 80
Fiske, John, 149–150
flame wars, 158
Flash Gordon, 101
Flora (character, *The Search for
Spock*), 93
flow, 9–11, 97, 145, 183n6, 193n13
Ford, Gerald, 6
Ford, Harrison, 80, 84
Fourteenth Amendment, 27
Franks, Jonathan, 91
Freejack, 87
Freiberger, Fred, 45, 47
French, 40, 106, 144
Freud, Sigmund, 118
Freudianism, 113
"Friday's Child," 52
Fu Manchu (character, movie serial),
62, 89, 101–102, 131, 168

"Galileo Seven, The," 55
"Game, The," 192n19
Gates, Henry Louis Jr., 14

Gatti, Jennifer, 126
Gay & Lesbian Star Trek/Sci Fi home
page, 191n14
Gaylaxions, 116, 152–153
Gemini mission, 33
gender, 13, 31, 35, 63–66, 72, 115–
116, 152–153, 178, 191n12,
194n27
Generations, 10, 70, 77, 97
"Genesis," 123, 129
Genesis Project, 93
genetics, 14, 122–123
geopolitics, 24, 91; as topic of fan dis-
cussion, 159–163
Geordi. *See* LaForge, Lieutenant J.G.
Geordi
Gingrich, Newt, 114
gods, 34, 120, 125, 134, 136
Goldberg, David Theo, 32, 130
Goldberg, Whoopi, 106, 122
Gorbachev, Mikhail, 100
Gorkin, Chancellor (character, *The
Undiscovered Country*), 98, 100,
101
Gorshin, Frank, 26
Gossett, Louis Jr., 85–86, 94
Gramsci, Antonio, 16–19
Grier, David Allan, 1
Gray, Herman, 21, 185n30
Great Bird of the Galaxy, The. *See*
Roddenberry, Gene
Greek romance novel, 91, 93
Griffith, D. W., 86
Guess Who's Coming to Dinner, 101
Guinan (character, *The Next Genera-
tion*), 106, 122, 178; in "Best of
Both Worlds, Part II," 128

Hagon (character, *The Next Generation*), 110–111
Haiti, 159–163, 181
half-breeds, 3, 35, 37, 43, 62, 97, 106,
126, 128, 156, 165
Hall, Stuart, 16–18, 148–151
Hamill, Mark, 80

Hamlet, 98
Hard Copy, 21
Hardin, Jerry, 122
Harlem, 91
Hawking, Stephen, 8, 25, 68, 102,
105, 118, 134–135
Heartbeat, 116
"Heart of Glory," 132–134
hegemony, 16–19, 21–22, 57, 80,
111, 140, 148–150, 180; counter-,
58–59
Henn, Carrie, 82
Herman, Pee Wee, 176
Herrnstein, Richard J., 183–184n9
heterosexism, 116–117, 191n12,
191n14
heterosexuality, 116–117
Hilton Hotels, 8
Hiroyuki, Cary, 121
historicity, 75, 96, 100, 104, 137, 143,
156
historiography, 96, 100, 104, 117–
122, 181
history, 12, 16, 44, 75, 78, 84, 91,
160, 168, 179; representation of, 27,
97–102, 112, 120, 131, 134–135,
157
Hitler, Adolf, 175
Hollywood, 11–12, 20–21, 57, 64,
70, 81–82, 84–86, 104, 144–145,
188n13
Holocaust, 172
holographic characters, 125, 128
homophobia, 89–90
homosexuality, 116–117, 139, 152–
153, 191n14
Hop Sing (character, Bonanza), 33
Horta (characters, Star Trek), 60–61
"Host, The," 116–117
Houston, Beverle Ann, 145, 193n13
Hubbell, Edwin, 8
Hudec, M. Leigh. See Barrett, Majel
Humanist, The, 34
humanist ideals, 101, 126, 161
humanocentrism, 101, 104

humanoids, 2, 26, 36, 47, 55–57, 62,
80, 86, 106–107, 115, 124–125,
166
Hyman, Charles H., 133
hypothetical spectator. See cognitive
model of readership

I Am Not Spock, 140
I Am Spock, 140
"Icarus Factor, The," 123, 131, 134,
192n20
ideology, 16, 18, 24, 29–30, 49, 75,
104, 115, 144, 152, 182; of alien
chronotope, 86; of coercion and
consent, 17–23, 148; of gender,
82, 115–116, 191n12; of neoconservatism, 115; patriarchal,
145
I Love Lucy, 36
imaginary time, theory of, 118
immigration, 115
imperialism, 78, 175, 178
Independence Day, 90
India, 158
infant mortality, 114
In Living Color, 1–3
integration, 3, 33, 35, 68, 115
Internet, 7–8, 24, 154–155,
194nn32–35
interracial characters, 38–39, 128–
130, 186n19
intertext, 7, 115, 117, 120, 131, 134–
135, 155, 158, 181, 190–191n7; of
biological determinism, 117, 132; of
evolution, 123–127, of history, 118;
of miscegenation, 130; of species,
126–127
intertextuality, 3, 22, 24, 111–112,
175, 190n3, 190n5
"In Theory," 192n20
Invasion of the Body Snatchers, 82
Iraqis, 166–168
Irish, 106
Ishikawa, Keiko (character, The Next
Generation), 130

Trek (*continued*)
97, 100, 181; history in, 100, history of, 168, 182; universe, 11, 50, 68, 97, 166
Trekkers, 5, 138–143, 150, 154–177, 193n7. *See also* fans of Trek
Tribbles (characters, *Star Trek*), 142
Trills (characters, *The Next Generation*), 116
Trimble, Bjo, 192n1
Trip to the Moon, A, 76, 81
Troi, Lieutenant Commander Deanna (character, *The Next Generation*), 106, 116, 126; in "Code of Honor," 106–108; in "Genesis," 123; in "Masterpiece Society," 128; in "Parallels," 129–130; in "Samaritan Snare," 124
"Trouble with Tribbles, The," 52
Troyius (planet), 64
Tucker, Chris, 89
Tulloch, John, 194n27
Twain, Mark, 122
Tyler, José "Joe" (character, *Star Trek*), 35

UCLA Hillel Jewish Center, 140–141
Uhura, Lieutenant (character, *The Next Generation*), 30, 40–42, 80, 91, 191n12; in "Balance of Terror," 53; in "The Cage," 36–37; in "Mirror, Mirror," 42, 67; parody of, 1–2; in "Plato's Stepchildren," 38–39, 130
uncertainty principle, 25
Undiscovered Country, The, 3, 10, 70, 77, 92, 97–98, 100–101, 131–132
unemployment, 114
United Federation of Planets, 11, 23, 30, 32, 63, 75, 97, 100, 106, 117, 130–131, 159, 166, 178, 181. *See also* diegetic logics
United States, 4, 16, 19, 22, 79, 82,

97, 100, 114, 131, 153, 155–156, 158–160
United States of Africa, 36
"Unnatural Selection," 122–123
UPN (United Paramount Network), 137, 187n1. *See also* Paramount Studios
Uses and Gratifications model of readership, 146–148, 150
U.S.S. *Crazy Horse*, 118
U.S.S. *Enterprise. See Enterprise*, U.S.S.
U.S.S. *Gandhi*, 118
U.S.S. *Potemkin*, 118
USSR. *See* Soviet Union
U.S.S. *Zapata*, 118
utopian vision of the future, 156–157, 176

Vader, Darth (character, *Star Wars* trilogy), 80
Vande Berg, Leah R., 132
Vanderbilt, Cornelius, 174
Vengeance of Fu Manchu, The, 63
versimilitude, 12
V'ger (character, *The Motion Picture*), 94, 125
Vietnam, 33, 64–65, 75, 79, 187n47
viewing environment, 145, 147, 149
"Visual Pleasure and Narrative Cinema," 72
visual style, 62, 86; in "Balance of Terror," 53–55; in "Elaan of Troyius," 65–67; in "Encounter at Farpoint," 120; in "Heart of Glory," 133–134; in "Let That Be Your Last Battlefield," 28–29; in "Mirror, Mirror," 42, 67; in *The Motion Picture*, 70–72; in "Omega Glory," 59–60; in "Plato's Stepchildren," 38–39
Vodrey, William F. B., 189–190n2, 192n18
Voting Rights Act of 1965, 33
Voyage Home, The, 10, 70, 76–77, 80, 92, 96–100, 189n25

About the Author

Daniel Bernardi is a visiting assistant professor in the Department of Comparative Literature and Foreign Languages, University of California–Riverside. He also teaches in the Department of Film and Television at UCLA, where he earned his doctorate. Bernardi has published in *The Encyclopedia of Knowledge, The Encyclopedia of Television, Film & History, The Journal of American History,* and *Science Fiction Studies.* He is the editor of *The Birth of Whiteness: Race and the Emergence of U.S. Cinema* (Rutgers University Press, 1996), and *Classic Whiteness: Race and the Hollywood Studio System* (University of Minnesota Press, forthcoming). Bernardi is also a creative consultant for the Sci-Fi Channel, and is currently working on a book that addresses the increasingly intimate yet blurry distinction between science fact and science fiction, entitled *Thinking Science/Living Fiction.*